MW00593990

México

ESTADOS UNIDOS
Río Colorado
Río Gila
Tijuana
Mexicali
Nogales
Nogales
El Paso
Ciudad Juárez
Río Grande
Río Misisipí
Houston
San Antonio
Hermosillo
Chihuahua
Río Conchos
Río Bravo
BAJA CALIFORNIA
Golfo de California
SIERRA MADRE OCCIDENTAL
SIERRA MADRE ORIENTAL
Laredo
Nuevo Laredo
Reynosa
Brownsville
Matamoros
Monterrey
Saltillo
Torreón
Golfo de México
La Paz
Trópico de Cáncer
Ciudad Victoria
Mazatlán
Cabo San Lucas
Tula
Zacatecas
Tampico
San Luis Potosí
Aguascalientes
León
Guanajuato
Canal de Yucatán
Tizmín
Cancún
Mérida
Chichén Itzá
Cozumel
OCÉANO PACÍFICO
Puerto Vallarta
Guadalajara
Bahía de Campeche
Uxmal
Campeche
YUCATÁN
Teotihuacán
Morelia
México, D.F.
Jalapa
Veracruz
Islas Revillagigedo
Uruapan
Toluca
Cuernavaca
Puebla
Orizaba
Taxco
Río Balsas
Villahermosa
Belmopan
BELICE
Lago Petén Itzá
Tlapa
Oaxaca
ISTMO DE TEHUANTEPEC
Acapulco
Lago Isabel
GUATEMALA
San Pedro Sula
HONDURAS
Copán
Golfo de Tehuantepec
Guatemala
Tegucigalpa
San Salvador
EL SALVADOR
0 100 200 300 400 Km.
0 100 200 300 400 Mi.

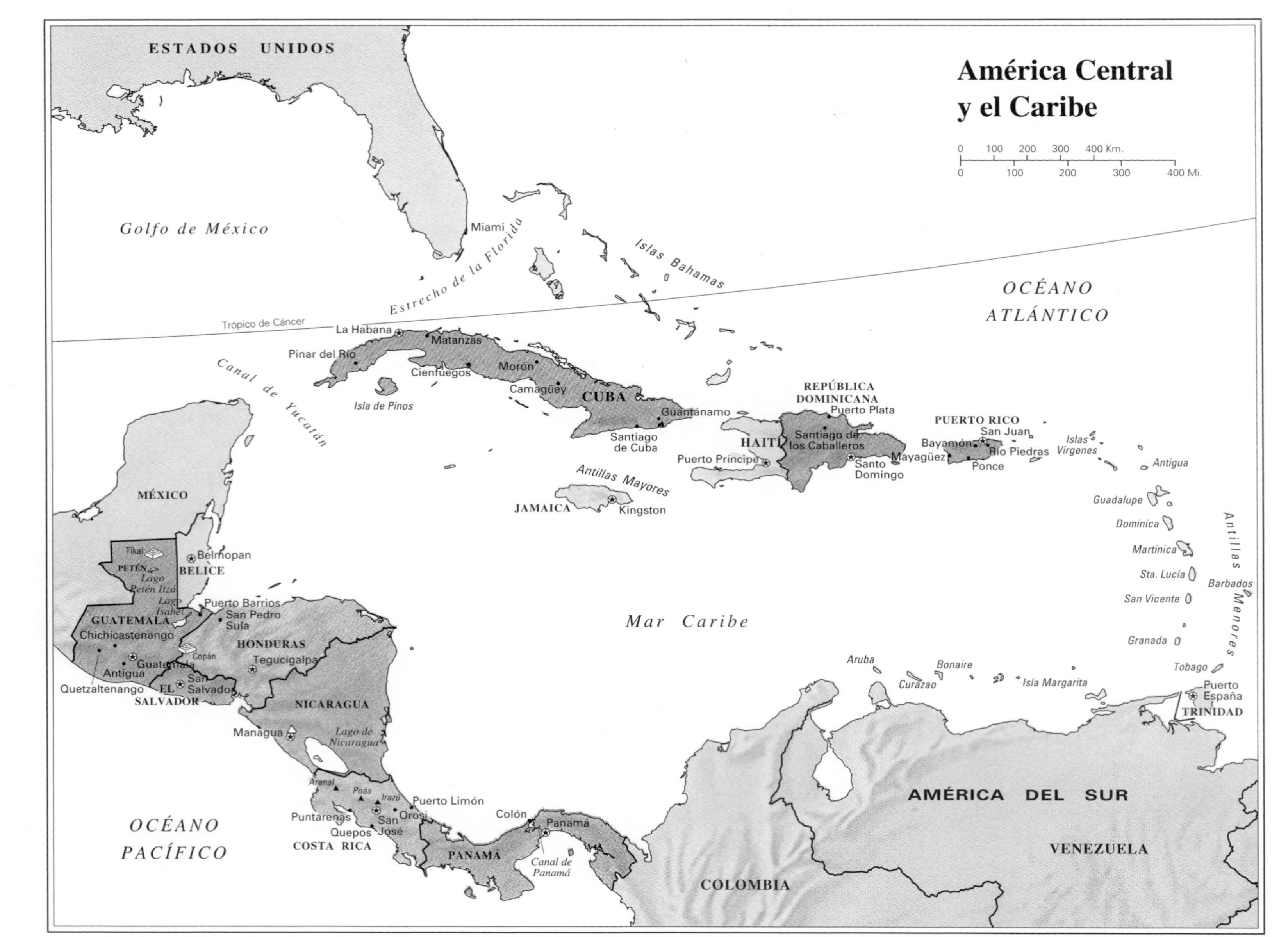
América Central
y el Caribe
0 100 200 300 400 Km.
0 100 200 300 400 Mi.
ESTADOS UNIDOS
Golfo de México
Miami
Estrecho de la Florida
Islas Bahamas
Trópico de Cáncer
OCÉANO ATLÁNTICO
La Habana
Matanzas
Pinar del Río
Cienfuegos
Morón
Camagüey
CUBA
Isla de Pinos
Canal de Yucatán
Guantánamo
Santiago de Cuba
REPÚBLICA DOMINICANA
Puerto Plata
Santiago de los Caballeros
Santo Domingo
HAITÍ
Puerto Príncipe
PUERTO RICO
San Juan
Bayamón
Río Piedras
Mayagüez
Ponce
Islas Vírgenes
Antigua
Guadalupe
Dominica
Martinica
Sta. Lucía
Barbados
San Vicente
Granada
Tobago
Antillas Menores
Antillas Mayores
JAMAICA
Kingston
MÉXICO
Tikal
PETÉN
Lago Petén Itzá
Belmopan
BELICE
Lago Isabel
GUATEMALA
Chichicastenango
Guatemala
Antigua
Quetzaltenango
Copán
EL SALVADOR
San Salvador
Puerto Barrios
San Pedro Sula
HONDURAS
Tegucigalpa
NICARAGUA
Managua
Lago de Nicaragua
Mar Caribe
Aruba
Curazao
Bonaire
Isla Margarita
Puerto España
TRINIDAD
Arenal
Poás
Irazú
Puerto Limón
Puntarenas
San José
Orosi
Quepos
COSTA RICA
Colón
Panamá
PANAMÁ
Canal de Panamá
OCÉANO PACÍFICO
COLOMBIA
AMÉRICA DEL SUR
VENEZUELA

THE BASIC SPANISH SERIES

BASIC SPANISH FOR TEACHERS

ENHANCED SECOND EDITION

Ana C. Jarvis
Chandler-Gilbert Community College

Raquel Lebredo
California Baptist University

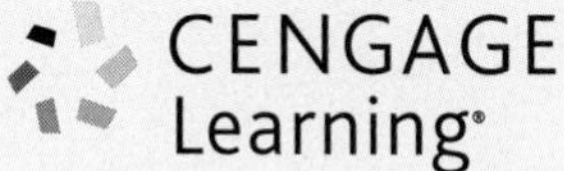

Australia • Brazil • Japan • Korea • Mexico • Singapore • Spain • United Kingdom • United States

Basic Spanish for Teachers,
Second Edition
Ana C. Jarvis and Raquel Lebredo

Product Director: Beth Kramer

Product Team Manager: Heather Bradley Cole

Product Manager: Mark Overstreet

Product Development Manager: Katie Wade

Associate Content Developer: Julie Allen

Marketing Director: Michelle Williams

Print Buyer: Betsy Donaghey

Cover Designer: Riezebos Holzbaur Design Group

Cover Image: istock

Art and Design Direction, Production Management, and Composition: Lumina Datamatics

Library of Congress Control Number: 2009941683

ISBN: 978-1-305-88599-8

Cengage Learning
20 Channel Center Street
Boston, MA 02210
USA

Cengage Learning is a leading provider of customized learning solutions with office locations around the globe, including Singapore, the United Kingdom, Australia, Mexico, Brazil, and Japan. Locate your local office at **international.cengage.com/region**

Cengage Learning products are represented in Canada by Nelson Education, Ltd.

For your course and learning solutions, visit **www.cengage.com.**

Purchase any of our products at your local college store or at our preferred online store **www.cengagebrain.com.**

Printed in the United States of America
Print Number: 01 Print Year: 2015

CONTENTS

PREFACE

Designed to fit multiple classroom styles, ***The Basic Spanish Series*** offers a flexible, concise introduction to Spanish grammar and communication with state-of-the-art online learning tools to better address the needs of today's students and professionals who need a working knowledge of Spanish.

Basic Spanish for Teachers

As a component of *The Basic Spanish Series, Basic Spanish for Teachers* is a career manual designed to serve those in the teaching professions who seek basic conversational skills in Spanish. Written for use in two-semester or three-quarter courses, it presents everyday situations that teachers may encounter at work settings such as public and private elementary, middle, and high schools when dealing with Spanish-speaking students and parents/guardians in the United States.

Basic Spanish for Teachers introduces practical vocabulary, everyday on-the-job situations, and culture notes (*Notas culturales*) written from a cross-cultural perspective. It provides students with opportunities to apply, in a wide variety of practical contexts, the grammatical structures presented in the corresponding lessons of the *Basic Spanish* core text.

Organization of the Text

Basic Spanish for Teachers contains one preliminary lesson *(Lección preliminar)*, twenty regular lessons, four reading sections *(Lecturas)*, and four review sections *(Repasos)*.

Each lesson contains the following sections:

- A **lesson opener** consists of the lesson objectives divided into two categories: Structures practiced from *Basic Spanish* and Communication.
- A **Spanish dialogue** introduces and employs key vocabulary and grammatical structures in the context of the lesson theme. Divided into manageable segments, the dialogue features contexts specific to the teaching professions. Audio recordings of the dialogues are available through the iLrn website. Translations of the dialogues can be found in the Instructor Resources folder on the iLrn website.
- The ***¡Escuchemos!*** activity and dialogue recording (available through iLrn) allow students to listen to the conversation and check their comprehension with true/false questions.
- The ***Vocabulario*** section summarizes new, active words and expressions presented in the dialogue, and categorizes them according to their parts of speech. The vocabulary highlights the most important communication tools needed in a variety of professional situations. A special subsection of cognates heads up the vocabulary list so students can readily identify these terms. The *Vocabulario adicional* subsection supplies supplementary vocabulary related to the lesson theme.
- ***Notas culturales,*** related to the lesson theme, give students up-to-date information that highlights Hispanic customs and traditions.
- ***Dígame...*** questions check students' comprehension of the dialogue.
- The ***Hablemos*** section provides personalized questions spun off from the lesson theme, where students are encouraged to work in pairs, asking and answering each of the questions presented.

- ***Vamos a practicar*** activities review grammar topics that students need to know before proceeding in the lesson.
- ***Conversaciones breves*** activities practice the lesson's vocabulary.
- The ***En estas situaciones*** section develops students' communication skills through role-playing in pairs or small groups and encourages more interactive speaking practice.
- The ***Casos*** activity establishes professional situations such as conversations between a teacher and student, between a teacher and parent, or between two teachers. The entire class participates in open-ended role-playing that re-creates and expands on the situations introduced in the dialogue and the *En estas situaciones* section.
- ***Un paso más*** features activities that practice the supplementary words and expressions in the *Vocabulario adicional* section, some through realia.
- Pair and group icons indicate pair and group activities.
- Audio icons show what is available either as downloadable In-text Audio MP3s or in audio flashcards on the iLrn website.
- Quiz Quiz icons indicate available resources on the *Basic Spanish for Teachers* iLrn website.
- **Five maps** of the Spanish-speaking world are included in the front and back of the text.
- For easy reference and to aid in lesson planning, the table of contents lists the **grammar structures** presented in the corresponding *Basic Spanish* text and practiced in *Basic Spanish for Teachers,* plus the communication objective for each lesson.
- The text's grammatical sequence parallels the core text of the series, *Basic Spanish.*

Organization of the *Lecturas*

A short reading section appears after every five lessons, containing the following materials:

- ***Lecturas*** present forms and handouts, such as a permission slip for a field trip, and rules of conduct.
- ***Dígame...*** activities check students' comprehension of the *Lectura.*

Organization of the *Repasos*

After every five lessons, a review section contains the following materials:

- ***Práctica de vocabulario*** exercises check students' cumulative knowledge and use of active vocabulary in a variety of formats: selecting the appropriate word to complete a sentence, identifying related words, matching, true/false, and puzzles.
- A ***Práctica oral*** section features questions that review key vocabulary and structures presented in the preceding five lessons. To develop students' aural and oral skills, the questions are available on the *Basic Spanish for Teachers* iLrn Language Learning Center.

Appendixes

The appendixes of this book include the following:

- **Appendix A, Introduction to Spanish Sounds and the Alphabet,** presents the alphabet and briefly explains vowel sounds, consonant sounds, linking, rhythm, intonation, syllable formation, and accentuation.
- **Appendix B, Verbs,** presents charts of the three regular conjugations and of the **-ar, -er**, and **-ir** stem-changing verbs, as well as lists of orthographic-changing verbs and some common irregular verbs.
- **Appendix C, Useful Classroom Expressions,** consists of a list of the most common expressions and directions used in the introductory Spanish-language class.
- **Appendix D, Weights and Measures,** features conversion formulas for temperature and metric weights and measures, as well as Spanish terms for U.S. weights and measures.

End Vocabularies

Comprehensive Spanish-English and English-Spanish vocabularies contain all words and expressions from the *Vocabulario* sections. Each term is followed by the lesson number where the active vocabulary is introduced. All passive vocabulary items found in the *Vocabulario adicional* sections, in marginal glosses to readings, and in glosses of direction lines or exercises are also included.

New to the Enhanced Second Edition

For this enhanced second edition, we are proud to offer an extensive technology program, which will give students easier access to required materials and give instructors the freedom to design their courses in the way that best meets their students' needs.

Basic Spanish for Teachers **iLrn Language Learning Center**, new to the enhanced second edition, allows students and instructors to access all the materials they need to prepare for class.

- Online, the core text *Basic Spanish* is transformed into a sophisticated, interactive eBook with built-in audio, note-taking features, and more.
- Students can **complete assignments** from *Basic Spanish for Teachers* entirely online. Many activities can be graded automatically, giving students instant results and saving the instructor hours of correcting time.
- Results from completed activities flow into the instructor **gradebook**, a customizable tool that allows instructors to grade open-ended writing activities—**including communicative and role-playing activities**—and assign scores according to his/her own schema.
- **Diagnostic tests** appear in every chapter in iLrn, and automatically design an individualized review plan based on student responses.
- New **Más práctica grammar activities** provide plenty of extra practice outside of class, freeing up precious class time for more high-level discussion.
- All-new **video content from National Geographic™** along with corresponding activities introduce students to the cultures and landscapes of twenty-one different Spanish-speaking countries.

Assets

Available on ***The Basic Spanish for Teachers* iLrn Language Learning Center**

For Students

- The **in-text audio** is available for listening online and in downloadable MP3 format.
- Brief **grammar videos** feature a professor teaching specific grammar topics presented in the core text; Flash-based **grammar tutorials** help students learn and understand Spanish grammar through succinct, interactive explanations and quizzes.
- An **answer key** for *Basic Spanish for Teachers* exercises is available to help students review for exams.
- **Text glossaries** provide support for learning and practicing vocabulary.
- The **iLrn website** includes access to additional quizzes, downloadable In-text Audio MP3s, audio-enabled flashcards, and Spanish pronunciation help.

For Instructors

- Instructors have access to **all iLrn content,** including resources for students. Instructor specific content is password-protected and is not available to students.
- For instructors transitioning to *The Basic Spanish Series* from a different text, a **sample syllabus** offers suggestions for dividing the material evenly through the course of a typical semester.
- A series of **PowerPoint presentations** reviews Spanish grammar and correlates to each chapter of *Basic Spanish*. An additional set of PowerPoints presents Spanish vocabulary from each chapter of *Basic Spanish for Teachers* and content from the *lecturas* as well.
- **Translations** for dialogues in *Basic Spanish for Teachers* are available for download.
- **Answer keys** are provided for exercises in *Basic Spanish for Teachers*, as well as for the self-directed tests.

Acknowledgments

We wish to thank our colleagues who have used previous editions of *Basic Spanish for Teachers* for their many constructive comments and suggestions:

Lupe V. Casillas, *Logan Elementary, El Paso, TX*
Julio Cordero-Ávila, *Boston Public Schools, Boston, MA*
Miguel Domínguez, *California State University, Dominguez Hills*
James Fonseca, *Molloy College*
Amarilis Hidalgo-De Jesus, *Bloomsburg University of Pennsylvania*
Robert Mena, *Cochise College*
Hugo Muñoz-Ballesteros, *Tarleton State University*
Loretta Salazar, *New Mexico Highlands University*
Elizabeth Ely Tolman, *University of North Carolina at Chapel Hill*

We wish to recognize the contributions of Sarah Link to this edition.

Finally, we extend our sincere appreciation to the World Languages team at Heinle Cengage Learning: Product Director, Beth Kramer; Product Team Manager, Heather Bradley Cole; Product Manager, Mark Overstreet; Product Development Manager, Katie Wade; and Assistant Content Developer, Julie Allen.

Ana C. Jarvis
Raquel Lebredo

Lección Preliminar: En el salón de clase

Objectives

Structures and Communication

- Greetings and farewells
- The alphabet
- Gender and number
- The definite and indefinite articles
- Cardinal numbers 0–39
- The present indicative of **ser**
- Uses of **hay**

iLrn™

The following illustration shows the names of people and things one sees in a classroom. Learn to say them in Spanish.

Nombre ______________________ Sección ______________ Fecha ______________

Conversaciones breves (*Brief conversations*)

A. —Buenos días, señorita Vega. ¿Cómo está usted?
—Muy bien, gracias, señor Pérez. ¿Y usted?
—Bien, gracias.
—Hasta mañana.
—Adiós.

B. —Buenas tardes, doctora Ramírez. Con permiso.
—Buenas tardes, señorita Soto. Pase y tome asiento, por favor.
—Gracias.

C. —Profesora Ortiz: el señor Méndez.
—Mucho gusto.
—El gusto es mío.
—¿De dónde es usted, señor Méndez?
—Soy de la Ciudad de México. ¿Y usted?
—Yo soy de Nicaragua.

D. —¿Qué fecha es hoy?
—Hoy es el cuatro de enero.
—¿Hoy es martes?
—No, hoy es lunes.

Nombre ______________________ Sección ____________ Fecha ____________

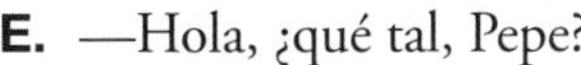

E. —Hola, ¿qué tal, Pepe?
—Bien, ¿y tú? ¿Qué hay de nuevo?
—No mucho.
—Hasta la vista.
—Chau.

F. —Hasta luego, Marisa.
—Adiós, Jorge. Saludos a María Isabel.

VOCABULARIO (*Vocabulary*)

Saludos y despedidas (*Greetings and farewells*)

Adiós. *Good-bye.*
Buenas noches. *Good evening, Good night (when leaving).*
Buenas tardes. *Good afternoon.*
Buenos días. *Good morning.*
Chau. *Bye.*
¿Cómo está usted? *How are you?*
Hasta la vista. *See you around.*
Hasta luego. *I'll see you later.*
Hasta mañana. *I'll see you tomorrow.*
Hola. *Hello. (Hi.)*
Muy bien, ¿y usted? *Very well, and you?*
¿Qué hay de nuevo? *What's new?*
¿Qué tal? *How's it going? (informal)*
Saludos a... *Say hello to . . .*

Expresiones de cortesía (*Polite expressions*)

Con permiso. *Excuse me.*
El gusto es mío. *The pleasure is mine.*
Gracias. *Thank you.*
Mucho gusto. *It's a pleasure (to meet you).*
Por favor. *Please.*

Palabras y expresiones útiles (*Useful words and expressions*)

el aula, el salón de clase *classroom*
bien *well, fine*
las conversaciones breves *brief conversations*
de *from*
¿De dónde...? *(From) where?*
hoy *today*

Nombre ______________________ Sección ______________ Fecha ______________

mucho *much*
muy *very*
no *no, not*
Pase. *Come in.*
¿Qué fecha es hoy? *What's the date today?*
soy *I am*
Tome asiento. *Have a seat.*
y *and*

Títulos (*Titles*)

doctor(a) (Dr./Dra.) *doctor*
profesor(a) *professor, teacher, instructor*
señor (Sr.) *Mr., sir, gentleman*
señora (Sra.) *Mrs., madam, lady*
señorita (Srta.) *Miss, young lady (unmarried)*

VOCABULARIO ADICIONAL (*Additional vocabulary*)

Algunas expresiones útiles (*Some useful expressions*)

When speaking to one student	*When speaking to the whole class*	*English equivalent*
1. Abre (Cierra) el libro.	Abran (Cierren) los libros.	*Open (Close) your books.*
2. Entrega la tarea (los exámenes).	Entreguen la tarea (los exámenes).	*Turn in your homework (exams).*
3. Escribe.	Escriban.	*Write.*
4. Escucha.	Escuchen.	*Listen.*
5. Estudia la lección ____.	Estudien la lección ____.	*Study lesson ____.*
6. Levanta la mano.	Levanten la mano.	*Raise your hand(s).*
7. No corras.	No corran.	*Don't run.*
8. No empujes.	No empujen.	*Don't push.*
9. Presta atención.	Presten atención.	*Pay attention.*
10. Siéntate.	Siéntense.	*Sit down.*
11. Silencio, por favor.	Silencio, por favor.	*Silence, please.*
12. Ve a la página ____.	Vayan a la página ____.	*Go to page ____.*
13. Ve a la pizarra.	Vayan a la pizarra.	*Go to the board.*
14. Vuelve a tu asiento.	Vuelvan a sus asientos.	*Go back to your seat(s).*

Notas Culturales

- Both **tú** and **usted** mean *you*. The **tú** form is used as the equivalent of *you* to address a friend, a coworker, a relative, or a child. The **usted** form is generally used to express deference or respect. In most Spanish-speaking countries today, young people tend to call each other **tú** even if they have just met. When in doubt, use **usted**.

Nombre ______________________ Sección ____________ Fecha ____________

- María is a very popular name in Spain and Latin America. It is frequently used in conjunction with other names: María Isabel, Ana María, María Teresa, María Inés, and so on. It is also used as a middle name for men: for example, José María, Luis María, and Jesús María.
- Cognates (**Cognados**) are words that are similar in spelling and meaning in two languages. Some Spanish cognates are identical to English words. In other instances, the words differ only in minor or predictable ways. There are many Spanish cognates related to education and the teaching profession, as illustrated in the following list. Learning to recognize and use cognates will help you to acquire vocabulary more rapidly and to read and speak Spanish more fluently.

el arte	*art*	**las instrucciones**	*instructions*
la atención	*attention*	**la literatura**	*literature*
la cafetería	*cafeteria*	**las matemáticas**	*mathematics*
las ciencias	*science(s)*	**la multiplicación**	*multiplication*
la clase	*class*	**la música**	*music*
la comprensión	*comprehension*	**la participación**	*participation*
la división	*division*	**el problema**	*problem*

Actividades

Dígame... (*Tell me . . .*) Write appropriate responses to the following.

1. Buenos días, señora.

____

2. Hola, ¿qué tal?

____

3. ¿Cómo está usted?

____

4. Mucho gusto, señor.

____

5. ¿Qué fecha es hoy?

____

6. ¿Qué día es hoy?

____

7. ¿Qué hay de nuevo?

____

8. ¿De dónde es usted?

____

9. Hasta la vista.

____

10. Hasta mañana.

____

Quiz

Vamos a practicar (*Let's practice*)

A Write how many of the following items there are in your classroom.

Modelo doors
Hay dos puertas.

1. teachers: ____________________
2. desks: ____________________
3. windows: ____________________
4. chalkboards: ____________________
5. students: ____________________
6. books: ____________________
7. lights: ____________________

B You are responsible for scheduling parent-teacher conferences. In order to verify that you have written the following names correctly in the appointment book, spell each one in Spanish.

Modelo Rojas
ere - o - jota - a - ese

1. Sandoval ____________________
2. Fuentes ____________________
3. Varela ____________________
4. Ugarte ____________________
5. Barrios ____________________
6. Zubizarreta ____________________

Nombre ______________________ Sección ____________ Fecha ____________

C Write the definite article before each noun and then write the plural form.

MODELO __________ bolígrafo
el bolígrafo **los bolígrafos**

1. __________ silla __________________
2. __________ maestro __________________
3. __________ señor __________________
4. __________ conversación __________________
5. __________ fecha __________________
6. __________ doctor __________________
7. __________ borrador __________________
8. __________ tiza __________________
9. __________ cuaderno __________________
10. __________ regla __________________

D Complete the following exchange, using the present indicative of the verb **ser.**

MODELO Tú __________ de Colorado.
Tú **eres** de Colorado.

—El señor Soto y la señora Arriola __________ profesores.

—¿De dónde __________?

—De México. ¿Y ustedes?

—Nosotros __________ de Guatemala. Yo __________ maestro y Carlos __________ profesor.

En estas situaciones (*In these situations*)

With two or more classmates, act out the following situations in Spanish.

1. You meet Dr. Pérez in the morning and ask how she is.
2. You are at an evening parent-teacher conference. You greet Mrs. Peña.
3. You see your professor in the afternoon. You greet him/her.
4. You greet your friend Carlos and ask what's new with him.
5. One of your relatives asks you how you are.
6. You are leaving your friend María, whom you're going to see again that same day.

7. You ask your professor where he/she is from.
8. You ask a third grade student where he/she is from.
9. You ask someone to say “hi” to your best friend.

Una actividad Name the people and objects in the following illustration.

1. ______________________________
2. ______________________________
3. ______________________________
4. ______________________________
5. ______________________________
6. ______________________________
7. ______________________________
8. ______________________________
9. ______________________________
10. ______________________________

Nombre ______________________ Sección ____________ Fecha ____________

11. ______________________
12. ______________________
13. ______________________
14. ______________________
15. ______________________
16. ______________________
17. ______________________
18. ______________________
19. ______________________
20. ______________________

Un paso más (*One step further*)

Review the **Vocabulario adicional** in this lesson and match the phrases in column **A** with their English equivalents in column **B**.

A	B
______ **1.** Escriban.	**a.** Sit down.
______ **2.** Ve a la pizarra.	**b.** Don't run.
______ **3.** Vayan a la página ______.	**c.** Listen.
______ **4.** Entreguen la tarea.	**d.** Go back to your seat.
______ **5.** Presten atención.	**e.** Write.
______ **6.** Escucha.	**f.** Open your books.
______ **7.** Levanta la mano.	**g.** Don't push.
______ **8.** No corras.	**h.** Go to the board.
______ **9.** Estudien la lección.	**i.** Study the lesson.
______ **10.** Siéntense.	**j.** Go to page ______.
______ **11.** Silencio, por favor.	**k.** Turn in your homework.
______ **12.** No empujes.	**l.** Pay attention.
______ **13.** Vuelve a tu asiento.	**m.** Silence, please.
______ **14.** Abran sus libros.	**n.** Raise your hand.

Conversaciones con la maestra

Objectives

Structures

- Subject pronouns
- The present indicative of regular **-ar** verbs
- Interrogative and negative sentences
- Forms and position of adjectives

Communication

- Talking to parents about their children

iLrn™

La maestra habla con la[1] señora Vera.

Maestra —María Inés es una niña muy inteligente, pero necesita estudiar más.
Sra. Vera —No trabaja mucho, ¿verdad?
Maestra —No, y siempre habla en clase.
Sra. Vera —¿Participa en clase?
Maestra —Muy poco. Y a veces no presta mucha atención.
Sra. Vera —¿Qué necesita estudiar?
Maestra —Necesita repasar las tablas de multiplicar. También necesita leer más.
Sra. Vera —Siempre lleva tarea a casa.
Maestra —Sí, porque nunca termina el trabajo aquí.
Sra. Vera —Bueno, la niña necesita mejorar.
Maestra —Sí, necesita ayuda.

A las cinco y cuarto de la tarde, la maestra habla con el señor Alba.

Sr. Alba —¿Hay algún problema con José?
Maestra —No, no hay problemas serios. José trabaja muy bien. Ya suma, resta y multiplica.

[1]When referring to a third person and using a title, the definite article is used.

Nombre ______________ Sección ______________ Fecha ______________

Sr. Alba —¿Y en lectura?
Maestra —Bueno... a veces no escucha las instrucciones y no participa mucho en las actividades de grupo.
Sr. Alba —José trabaja mejor independientemente.
Maestra —Sí, pero a veces necesita trabajar con los otros niños.
Sr. Alba —Sí. ¡Ah! ¿Qué significa la "O" en la libreta de calificaciones?
Maestra —La "O" significa "sobresaliente", la "S", "satisfactorio" y la "N", "necesita mejorar".
Sr. Alba —Muy bien. Muchas gracias. ¿Dónde firmo?
Maestra —Aquí, por favor.
Sr. Alba —¿Qué hora es, señorita?
Maestra —Son las cinco y media. Gracias por venir, señor Alba.

¡Escuchemos!

While listening to the dialogue, circle **V (verdadero)** if the statement is true and **F (falso)** if it is false.

1. María Inés no es muy inteligente. V F
2. María Inés habla en clase. V F
3. María Inés no participa mucho en clase. V F
4. María Inés siempre presta atención. V F
5. María Inés nunca lleva tarea a casa. V F
6. María Inés necesita mejorar. V F
7. José no siempre escucha las instrucciones. V F
8. José trabaja mejor con los otros niños. V F
9. En la libreta de calificaciones, la "O" significa "sobresaliente". V F
10. La "N" significa "satisfactorio". V F

Nombre ______________________ Sección ____________ Fecha ____________

VOCABULARIO

Cognados (*Cognates*)

la clase
independientemente
inteligente
la instrucción
el problema
satisfactorio(a)
serio(a)

Nombres (*Nouns*)

las actividades de grupo *group activities*
la ayuda *help*
la lectura *reading*
la libreta de calificaciones, la boleta de calificaciones (*Méx.*), **la tarjeta de notas** (*Puerto Rico*) *report card*
la materia *subject*
el (la) niño(a) *child*
la tarea *homework*
el trabajo *work*

Verbos (*Verbs*)

escuchar *to listen*
estudiar *to study*
firmar *to sign*
hablar *to speak*
llevar *to take, to carry*
mejorar *to improve, to get better*
multiplicar *to multiply*
necesitar *to need*
participar *to participate*
repasar *to review*
restar *to subtract*
significar *to mean, to stand for, to signify*
sumar *to add, to add up*
terminar, acabar *to finish*
trabajar *to work*

Adjetivos (*Adjectives*)

mucho(a) *much*
muchos(as) *many*
otro(a) *other, another*
sobresaliente *outstanding*

Otras palabras y expresiones (*Other words and expressions*)

a *at*
a casa *home*
a veces *sometimes*
algún *any*
aquí *here*
bueno... *well . . .*
con *with*
¿dónde? *where?*
en *in*
Gracias por venir. *Thanks for coming.*
leer más *to read more*
más *more*
mejor *better*
mucho *much, a lot*
muy poco *very little*
nunca *never*
pero *but*
porque[1] *because*
prestar atención *to pay attention*
¿qué? *what?*
¿Qué hora es? *What time is it?*
¿Qué significa...? *What does . . . mean?*
sí *yes*
siempre *always*
Son las (+ *time*).[2] *It's* (+ *time*).
las tablas de multiplicar *multiplication tables*
también *also*
¿verdad? *right?, true?*
ya *already*

[1] *why?* **¿Por qué?**
[2] **Es la una** is used to express *It's one o'clock.*

Nombre ______________________ Sección ______________ Fecha ______________

VOCABULARIO ADICIONAL

Lectura (*Reading*)

la comprensión *comprehension*
la lectura oral *oral reading*
los sonidos *sounds*

Aritmética, matemáticas (*Arithmetic, mathematics*)

la división *division*
la multiplicación *multiplication*
la resta *subtraction*
la suma *addition*

Lenguaje (*Language*)

la gramática *grammar*
la ortografía *spelling*

Otras materias (*Other subjects*)

el arte *art*
la educación física *physical education*
los estudios sociales *social studies*
la música *music*

Comportamiento (*Behavior*)

la conducta *conduct, citizenship*
la cooperación *cooperation*
el esfuerzo *effort*

Notas Culturales

- According to the United States Census Bureau, out of a total United States population of approximately 302 million, approximately 46.9 million are Latino. The largest Latino groups are Mexican Americans (64%), Puerto Ricans (9%), Cubans (3.5%), Salvadorean (3.1%), Dominican (2.9%), and other Central and South Americans (17.7%). The states with the highest Latino populations are California, Texas, New York, Florida, Illinois, Arizona, New Jersey, New Mexico, and Colorado. More than half of all Hispanic Americans live in Califonia and Texas alone. Over 90% of Hispanic Americans live in urban areas, compared to 73% of non-Hispanics.
- It is important to remember that Latinos in the United States do not constitute a homogeneous ethnic group. They have significant cultural, racial, and ethnic differences resulting from various combinations of Spanish, indigenous, African, European, and mestizo traditions. They have different immigration stories, even within a single national group: the term "Mexican American," for example, may identify both recent immigrants and persons whose families have lived in what is now the United States since the sixteenth century. Nevertheless, familiarity with certain underlying cultural traditions and values predominant in Spanish-speaking countries may provide teachers of less acculturated Latino students with insights into their students' assumptions regarding appropriate classroom behavior, actions, or attitudes that are likely to be rewarded, and expectations of teachers or other authority figures at school.

Nombre ______________________ Sección ____________ Fecha ____________

Actividades

Dígame... Answer the following questions, basing your answers on the dialogues.

1. Según (*According to*) la maestra, ¿cómo es[1] María Inés y qué necesita hacer (*to do*)?

2. ¿Participa María Inés en clase? ¿Trabaja mucho o habla mucho?

3. ¿Qué necesita repasar la niña?

4. ¿Necesita María Inés leer más también?

5. ¿María Inés lleva tarea a casa? ¿Por qué?

6. Según la señora Vera, ¿qué necesita María Inés? ¿Y según la maestra?

7. ¿Hay problemas serios con José? ¿Trabaja bien?

8. ¿Escucha José las instrucciones?

9. ¿José participa en las actividades de grupo? ¿Qué necesita hacer a veces?

10. ¿Qué significa la "N" en la libreta de calificaciones? ¿Y la "O"? ¿Y la "S"?

Hablemos With a partner, take turns asking each other the following questions.

1. ¿Trabaja usted mucho?
2. ¿Trabaja usted mejor independientemente o con otros estudiantes?

[1] *What is she like?*

Nombre ______________________ Sección ____________ Fecha ____________

3. ¿Necesita usted estudiar más?
4. ¿Presta usted atención en clase?
5. ¿Lleva usted tarea a casa?
6. ¿Necesita usted repasar la lección preliminar?
7. ¿Terminamos la tarea de español en la clase?
8. ¿Participan ustedes en clase?
9. ¿Necesitan ustedes ayuda?
10. ¿Qué hora es?

Quiz

VAMOS A PRACTICAR

A Rewrite the following sentences or questions using the new subjects. Be sure to make all necessary changes.

MODELO Yo hablo con Eva. (Nosotros)
Nosotros hablamos con Eva.

1. ¿Roberto ya suma, resta y multiplica?

   ¿Ellos ______________________________?

2. ¿Dónde firmo?

   ¿ ______________________________ usted?

3. Elena termina la tarea a las doce de la noche.

   Nosotros ______________________________.

4. Juan no presta atención en clase.

   Tú ______________________________.

5. Mejoramos porque repasamos las lecciones.

   La niña ______________________________.

6. Tú escuchas las instrucciones.

   Yo ______________________________.

7. Yo estudio mucho.

   Roberto y yo ______.

8. La niña no necesita ayuda.

   Tú ______.

B Write negative sentences using the subject and verb cues provided. Add words from the dialogue to provide as much information as possible.

MODELO ella / llevar
Ella no lleva tarea a casa.

1. ellos / terminar

   ______

2. nosotros / participar

   ______

3. yo / hablar

   ______

4. él / trabajar

   ______

5. tú / necesitar

   ______

C Rewrite the following, making the adjectives agree with the new noun or pronoun.

MODELO otro niño (niñas)
otras niñas

1. señor inteligente (señoritas)

   ______

2. muchos libros (plumas)

   ______

3. problema serio (problemas)

   ______

Nombre ______________ Sección ______________ Fecha ______________

4. otra tarea (trabajos)

____

5. mucho trabajo (atención)

____

Conversaciones breves

Complete the following dialogue using your imagination and the vocabulary from this lesson.

Una conversación.

Sra. Paz —____

Maestra —No, señora, la niña nunca termina la tarea.

Sra. Paz —____

Maestra —Sí, señora, habla mucho en clase.

Sra. Paz —____

Maestra —No, no participa mucho en clase y no presta atención.

Sra. Paz —____

Maestra —Sí, señora, suma y resta bien, pero no multiplica bien.

Sra. Paz —____

Maestra —Lleva tarea a la casa porque no termina el trabajo aquí.

Sra. Paz —____

Maestra —Sí, trabaja bien con los otros niños, pero a veces no escucha las instrucciones.

Sra. Paz —____

Maestra —Sí, la niña necesita mucha ayuda.

Sra. Paz —____

Maestra —Sí, también necesita mejorar en lectura.

Sra. Paz —____

Maestra —Aquí, por favor.

Sra. Paz —____

En estas situaciones

With two or more classmates, act out the following situations in Spanish.

1. You are talking to Diego's father. Tell him that Diego is very intelligent but that he does not pay attention. Tell him also that he needs to review the multiplication tables.
2. You are a parent. Ask your child's teacher if your child needs help. Tell him/her that your child always takes homework home. Ask if your child does not finish the work in class.

Nombre ______________ Sección ______________ Fecha ______________

3. You are explaining the grading system to a parent. Tell him/her what *O, S,* and *N* stand for.
4. You are a parent. Tell your child's teacher that Luis works well with other children, but he does not work very well independently.
5. You are talking with your child's teacher. Ask him/her if there is any serious problem with the child, and if he/she needs to improve. Then ask what time it is.

Casos (*Cases*)

With you and a partner playing the roles, work through the following scenarios.

1. A teacher holds a conference with the parent of a very good student.
2. A teacher holds a conference with the parent of a very poor student to discuss problems he/she is having in school.

Un paso más

Review the **Vocabulario adicional** in this lesson and write the Spanish equivalent of the following words.

1. subtraction ______________
2. vocabulary ______________
3. grammar ______________
4. reading ______________
5. citizenship ______________
6. addition ______________
7. comprehension ______________
8. spelling ______________
9. physical education ______________
10. art ______________
11. music ______________
12. multiplication ______________
13. effort ______________
14. division ______________
15. mathematics ______________

Actividad en grupo (*Group activity*)

Ana María Sánchez, a student in your class, is quite intelligent but does as little as possible and is quite talkative. She is very good in math and a great athlete. She generally does poorly in language arts, but does a decent job in art and music.

In groups of three or four, decide what grades (**sobresaliente, satisfactorio, necesita mejorar**) you are going to give Ana María in the subjects listed above.

Lección 2

En la escuela

Objectives

Structures

- The present indicative of regular **-er** and **-ir** verbs
- Possession with **de**
- Agreement of articles, nouns, and adjectives
- Possessive adjectives

Communication

- In the classroom: taking attendance
- Answering students' questions about an assignment

iLrn™

La Sra. Soto habla con sus alumnos en la clase. Primero pasa lista.

Sra. Soto —Buenos días, niños. ¿Cómo están?
Niños —Buenos días, maestra.
Sra. Soto —(*Pasa lista.*) José Flores.
José —Presente.
Sra. Soto —Ana Rodríguez.
Carlos —Ausente...

Después de pasar lista:

Sra. Soto —(*A Carlos.*) ¿Necesitas lápiz y papel?
Carlos —No, pero necesito el libro de lectura.
Sra. Soto —Siempre debes traer tu libro de lectura a la escuela, Carlos.
María —Maestra, ¿escribo la fecha en la pizarra?
Sra. Soto —Sí, María. Raúl, ¿qué fecha es hoy?
Raúl —Hoy es el veinticinco de septiembre.
Lupe —¿Qué páginas leemos hoy, señorita?[1]

[1]In most Latin American countries, students call their female teachers **señorita** regardless of their marital status.

Sra. Soto —Hoy deben leer las páginas trece, catorce y quince.
Lupe —¿Leemos en voz alta?
Sra. Soto —No, con la vista... ¡Silencio, niños! Por favor.

Después de la hora de la lectura todos trabajan en grupos. La maestra ayuda a los niños.

Julio —Maestra, Alicia y yo necesitamos lápices de colores.
Sra. Soto —Muy bien. Aquí hay lápices rojos, azules, amarillos, anaranjados, rosados y marrones para colorear.
Julio —¿Abro la ventana, maestra?
Sra. Soto —Sí, por favor.
Carmen —Necesito ir al baño, señora.
Sra. Soto —Debes esperar un minuto, Carmen.
Rosa —¿Borro las palabras de la pizarra?
Sra. Soto —No, todavía no. Todos deben copiar el vocabulario en el cuaderno de ejercicios.

Entra la secretaria.

Secretaria —Buenos días, Sra. Soto. Soy Amanda García, la nueva secretaria; perdone la molestia, pero necesito saber si algunos de sus estudiantes no comen en la cafetería hoy.
Sra. Soto —Aquí tiene la lista, señora.

La secretaria lleva la lista de la maestra a la dirección.

¡Escuchemos! While listening to the dialogue, circle **V (verdadero)** if the statement is true and **F (falso)** if it is false.

1.	Carlos necesita papel.	V	F
2.	Carlos no siempre trae su libro de lectura a la escuela.	V	F
3.	María escribe la fecha en la pizarra.	V	F
4.	Hoy es el quince de septiembre.	V	F
5.	Los niños deben leer con la vista.	V	F
6.	Los niños trabajan en grupos.	V	F
7.	La maestra necesita lápices de colores.	V	F
8.	La maestra necesita ir al baño.	V	F
9.	Los niños escriben en el cuaderno de ejercicios.	V	F
10.	La Sra. Soto es la nueva secretaria.	V	F

Nombre ______________ Sección ______________ Fecha ______________

VOCABULARIO

Cognados

la cafetería, el comedor (*Méx.*)
el grupo
la lista
el minuto
presente
el (la) secretario(a)
el silencio
el vocabulario

Nombres

el baño *bathroom*
el cuaderno de ejercicios *workbook*
la dirección *principal's office*
la escuela *school*
la fecha *date*
la hora de lectura *reading time*
los lápices de colores *colored pencils*
el libro de lectura *reading book*
los (las) niños(as) *children*
la página *page*
la palabra *word*
el papel *paper*

Verbos

abrir *to open*
ayudar *to help*
borrar *to erase*
colorear *to color*
comer *to eat*
copiar *to copy*
deber *must, should*
entrar (en) *to enter*
escribir *to write*
esperar *to wait*
saber *to know*[1]
ser *to be*
traer[2] *to bring*

Adjetivos

amarillo(a) *yellow*
anaranjado(a) *orange*
ausente *absent*
azul *blue*
marrón, café (*Méx.*), **carmelita** (*Cuba*) *brown*
nuevo(a) *new*
rojo(a) *red*
rosado(a), rosa *pink*

Otras palabras y expresiones

a la escuela *to school*
algunos(as) *some*
Aquí tiene... *Here is . . .*
¿Cómo están? *How are you? (when talking to more than one person)*
con la vista, en silencio *silently (reading)*
después (de) *after*
en *on, at*
en voz alta *aloud*
hay *there is, there are*
ir al baño *to go to the bathroom*
más tarde *later*
pasar lista *to take roll, to take attendance*
Perdone la molestia. *Excuse the interruption.*
primero(a) *first*
si *if*
todavía no *not yet*
todos(as) *all, everybody*

---

[1]Irregular first person: **yo sé**
[2]Irregular first person: **yo traigo**

Nombre ______________________ Sección ______________ Fecha ______________

VOCABULARIO ADICIONAL

Para hablar de los colores (*To talk about colors*)

azul celeste *sky blue*
azul marino *navy blue*
beige *beige*
blanco(a) *white*
claro(a) *light*
dorado(a) *golden*
gris *gray*
morado(a), violeta *purple*
negro(a) *black*
oscuro(a) *dark*
plateado(a) *silver, silvery*
verde *green*

Más palabras interrogativas (*More interrogative words*)

¿cómo? *how?*
¿cuál?, ¿cuáles? *which?, what?*
¿cuándo? *when?*
¿cuánto? *how much?*
¿cuántos(as)? *how many?*
¿para qué? *what for?*
¿por qué? *why?*
¿quién(es)? *who, whom?*

Personas que trabajan en la escuela (*People who work in schools*)

el (la) bibliotecario(a) *librarian*
el (la) conserje *janitor*
el (la) director(a) *principal*
el (la) enfermero(a) *nurse*
el (la) psicólogo(a) *psychologist*
el (la) subdirector(a) *vice principal*

Notas Culturales

In most Spanish-speaking countries, the numeral indicating the day is written before the month. For example, 3/10/10 refers to **el 3 de octubre de 2010**, *not* March 10, 2010. To avoid misunderstandings, dates are best spelled out rather than indicated numerically in notices sent home to inform parents of important upcoming events.

Actividades

Dígame... Answer the following questions, basing your answers on the dialogue.

1. ¿Con quiénes habla la Sra. Soto? ¿Pasa lista?

____

2. ¿Carlos necesita lápiz y papel? ¿Qué necesita?

____

Nombre ______________________ Sección ____________ Fecha ____________

3. ¿Quién escribe la fecha en la pizarra? ¿Qué fecha es?

____

4. ¿Qué páginas deben leer los alumnos de la Sra. Soto?

____

5. ¿Deben los niños leer en voz alta? ¿Cómo deben leer?

____

6. ¿Cómo trabajan los niños? ¿La maestra ayuda a sus alumnos?

____

7. ¿Qué hay para colorear? ¿De qué colores son los lápices?

____

8. ¿Qué abre Julio?

____

9. ¿Qué necesita Carmen? ¿Cuánto debe esperar?

____

10. ¿Dónde deben copiar los niños el vocabulario?

____

11. ¿Quién entra en la clase? ¿Qué necesita saber?

____

12. ¿Qué lleva la Sra. García a la dirección?

____

Hablemos With a partner, take turns asking each other the following questions.

1. ¿Quién es Ud.?
2. ¿Es Ud. maestro(a)?
3. ¿Escribe Ud. con lápiz o con pluma?
4. ¿Qué copia Ud. en su cuaderno de ejercicios?
5. ¿Lee Ud. en silencio o en voz alta?
6. ¿Pasa el profesor (la profesora) lista en la clase de español?
7. ¿A qué hora entra Ud. en la clase de español?

Nombre ______________________ Sección ____________ Fecha ____________

8. ¿Qué libros debemos traer a la clase de español?
9. ¿Con qué escribe Ud. en la pizarra? ¿Y en su cuaderno?
10. ¿Hay muchos estudiantes ausentes hoy?
11. ¿Come Ud. en la cafetería mañana? ¿A qué hora come?
12. ¿Qué fecha es hoy? ¿Qué día es hoy?

Quiz

VAMOS A PRACTICAR

A Complete the following sentences with the Spanish equivalent of the words in parentheses.

MODELO Ellos necesitan __________ (*the red pens*).
Ellos necesitan **las plumas rojas.**

1. Yo necesito __________ (*the black pencil*) y ella necesita __________ (*the white chalks*).
2. Yo llevo __________ (*my students*) a la cafetería y ella ayuda __________ (*the other children*) en la clase.
3. __________ (*Miss Alvarado's students*) no participan mucho en clase.
4. Necesitas traer __________ (*Ernesto's reading book*) a la clase mañana.

B Write sentences, using the subjects and verbs given and adding any necessary words.

MODELO yo / escribir
Yo escribo en la pizarra.

1. nosotros / comer ______________________________
2. tú / traer ______________________________
3. Armando / leer ______________________________
4. los niños / abrir ______________________________
5. yo / deber ______________________________
6. Uds. / escribir ______________________________

Nombre ______________________ Sección ____________ Fecha ____________

C Complete the following, using the appropriate possessive adjectives that refer to the subject of each sentence.

Modelo Arturo necesita ____________ libro.
Arturo necesita **su** libro.

1. Yo necesito ____________ cuadernos y ella necesita ____________ bolígrafo.
2. Nosotros hablamos con ____________ maestra y tú hablas con ____________ profesor.
3. Los niños esperan a ____________ maestro.
4. Ana y yo ayudamos a ____________ profesores.
5. ¿Tú necesitas ____________ lápices de colores?

Conversaciones breves

Complete the following dialogue, using your imagination and the vocabulary from this lesson.

La maestra habla con Rosita y con Carlos.

Maestra —Rosita, es la hora de lectura.

Rosita —____

Maestra —¿Necesitas el libro de lectura? Pero Rosita, siempre debes traer tu libro a clase.

Rosita —____

Maestra —Primero debes leer la página 15 y después la página 16.

Rosita —____

Maestra —No. Debes leer en voz alta.

Carlos —____

Maestra —No, todavía no debes borrar la pizarra. Debes esperar un minuto.

Carlos —____

Maestra —Sí, necesitas repasar el vocabulario.

Carlos —____

Maestra —Hoy es el 12 de mayo.

En estas situaciones

With two or more classmates, act out the following situations in Spanish.

1. Greet your students and ask them how they are. Respond to a student who volunteers to erase the chalkboard.
2. Tell your students that they must write the date in their notebook. Today is May second.

Nombre ______________________ Sección ____________ Fecha ____________

3. You are in your Spanish class. The teacher is taking attendance. Respond when your name is called, and answer for a student who is not there. Then ask your teacher what pages you should study, and whether you should read aloud or silently.
4. Your students are being very noisy. One of them needs to go to the bathroom, and another needs a pen and some paper. You need to restore order and to tell them everybody must copy the vocabulary in the workbook.
5. One of your students always forgets to bring the reading book to class. Talk to him/her.
6. You need to interrupt Mr. Valenzuela's class. Apologize and identify yourself.

Casos With you and a partner playing the roles, work through the following scenarios.

1. A teacher converses in class with his/her students. (One partner will play the role of several students.)
2. Two students discuss the things they do in their classroom.

Un paso más

A Review the **Vocabulario adicional** in this lesson and then write the questions that elicited the responses given.

1. ______________________________

   Bien, gracias. ¿Y usted?

2. ______________________________

   Los niños estudian el vocabulario los lunes.

3. ______________________________

   Irma borra la pizarra.

4. ______________________________

   Necesito seis lápices.

5. ______________________________

   No aprende porque no presta atención.

6. ______________________________

   No necesito mucho dinero (*money*). Necesito cinco dólares.

Nombre ______________________ Sección ______________ Fecha ______________

B Complete the following sentences with the appropriate word.

1. El color rojo y el color azul forman (*form*) el color ___________.
2. No necesito un lápiz azul claro. Necesito un lápiz azul ___________.
3. El color negro y el color blanco forman el color ___________.
4. La secretaria trabaja con el director y con la ___________.
5. La ___________ trabaja en la escuela los lunes y en el hospital los martes.
6. El color amarillo y el color azul forman el color ___________.
7. El ___________ limpia (*cleans*) la escuela.
8. La ___________ trae los libros.
9. El ___________ habla de psicología.
10. No necesitamos papeles plateados; necesitamos papeles ___________.
11. El uniforme no es azul celeste; es azul ___________.
12. El ___________ es un color marrón muy, muy claro.

Actividad en grupo In groups of three or four, come up with a list of activities for your class today. Decide also what items you are going to need to complete the activities.

Lección 3

Una lección de lenguaje

Objectives

Structures

- The irregular verbs **ir, dar,** and **estar**
- **Ir a** + infinitive
- Uses of the verbs **ser** and **estar**
- Contractions

Communication

- A grammar lesson: explaining grammar to students

iLrn™

Los alumnos del Sr. Mena repasan el material para el examen de lenguaje.

Maestro —Hoy vamos a repasar las partes de la oración.
Antonio —¿En qué página están los ejercicios, maestro?
Maestro —En la página cuarenta. Deben subrayar los verbos, los nombres y los adjetivos.
Teresa —¿Vamos a escribir oraciones con las palabras nuevas?
Maestro —Sí, deben escribir una oración con cada palabra nueva.
Tomás —¿Cómo se escribe "Phoenix", maestro?
Maestro —Pe-hache-o-e-ene-i-equis.
Tomás —¿Con *P* mayúscula o con *p* minúscula?
Maestro —Siempre debes escribir los nombres propios con letra mayúscula.
Jorge —¿Cuándo es el examen de ortografía? ¿Va a ser fácil o difícil?
Maestro —El viernes, y no va a ser muy difícil. ¡Ah, Jorge! ¿Dónde está tu composición?
Jorge —Está en mi casa. No está terminada todavía.
Alicia —¿Cuáles son las palabras que debemos aprender para el examen de ortografía?
Maestro —Todas. También deben dar el significado de cada una.
Teresa —Aquí están mis oraciones. ¿Están bien así?
Maestro —Sí, muy bien. Tu letra es muy bonita y muy clara.
Oscar —Mi trabajo está mal, ¿verdad?
Maestro —No, tus oraciones están bien, pero debes escribir con más cuidado.

Olga —Maestro, necesito usar el sacapuntas.
Maestro —Está roto. Debes ir a la oficina para usar el sacapuntas de la secretaria.
Olga —¿Voy ahora o después?
Maestro —Ahora.
Rafael —Señor, ¿cómo se dice "regla" en inglés?
Maestro —*Ruler.* Rafael, debes aprender a[1] buscar las palabras en el diccionario.

Regresa Olga.

Olga —Disculpe, Sr. Mena. Llaman a Jorge Rodríguez por teléfono. ¡Es una emergencia!
Jorge —¿Adónde debo ir?
Maestro —Debes ir a la dirección ahora mismo.

Los alumnos terminan el repaso y guardan los libros. Es la hora del recreo y todos van al patio.

¡Escuchemos!

While listening to the dialogue, circle **V (verdadero)** if the statement is true and **F (falso)** if it is false.

1.	Los estudiantes van a repasar la página cuarenta.	V	F
2.	Los niños deben escribir oraciones.	V	F
3.	Debemos escribir los nombres propios con letra minúscula.	V	F
4.	La composición de Jorge está en su casa.	V	F
5.	Para el examen, los niños no necesitan aprender todas las palabras.	V	F
6.	El sacapuntas está roto.	V	F
7.	Rafael necesita aprender a buscar las palabras en su libro de lenguaje.	V	F
8.	Llaman a Jorge por teléfono.	V	F
9.	Jorge debe ir a la dirección mañana.	V	F
10.	A la hora del recreo, los alumnos van a su casa.	V	F

[1]After **aprender,** the preposition **a** is used before the infinitive.

Nombre ______________ Sección ________ Fecha ________

VOCABULARIO

Cognados

el adjetivo
la composición
el diccionario
el ejercicio
la emergencia
el examen
el material
la oficina
la parte
el verbo

Nombres

la hora del recreo *recess time*
el inglés *English (language)*
la lección *lesson*
la letra *handwriting, letter*
el nombre, el sustantivo *noun*
los nombres propios *proper nouns*
la oración *sentence*
la ortografía *spelling*
el patio *school yard*
el repaso *review*
el significado *meaning*

Verbos

aprender *to learn*
buscar *to look for*
dar *to give*
estar *to be*
guardar *to put away, to keep*
ir *to go*
llamar *to call*
regresar *to return, to go (come) back*
subrayar *to underline*
usar *to use*

Adjetivos

bonito(a) *pretty, beautiful*
claro(a) *clear*
difícil *difficult*
fácil *easy*
mayúscula *uppercase (capital) letter*
minúscula *lowercase (small) letter*
roto(a) *broken*
terminado(a) *finished*

Otras palabras y expresiones

¿adónde? *where (to)?*
ahora *now*
ahora mismo *right now*
así *like this*
cada *each*
¿Cómo se dice...? *How do you say . . . ?*
¿Cómo se escribe(n)...? *How do you spell . . . ?*
con más cuidado *more carefully, with more care*
disculpe *excuse me*
en mi casa *at home (lit. at my house)*
la lección para hoy *today's lesson*
llamar por teléfono *to call on the telephone*
mal *badly, wrong*
para *for*
¿Voy ahora? *Shall I go now?*

Nombre ______________________ Sección ______________ Fecha ______________

VOCABULARIO ADICIONAL

Otras partes de la oración
(*Other parts of speech*)

el adverbio *adverb*
el artículo definido *definite article*
el artículo indefinido *indefinite article*
la conjunción *conjunction*
la interjección *interjection*
los nombres comunes *common nouns*
la preposición *preposition*

Palabras relacionadas con el lenguaje
(*Words related to language*)

la abreviatura *abbreviation*
el antónimo *antonym*
el complemento *object*
la definición *definition*
en orden alfabético *in alphabetical order*
el futuro *future*
el pasado *past*
el predicado *predicate*
el presente *present*
el sinónimo *synonym*
el sujeto *subject*
el tiempo *tense*

Notas Culturales

- In Spanish-speaking countries people generally use two surnames: the father's last name followed by the mother's maiden name. For example, the children of Isabel Vargas and Carlos Reyes will use the surnames Reyes Vargas.
- In a telephone directory, the names are alphabetized according to both last names. For example:
  Pérez Acosta, Rosa María
  Pérez Acosta, Sara Victoria
  Pérez González, José María
  Quintana Álvarez, Héctor Daniel
  Quintana Álvarez, Mario Enrique
  Quintana Centurión, Sergio Rafael
- Just like American students take Engish as a school subject, students in Spanish-speaking countries take Spanish. As a school subject, it is called **castellano,** not **español.**

Nombre ____________________ Sección ____________ Fecha ____________

Actividades

Dígame... Answer the following questions, basing your answers on the dialogue.

1. ¿Qué van a repasar los alumnos del Sr. Mena? ¿Para qué?

2. ¿En qué página están los ejercicios?

3. ¿Qué deben subrayar los niños?

4. ¿Qué más (*What else*) escriben los alumnos?

5. ¿Cómo se escriben los nombres propios?

6. ¿Qué día es el examen de ortografía? ¿Va a ser muy difícil?

7. ¿Dónde está la composición de Jorge? ¿Está terminada?

8. ¿Están mal las oraciones de Oscar? ¿Qué debe hacer (*do*) él?

9. ¿Qué debe aprender Rafael?

10. ¿Adónde va Olga? ¿Qué necesita?

11. ¿A quién llaman por teléfono? ¿Adónde debe ir el niño ahora mismo?

12. ¿Adónde van todos los alumnos? ¿Por qué?

Nombre ______________________ Sección ____________ Fecha ____________

Hablemos With a partner, take turns asking each other the following questions.

1. ¿Qué debe aprender Ud. hoy?
2. ¿Busca Ud. todas las palabras nuevas en el diccionario?
3. ¿Su profesor(a) da un examen el viernes?
4. ¿En qué página está la lección para hoy?
5. ¿Hay sacapuntas en su salón de clase?
6. La palabra "aprender", ¿es un nombre, un adjetivo o un verbo?
7. ¿Cuál es el significado en inglés del verbo "subrayar"?
8. ¿Es clara su letra o debe escribir con más cuidado?
9. ¿Cómo se dice "respuesta" en inglés?
10. ¿Dónde guarda Ud. sus papeles?

Quiz

VAMOS A PRACTICAR

A Complete the following sentences or questions, using the present indicative of **ser, ir, dar,** or **estar.**

MODELO El examen __________ fácil.
El examen **es** fácil.

1. El examen __________ hoy. __________ a las dos.
2. Los ejercicios __________ en la página dos. No __________ muy difíciles.
3. El maestro __________ a la oficina y los alumnos __________ a la clase.
4. Hoy el maestro __________ un examen de inglés.
5. El verbo y el adjetivo __________ dos partes de la oración.
6. Nosotros __________ de Colombia.
7. La clase de lenguaje __________ en el aula 220, pero yo no __________ a la universidad hoy.
8. ¿Tú __________ la lección de lenguaje hoy?
9. Nosotros __________ bien. ¿Cómo __________ Uds.?
10. ¿Dónde __________ la secretaria?

Nombre ______________________ Sección ____________ Fecha ____________

B Using the expression **ir a** + ***infinitive,*** say what everybody is going to do, according to each situation.

Modelo I have a difficult exam tomorrow.
Yo **voy a estudiar.**

1. The students have a quiz on the multiplication tables after lunch.

   Los estudiantes ______________________________.

2. Carlos needs help and you are his teacher.

   Ud. ______________________________.

3. Miss Ortega is going to be late.

   Nosotros ______________________________.

4. You see a Spanish word you don't understand.

   Tú ______________________________.

5. I cannot read aloud.

   Yo ______________________________.

C Complete each sentence, using one of the following phrases.

de la   a la   de las   a las   del   al   de los   a los

Modelo El libro es __________ Sr. Díaz.
El libro es **del** Sr. Díaz.

1. Llevo __________ niños __________ patio.
2. Voy __________ clase __________ profesor Salgado.
3. El maestro __________ niños lleva __________ señoras __________ salón de clase.
4. Los libros son __________ maestra y los cuadernos son __________ alumnas.

Nombre ______________________ Sección ______________ Fecha ______________

Conversaciones breves

Complete the following dialogue, using your imagination and the vocabulary from this lesson.

El maestro habla con sus alumnos.

Maestro —______________________________

Jorge —Sí, señor, mi composición está terminada.

Maestro —______________________________

Jorge —Está en su escritorio.

Raúl —¿Cuándo es el repaso para el examen de lenguaje, Sr. Rodríguez?

Maestro —______________________________

Raúl —¿El jueves? ¿Y debemos dar el significado de las palabras nuevas en el examen?

Maestro —______________________________

Rita —¿Cuántas oraciones debemos escribir con cada palabra?

Maestro —______________________________

Rita —Señor, ¿cómo se escribe "bien" en inglés?

Maestro —______________________________

Tomás —Señor, ¿mi trabajo está bien así?

Maestro —______________________________

Ignacio —¿Va a ser muy difícil el examen?

Maestro —______________________________

En estas situaciones

With two or more classmates, act out the following situations in Spanish.

1. Tell your students to what page they must open their language arts books. Today's lesson is a review of parts of the sentence.
2. Tell your students to underline the verbs, nouns, and adjectives in all the sentences on the page.
3. Ask your Spanish teacher if "**abril**" is spelled with an uppercase "*a*" or a lowercase "*a*."
4. Tell your students that the spelling test is on Thursday. Tell them they must learn all the new words and give the meaning of each one. Tell them also that they should look up the words in the dictionary.
5. Tell one of your students that his/her sentence is fine but that his/her handwriting is not clear, and that he/she must write more carefully.
6. Tell your Spanish teacher that your composition is in your notebook, but it is not finished yet.
7. Tell your students that the pencil sharpener, the ruler, and the dictionary are on your desk. Tell them also that they must put their books and notebooks away because it is time for recess.
8. Instruct one of your students to go to the principal's office right away.

Nombre ______________________ Sección ____________ Fecha ____________

Casos

Casos With you and a partner playing the roles, work through the following scenarios.

1. A student asks his/her teacher questions about assignments, spelling, dates of tests, where things are, etc.
2. Two students studying for a spelling test take turns asking each other how to spell various words.

Un paso más

A Review the **Vocabulario adicional** in this lesson and identify the parts of speech that correspond to the following words.

1. los ______________________
2. ¡Ah! ______________________
3. con ______________________
4. libro ______________________
5. la ______________________
6. mal ______________________
7. y ______________________
8. una ______________________
9. independientemente ______________________

B Complete the following sentences, using the new words.

1. Necesito buscar el ____________ de las palabras en el diccionario.
2. En la oración "Juan es maestro", la palabra "Juan" es el ____________ y "es maestro" es el ____________.
3. En el diccionario, todas las palabras están en ____________.
4. "*I go*" está en ____________ presente. "*I went*" está en tiempo ____________. "*I will go*" está en tiempo ____________.
5. La ____________ de "usted" es "Ud."
6. En la oración "Yo llamo a Luis", "Luis" es el ____________.
7. "Bien" y "mal" no son sinónimos; son ____________.
8. "Estudiante" y "alumno" son ____________.

Actividad en grupo

Actividad en grupo In groups of three or four, design a short quiz for your language class.

Lección 4

En la clase de geografía

Objectives

Structures

- The irregular verbs **tener** and **venir**
- Expressions with **tener**
- Comparative forms
- Irregular comparative forms

Communication

- Geography class: teaching and answering questions about U.S. geography

iLrn™

Hoy la maestra viene a clase con mapas, carteles y láminas. También tiene un globo terráqueo. La lección de hoy es sobre la geografía de los Estados Unidos.

Maestra —¿En qué continente está situado nuestro país?
César —En el continente americano.
Maestra —¿Cuáles son los límites de los Estados Unidos?
Lupe —Al norte limita con Canadá, al sur con México y con el golfo de México, al este con el océano Atlántico y al oeste con el océano Pacífico.
Maestra —¡Muy bien! Sabes mucho. Y, ¿cuál es el río más largo de los Estados Unidos?
Roberto —¿El río Misisipí?
Maestra —No, el río Misuri es más largo que el río Misisipí. Es el más largo de todos.
Sara —¡Señorita! La montaña más alta es el monte McKinley, ¿verdad?
Maestra —Sí. ¿Cuántos estados tiene nuestro país y cuál es su población?
José —Tiene cincuenta estados, pero no estoy seguro del número de habitantes.
Maestra —Más o menos doscientos noventa y seis millones. ¿Cuál es la capital de los Estados Unidos?
Eva —¿Nueva York?
Marta —¡No! Washington, D.C. Allí vive el presidente.
Maestra —Tienes razón, Marta. También tenemos un estado que no está dentro del continente. ¿Cuál es?
Rafael —Hawai. Mi tío vive allí en la isla de Maui, y viene la semana próxima.

Nombre ______________________ Sección ____________ Fecha ____________

Maestra —¡Qué bien! Y, ¿saben Uds. cuál es el producto principal que tiene Hawai?
Rafael —El azúcar... Y tiene muchos volcanes.
Maestra —Es verdad. Mario, ¿cuál es la superficie de los Estados Unidos?
Mario —¿Un millón de millas cuadradas?
Maestra —No, mucho más. Tiene tres millones, seiscientas ochenta y siete mil, cuatrocientas veintiocho millas cuadradas.
Olga —¡Uy! ¿Es el país más grande del mundo?
Maestra —No, pero es uno de los más grandes. Tiene muchas fuentes de riqueza: la agricultura, la ganadería, la industria, la pesca y la minería. Bueno, ahora tenemos que guardar los libros porque tenemos la práctica de incendios.
Mario —Y después vamos a la cafetería, ¿verdad? ¡Yo tengo mucha hambre!
Maestra —No, Mario, tenemos que esperar hasta las doce.

¡Escuchemos!

While listening to the dialogue, circle **V (verdadero)** if the statement is true and **F (falso)** if it is false.

1. La maestra no tiene mapas. V F
2. Al norte, Estados Unidos limita con México. V F
3. El río más largo de Estados Unidos es el Misuri. V F
4. José no sabe cuál es la población de los Estados Unidos. V F
5. Hawai no está dentro del continente. V F
6. Mario sabe cuál es la superficie de los Estados Unidos. V F
7. Estados Unidos es el país más grande del mundo. V F
8. La ganadería es una de las fuentes de riqueza de los Estados Unidos. V F
9. Los niños tienen que guardar los libros. V F
10. Mario no tiene hambre. V F

Nombre ____________________ Sección ____________ Fecha ____________

VOCABULARIO

Cognados

la agricultura
americano(a)
Atlántico
la capital
el continente
la geografía
la industria
la isla
el millón
el monte
el número
el océano
Pacífico
el presidente
el producto

Nombres

el azúcar *sugar*
el cartel *poster, chart*
el estado *state*
los Estados Unidos *United States*
el este *east*
la ganadería *livestock*
el globo terráqueo *globe*
el golfo *golf*
el (la) habitante *inhabitant*
el incendio, el fuego *fire*
la lámina, la ilustración *picture, illustration*
el límite *boundary*
la milla *mile*
la minería *mining*
la montaña *mountain*
el mundo *world*
el norte *north*
el oeste *west*
el país *country (nation)*
la pesca *fishing*
la población *population*
la práctica, el simulacro (*Méx., Puerto Rico*) *drill*
el río *river*
la semana *week*
la superficie, el área *area*
el sur *south*
la tía *aunt*
el tío *uncle*
el volcán *volcano*

Verbos

limitar (con), colindar (con) (*Méx.*) *to border*
tener *to have*
venir *to come*
vivir *to live*

Adjetivos

alto(a) *high, tall*
grande *big, large*
largo(a) *long*
principal *main*
próximo(a) *next*
seguro(a) *sure*
situado(a) *located, situated*

Otras palabras y expresiones

allí *there*
¿cuántos(as)? *how many?*
dentro *in, inside*
después *afterwards*
las fuentes de riqueza *sources of income*
hasta *until*
la semana próxima *next week*
mañana *tomorrow*
más o menos *about, more or less*
Norteamérica (América del Norte) *North America*
que *that, than*
¡qué bien! *how nice!*
¡qué contento! *how happy!*
sobre *about*
tener hambre *to be hungry*
tener que (+ *inf.*) *to have to (do something)*
tener razón *to be right*
¡uy! *wow!*

Nombre ______________ Sección __________ Fecha __________

VOCABULARIO ADICIONAL

Otros lugares (*Other places*)

África *Africa*
Antártida *Antarctica*
Asia *Asia*
Australia[1] *Australia*
Centroamérica (América Central) *Central America*
Europa *Europe*
Sudamérica (América del Sur) *South America*

Palabras relacionadas con la geografía (*Words related to geography*)

el archipiélago *archipelago*
el cabo *cape*
la cordillera *chain of mountains*
el desierto *desert*
el lago *lake*
el mar *sea*
el meridiano *meridian*
el paralelo *parallel*
la península *peninsula*
el polo *pole*

Palabras relacionadas con el clima (*Words related to weather*)

cálido(a) *warm, hot*
frío(a) *cold*
templado(a) *temperate*

Fenómenos naturales (*Natural phenomena*)

el ciclón *cyclone*
el huracán *hurricane*
la inundación *flood*
la lluvia torrencial *cloudburst*
el terremoto, el temblor *earthquake*
la tormenta de nieve (*snow*) *blizzard*
el tornado *tornado*

Notas Culturales

Most Latino children are taught from an early age that the family comes first. Knowing one's place in a hierarchical, often-authoritarian family structure and showing appropriate deference and respect to older family members are of great importance, as is recognizing the interdependence of family members and the necessity of placing the family's well-being ahead of one's own needs or desires.

[1]The continent is called **Oceanía,** and it includes Australia and New Zealand.

Nombre ______________________ Sección ____________ Fecha ____________

Actividades

Dígame... Answer the following questions, basing your answers on the dialogue.

1. ¿Qué tiene la maestra para enseñar (*to teach*) a la clase de hoy?

2. ¿Sobre qué es la lección de hoy?

3. ¿Con qué países limitan los Estados Unidos?

4. ¿Cuántos habitantes hay en los Estados Unidos?

5. ¿Cuál es la montaña más alta y cuál es el río más largo de los Estados Unidos?

6. ¿Cuál es el estado que no está dentro del continente y cuál es su producto principal?

7. ¿Qué fuentes de riqueza tiene nuestro país?

8. ¿Por qué tienen que guardar los libros los estudiantes?

9. ¿Por qué necesita ir Mario a la cafetería?

10. ¿Hasta qué hora tiene que esperar él?

 **Hablemos** With a partner, take turns asking each other the following questions.

1. ¿En qué estado vive Ud.? ¿En qué ciudad?
2. ¿Con qué limita al oeste el estado donde Ud. vive? ¿Y al norte?
3. Más o menos, ¿cuántos habitantes tiene su ciudad?
4. ¿Con qué limitan los Estados Unidos al este? ¿Y al sur?

5. ¿Está situado nuestro país en Sudamérica?
6. ¿Están dentro del continente todos los estados de los Estados Unidos?
7. ¿Cuál es la capital de su estado? ¿Cuáles son sus fuentes de riqueza?
8. ¿Tiene Ud. muchas láminas en su clase? ¿Y carteles?

Quiz

VAMOS A PRACTICAR

A Complete the following exchanges, using the present indicative of **tener** or **venir.**

MODELO —¿A qué hora ____________ ella? —Ella ____________ a las ocho.
—¿A que hora **viene** ella? —Ella **viene** a las ocho.

1. —¿Ud. ____________ los mapas?

   —Sí, y también ____________ las láminas.

2. —¿Ellos ____________ mañana?

   —Sí, y nosotros ____________ la semana próxima.

3. —¿De qué país ____________ que hablar Uds.?

   —Nosotros ____________ que hablar de los Estados Unidos.

4. —¿Tú ____________ con tu tío?

   —No, ____________ con mi tía.

B Using expressions with **tener,** say how these people feel according to each circumstance.

MODELO I haven't eaten for ten hours.
Yo **tengo hambre.**

1. You are in Alaska in December.

   Tú ____.

2. We are going through a dark alley.

   Nosotros ____.

3. Raquel's throat is very dry.

   Raquel ____.

4. They have one minute to get to their next class.

   Ellos ____.

Nombre ______________________ **Sección** ____________ **Fecha** ____________

C Establish comparisons using the adjectives in parentheses. Add the corresponding definite articles whenever necessary.

MODELO (alta) ella / tú
Ella ***es menos alta que*** **tú.**
or
Ella ***es más alta que*** **tú.**

1. (alto) el profesor / yo

   ____

2. (largo) río Colorado / río Misuri

   ____

3. (interesante) Lección 4 / Lección 3

   ____

4. (pequeño [*small*]) océano Atlántico / océano Pacífico

   ____

5. (grande / el más grande) Vermont / Arizona / Texas

   ____

Conversaciones breves

Complete the following dialogue, using your imagination and the vocabulary from this lesson.

En la clase de geografía:

Maestra —Hoy nuestra lección es sobre los Estados Unidos.

Rita —____

Maestra —No, Estados Unidos no es el más grande de todos.

Marcos —____

Maestra —Tiene más o menos doscientos noventa y seis millones de habitantes. ¿Cuántos estados tiene nuestro país, Raúl?

Raúl —____

Maestra —¿Qué estado tiene muchos volcanes?

Carmen —____

Maestra —¿Es Hawai una isla o un continente?

Irene —____

Maestra —____

Clara —La pesca, la ganadería, la industria, etc.

Maestra —¡Qué bien! Uds. estudian mucho.

Nombre ______________________ Sección ____________ Fecha ____________

En estas situaciones

With two or more classmates, act out the following situations in Spanish.

1. The topic of today's class is the geography of the United States. You want to make sure that your students know on which continent the United States is situated, what its boundaries are, its highest mountain, its longest river, its capital, and the number of states it has.
2. Ask your students to identify the population and area of the United States.
3. You and your students are discussing the major sources of income in the United States.
4. Your class is going to have a fire drill next week.
5. You want to know how old one of your students is.

Casos

With you and a partner playing the roles, work through the following scenarios.

1. A teacher asks students a variety of questions about the geography of the United States.
2. Students quiz one another on the geography of their state.

Un paso más

Review the **Vocabulario adicional** in this lesson and complete the following sentences with the appropriate word or phrase.

1. ___________ y ___________ son continentes.
2. El Hurón es un ___________.
3. Un ___________ es un grupo de islas.
4. Las líneas del globo terráqueo son los ___________ y los ___________.
5. El canal de Panamá está en ___________.
6. El Mediterráneo es un ___________.
7. El ___________ Cañaveral está en el estado de la Florida.
8. El Sahara es un ___________.
9. La Florida es una ___________.
10. Argentina está en ___________.
11. No es un huracán. Es un ___________.
12. El ___________ Norte tiene un clima muy frío.

13. Chile limita al este con la __________ de los Andes.

14. Frecuentemente hay __________ en California.

15. En Kansas a veces hay __________.

16. En el invierno hay tormentas de __________.

17. Llovió (*It rained*) mucho y ahora tienen muchas __________.

18. En los países tropicales a veces hay __________ torrenciales.

Actividad en grupo In groups of two or three, prepare a short lesson for a geography class giving information about South America.

____

____

____

____

____

EN LA CLASE DE ARTE

OBJECTIVES

Structures

- Stem-changing verbs (**e:ie**)
- The present progressive
- Ordinal numbers

Communication

- Art class: explaining an art project to students

iLrn™

Hoy los alumnos de segundo grado van a aprender a hacer un árbol de Navidad.

Maestra —Niños, hoy vamos a hacer varias cosas con papeles de colores.
Blanca —Señorita, yo no tengo tijeras. ¿Vamos a recortar algo?
Maestra —Sí. Hay tijeras y goma de pegar en el armario que está a la derecha.
Silvia —¿Dónde está el estambre, señorita?
Maestra —En el estante de arriba, a la izquierda. Bueno, vamos a empezar.
Elba —¿Qué color de papel vamos a usar?
Maestra —Verde. Primero vamos a doblar el papel por la mitad y dibujar el árbol.
Javier —Yo no tengo el modelo.
Maestra —Hay uno en el primer cajón de mi escritorio.
Javier —¿Aquí?
Maestra —Sí. (*A la clase*) Deben poner el modelo sobre el papel y trazar una línea alrededor del árbol.
Hilda —Yo no entiendo, maestra.
Maestra —Así, con el papel doblado. (*A la clase*) Ahora deben cortar, siguiendo la línea del dibujo.
Rubén —¿Ya está listo?
Maestra —No, ahora vamos a recortar círculos pequeños de diferentes colores. ¿Qué colores quieren?
Gloria —Yo quiero dorado y rojo.
Javier —Yo prefiero azul y plateado.
Maestra —Vamos a pegar los círculos en el árbol.

Nombre ______________________ **Sección** ____________ **Fecha** ____________

Yolanda —¡Es un árbol de Navidad! ¡Qué bonito![1]
Maestra —Ahora vamos a hacer un Santa Claus[2] de fieltro y algodón.

Después del recreo, los niños regresan al salón de clase y continúan la clase de arte. Jaime está mascando chicle.

Maestra —¡Jaime! ¡No debes mascar chicle aquí! (*A la clase*) ¡Ah, niños, ya son las tres menos veinte!
Jaime —¿Vamos a terminar el Santa Claus hoy?
Maestra —No, el lunes. Ahora van a recoger todas las cosas y a limpiar las mesas. Es la hora de salida.

Los niños empiezan a recoger las tijeras y los papeles y la maestra cierra la ventana.

¡Escuchemos!

While listening to the dialogue, circle **V (verdadero)** if the statement is true and **F (falso)** if it is false.

1.	Los niños van a usar papeles de colores.	V	F
2.	La maestra no tiene goma de pegar.	V	F
3.	Van a usar papel amarillo.	V	F
4.	Hay un modelo en el escritorio de la maestra.	V	F
5.	Los niños deben cortar el papel.	V	F
6.	Gloria quiere papeles de color blanco.	V	F
7.	Los niños pegan los círculos en el libro.	V	F
8.	Los niños usan fieltro y algodón para hacer un Santa Claus.	V	F
9.	La maestra masca chicle.	V	F
10.	Los niños limpian la mesa.	V	F

---

[1]Spanish **qué** + adjective: English ***how*** + adjective.
[2]**Santa Clos,** in Mexico and Puerto Rico.

Nombre ______________________ Sección __________ Fecha __________

VOCABULARIO

Cognados

el arte
el color
el grado
la línea

Nombres

el algodón *cotton*
el árbol *tree*
el armario, el gabinete (*Méx.*) *cabinet*
el cajón, la gaveta (*Cuba, Puerto Rico*) *drawer*
el chicle, la goma de mascar *chewing gum*
el círculo *circle*
la cosa *thing*
el dibujo *drawing*
el estambre, la lana de tejer *yarn*
el estante *shelf*
el fieltro *felt*
la goma de pegar *glue*
la hora de salida *time to go*
la mesa *table*
la mitad *half*
el modelo, el patrón *pattern, model*
la Navidad *Christmas*
las tijeras *scissors*

Verbos

cerrar (e:ie) *to close*
continuar *to continue*
cortar *to cut*
dibujar *to draw*
doblar *to fold*
empezar (e:ie), comenzar (e:ie) *to begin, to start*
entender (e:ie) *to understand*
hacer[1] *to do, to make*
limpiar *to clean*
mascar, masticar *to chew*
pegar *to glue*
poner[2] *to put*
preferir (e:ie) *to prefer*
querer (e:ie) *to want, to wish*
recoger[3] *to pick up*
recortar *to cut, to trim*
tomar *to drink*
trazar *to draw* (*i.e., a line*)

Adjetivos

diferente *various, different*
doblado(a) *folded*
listo(a) *ready*
pequeño(a) *small, little*
varios(as) *several, various*

Otras palabras y expresiones

a la derecha *to the right*
a la izquierda *to the left*
algo *something*
alrededor (de) *around*
de arriba *top, upper*
por la mitad *in half*
¡qué bonito(a)! *how pretty!*
siguiendo *following*
sobre *on, on top of*

---

[1]Irregular first person: **yo hago**
[2]Irregular first person: **yo pongo**
[3]Orthographic change in the first person: **yo recojo**

Nombre ______________________ Sección ____________ Fecha ____________

VOCABULARIO ADICIONAL

Palabras útiles para la clase de arte (*Useful words for art class*)

la acuarela *watercolor*
la aguja *needle*
calcar *to trace*
el cartón *cardboard*
la cartulina *construction paper*
el compás *compass*
coser *to sew*
desdoblar *to unfold*
el hilo *thread*
la línea de puntos *dotted line*
el pincel *brush*
pintar *to paint*
la pintura *paint*
el trabajo manual *arts and crafts*
unir los puntos *connect the dots*

Palabras útiles para describir dónde está algo (*Useful words for describing where something is*)

abajo *down, downstairs*
adentro *inside*
afuera *outside*
arriba *up, upstairs*
debajo de *under*
delante (de) *in front of*
detrás (de) *behind*
encima de *on top of*

Días festivos (*Holidays*)

el Día de Acción de Gracias *Thanksgiving*
el Día de la Independencia *Independence Day*
el Día de la Madre *Mother's Day*
el Día de los Enamorados *Valentine's Day*
el Día de los Trabajadores *Labor Day*
el Día de los Veteranos *Veterans' Day*
el Día del Padre *Father's Day*
la Nochebuena *Christmas Eve*
la Pascua Florida *Easter*

Notas Culturales

- Thanksgiving Day is not celebrated in Spanish-speaking countries. It is celebrated in Puerto Rico, which is a U.S. territory.
- Labor Day is celebrated on May 1.
- People in Spanish-speaking countries generally celebrate Christmas Eve. The **Posadas** are a Mexican tradition, while Paraguayans, for example, have very elaborate manger scenes called **pesebres.** However, the Christmas tree is becoming more and more popular.
- Although Santa Claus is now more visible in Spain and Latin America, especially in stores, children continue to wait for the Three Wise Men **(Los Reyes Magos)** to bring them toys, candy, and other presents on the night of January 5.

Nombre ______________________ Sección ____________ Fecha ____________

ACTIVIDADES

Dígame... Answer the following questions, basing your answers on the dialogue.

1. ¿Qué van a aprender hoy los alumnos de segundo grado?

2. Blanca va a necesitar tijeras. ¿Por qué?

3. ¿Dónde están las tijeras y la goma de pegar? Y el armario, ¿dónde está?

4. ¿Dónde está el estambre?

5. ¿Qué color de papel van a usar los niños para hacer los árboles?

6. ¿Qué van a hacer los niños primero?

7. ¿Qué colores quiere usar Gloria? ¿Qué colores prefiere Javier?

8. ¿Qué está mascando Jaime?

9. Es la hora de salida. ¿Qué deben hacer los niños antes de (*before*) ir a casa?

10. ¿Qué recogen los niños? ¿Qué cierra la maestra?

 **Hablemos** With a partner, take turns asking each other the following questions.

1. ¿Tiene Ud. clases de arte en su escuela? ¿Qué días de la semana?
2. ¿Qué materiales usan sus alumnos en la clase de arte?
3. Después de una clase de trabajo manual (*arts and crafts*), ¿quién recoge todas las cosas?
4. ¿Limpia Ud. las mesas después de la clase de trabajo manual?

Nombre ______________________ Sección ____________ Fecha ____________

5. Quiero hacer un árbol de Navidad. Después de poner el modelo sobre el papel, ¿qué debo hacer?
6. ¿Qué cosas tiene Ud. en los gabinetes en su salón de clase?
7. ¿Cuál es la hora de salida para los alumnos en su escuela? Y para los maestros, ¿es diferente?
8. ¿Sus alumnos mascan chicle en su clase?
9. ¿A qué hora empieza su clase de español? ¿A qué hora termina?
10. ¿Qué quiere hacer Ud. después de (*after*) la clase?

Quiz

VAMOS A PRACTICAR

A Write complete sentences, using the elements given. Add any necessary words.

MODELO yo / querer / recortar / árbol
Yo quiero recortar el árbol.

1. nosotros / no querer / limpiar / mesas

____

2. yo / preferir / regresar / cuatro y media

____

3. Roberto / cerrar / ventanas

____

4. niños / empezar / cortar / patrón

____

5. clases / comenzar / semana / próxima

____

6. ¿tú / entender / lección?

____

B Rewrite the following sentences, using the present progressive.

1. Ellos mastican chicle.

____

2. ¿Tú escribes con un lápiz rojo?

____

3. Nosotros estudiamos en la biblioteca.

____

4. Daniel come en la cafetería.

____

5. Yo leo la Lección 4.

____

C Complete the following, as appropriate.

MODELO Mayo es el __________ mes del año.
Mayo es el **quinto** mes del año.

1. Octubre es el __________ mes del año.
2. __________ es el primer mes del año.
3. Febrero es el __________ mes del año.
4. __________ es el noveno mes del año.
5. Julio es el __________ mes del año.
6. Marzo es el __________ mes del año.
7. __________ es el cuarto mes del año.
8. Junio es el __________ mes del año.

Conversaciones breves

Complete the following dialogue, using your imagination and the vocabulary from this lesson.

La maestra y Javier:

Maestra —Javier, vamos a hacer un árbol de Navidad. ¿Tienes goma de pegar?

Javier —____

Maestra —Hay goma de pegar en mi escritorio.

Javier —____

Maestra —En el cajón de arriba.

Javier —____

Maestra —Sí, y también necesitamos papel verde y papeles de colores.

Javier —____

Nombre ______________________ Sección ____________ Fecha ____________

Maestra —No, hoy no. Ahora vamos a recoger todas las cosas. Vamos a empezar la clase de lenguaje.

Javier —____

Maestra —Vamos a terminar el árbol la semana próxima.

En estas situaciones

With two or more classmates, act out the following situations in Spanish.

1. You want to teach your students how to make an apple tree in art class. Tell them what materials they will need, where they can be found in the classroom, and the steps they must follow to make the tree.
2. It's a hectic day in your classroom. One of your students is chewing gum in class, which is not allowed; another student leaves her supplies on her desk when it is time to go.

Casos

With you and a partner playing the roles, work through the following scenarios.

1. A teacher and a student discuss the student's choice of an art project, and how he/she will go about doing it.
2. A teacher and his/her students talk about what they are going to do to tidy up the classroom before they go home.

Un paso más

A Review the **Vocabulario adicional** in this lesson and answer the following questions in the negative, giving the opposite of what is asked.

1. ¿Estás *detrás de* la casa?

   ____

2. ¿El pincel está *arriba?*

   ____

3. ¿La cartulina está *debajo del* escritorio?

   ____

4. ¿Las acuarelas están *afuera?*

   ____

B Complete the following sentences with the appropriate word or phrase.

1. Para coser necesito ____________ y una ____________.
2. No vamos a usar ____________ para hacer el árbol; vamos a usar cartulina.
3. Para pintar necesitamos la ____________ y los ____________.

4. Para hacer un círculo necesito un ____________.
5. Debes firmar en la ____________.
6. La ____________ es una pintura de agua.
7. No vamos a calcar el árbol. Vamos a ____________.
8. Vamos a ____________ el papel y cortar por la línea de puntos.
9. En la clase de ____________ los alumnos pequeños aprenden a hacer muchas cosas.

Actividad en grupo In groups of three or four, prepare instructions to make a special art project for Mother's Day.

____

____

____

____

____

LECTURA 1

PERMISO PARA IR DE EXCURSIÓN

Read the following information from a permission slip for a field trip. Try to guess the meaning of all cognates.

DISTRITO ESCOLAR DE LOS ÁNGELES

PERMISO PARA IR DE EXCURSIÓN

He leído[1] la información contenida en este documento, y mi hijo(a) ______________________ tiene mi permiso para acompañar a la clase de ______________ a la excursión a ______________ el ____ de ______________ de ________ a ______________________.

Yo sé[2] que el seguro[3] del Distrito cubre solamente lesiones[4] causadas por negligencia de los maestros que acompañan a los niños, y que en otras circunstancias, el seguro médico del estudiante es el responsable.

Padre o tutor[5] (Escriba con letra de imprenta[6])

Nombre y apellido ______________________
Número de teléfono ______________________
Dirección ______________________
____

____
Firma del padre o tutor

[1]**He leído** *I have read*
[2]**Yo sé** *I know*
[3]**el seguro** *insurance*
[4]**lesiones** *injuries*
[5]**tutor** *legal guardian*
[6]**Escriba con letra de imprenta** *Print*

Nombre ______________________ Sección ____________ Fecha ____________

Dígame... Complete the permission slip on the previous page. Fill in the form according to the information below.

Daniel Peña, who is in the second grade, lives with Mrs. Alicia Barrios, his legal guardian. They live on 345 Alvarado Street in Los Angeles, and their phone number is (213) 792-4834. Daniel is going with his class to the Museum of Science on March 17, from 10 o'clock in the morning to 2 o'clock in the afternoon.

Nombre ______________________ Sección ____________ Fecha ____________

REPASO

Práctica de vocabulario (*Vocabulary practice*)

A Circle the word or phrase that does not belong in each group.

1. la agricultura la pesca el terremoto
2. terminar mascar acabar
3. el tío la página el papel
4. palabras vocabulario secretaria
5. estante patio armario
6. dibujar trazar regresar
7. recortar sumar multiplicar
8. sobresaliente doblado satisfactorio
9. rosado anaranjado listo
10. ¿Cómo se escribe...? baño ortografía
11. milla monte montaña
12. población habitantes mina
13. mapa globo terráqueo tijeras
14. aquí allí bueno
15. mitad algodón fieltro
16. clase maestro minería
17. ir entender venir
18. ¿Qué hora es? la hora de salida nuevo
19. acabar terminar escribir
20. adjetivo reloj verbo
21. salón de clase aula temblor
22. hasta la vista perdone la molestia disculpe
23. tornado dirección tormenta de nieve
24. fácil plateado difícil
25. bibliotecario psicólogo ciudad

Nombre ________________________ **Sección** ____________ **Fecha** ____________

B Circle the word or phrase that best completes each sentence.

1. El azúcar es (una lámina / un producto / un número) de Hawai.
2. Estoy muy contento. Hoy no (escucho / llevo / voy) a la escuela.
3. Ahora necesito (el árbol / la conversación / la lista) de los niños que están presentes.
4. No trabajamos mucho. Tenemos (muy bien / muy poco / muy bonito) trabajo.
5. Su hijo estudia, pero nunca (participa / dobla / pone) en clase.
6. El fieltro está en el cajón de (alrededor / arriba / agua).
7. Es la hora de lectura. Los niños (borran / llaman / leen).
8. Primero buscamos el significado de las palabras en (el material / el diccionario / la cosa).
9. Después deben copiar los números en el cuaderno de (láminas / ayudas / ejercicios).
10. Es la hora del recreo. ¿Quién necesita (nombres propios / ir al baño / más o menos)?
11. El veinticinco de diciembre es (la semana pasada / la tabla de multiplicar / la Navidad).
12. ¿Quiénes deben (firmar / limpiar / aprender) la libreta de calificaciones?
13. Si ya tienen la respuesta correcta, deben (pasar lista / levantar la mano / leer más).
14. No leemos porque no tenemos (secretario / oficina / libro de lectura).
15. Todos ustedes estudian mucho. ¡Qué (bonito / bien / largo)!
16. Debes escribir con más (cuidado / límite / dibujo).
17. Es la hora de salida. Debemos terminar (el repaso / el sustantivo / la atención).
18. ¿Qué color de (papel / lectura / tarea) necesitamos para la clase de trabajo manual?
19. Es una ciudad muy importante. Es la ciudad (segura / principal / diferente).
20. Debes (recoger / tomar / doblar) el papel por la mitad.
21. ¡Un momento! Todavía no está (nuevo / varios / terminado).
22. Ella siempre me llama por (instrucción / verdad / teléfono).
23. ¿Tiene (algún / sobre / cada) problema con Pepito?
24. Tu letra no es muy (así / clara / contenta).
25. Voy a (esperar / trabajar / vivir) a la maestra.
26. ¿Para qué (necesitas / estudias / entiendes) el fieltro?

Nombre ______________________ Sección ____________ Fecha ____________

C Match the questions in column **A** with the answers in column **B.**

A	B
_______ **1.** ¿Trabaja Ud. mejor con los demás?	**a.** Para subrayar los verbos.
_______ **2.** ¿Qué debo hacer para mejorar?	**b.** La lección para hoy.
_______ **3.** ¿Dónde estudiamos hoy?	**c.** Dentro de la gaveta.
_______ **4.** ¿Cómo se dice *until?*	**d.** Sí, un lápiz azul.
_______ **5.** ¿Por qué vas a tu casa?	**e.** El libro que está sobre la mesa.
_______ **6.** ¿Para qué necesitas el lápiz rojo?	**f.** Prestar más atención.
_______ **7.** ¿Cómo están?	**g.** A Europa.
_______ **8.** ¿Tienen práctica de incendios?	**h.** Está en su oficina.
_______ **9.** ¿Dónde está el director?	**i.** Sí, y Carlos también.
_______ **10.** ¿Qué debemos repasar?	**j.** No, no tengo hambre.
_______ **11.** ¿Cómo dibujamos el árbol?	**k.** Estamos bien, gracias.
_______ **12.** ¿Dónde guardan el estambre?	**l.** No, trabajo mejor independientemente.
_______ **13.** ¿Rosa debe continuar con el grupo?	**m.** Siguiendo la línea de puntos.
_______ **14.** ¿Necesitas algo?	**n.** Porque debo escribir una composición.
_______ **15.** ¿Cuál es tu libro?	**o.** Sí, a veces.
_______ **16.** ¿Qué debo traer?	**p.** En mi casa.
_______ **17.** ¿Es azul marino?	**q.** Sí, porque tiene muchos problemas.
_______ **18.** ¿Quieres comer?	**r.** Hasta.
_______ **19.** ¿Vas a ayudar a Rosita?	**s.** Las láminas.
_______ **20.** ¿Adónde van Uds.?	**t.** No, es dorado.

Nombre ______________________ Sección ____________ Fecha ____________

D Crucigrama

Horizontales

4. No deben leer en voz alta. Deben leer en __________.
7. fuego
8. mil × mil = un __________
11. California es un __________.
13. Los estudiantes comen en la __________.
15. dar color
17. Estados Unidos está situado en __________ del Norte.
18. patrón
20. El Pacífico y el __________ son océanos.
23. Hawai es una __________.
24. México es un __________.
26. opuesto de norte
27. opuesto de sumar
30. No está a la derecha; está a la __________.
33. El azul y el __________ forman el color verde.
34. Para pegar uso __________ de pegar.
35. Hoy es martes; __________ es miércoles.
36. No se escribe con letra mayúscula; se escribe con letra __________.
37. lana de tejer (*knit*)
38. opuesto de este
39. Los niños __________ chicle.

Verticales

1. ¿Qué significa la palabra "aprender"? Necesito un __________.
2. La ganadería es una __________ de riqueza.
3. opuesto de mal
5. empezar
6. Asia es un __________.
9. Los Estados Unidos __________ al norte con Canadá.
10. goma de mascar
12. El adjetivo es una parte de la __________.
14. El Misuri es un __________ muy largo.
15. Washington, D.C., es la __________ de los Estados Unidos.
16. ¿Qué __________ es hoy? El 3 de septiembre.
19. color café
20. **Pequeño** no es un verbo; es un __________.
21. superficie
22. Los maestros trabajan en la __________.
25. nombre
28. En la clase de __________ estudiamos los ríos de Europa.
29. Para cortar necesito __________.
31. El monte Everest es la __________ más alta del mundo.
32. Los niños estudian mucho porque tienen un __________.
34. cajón

Nombre ______________________ **Sección** ____________ **Fecha** ____________

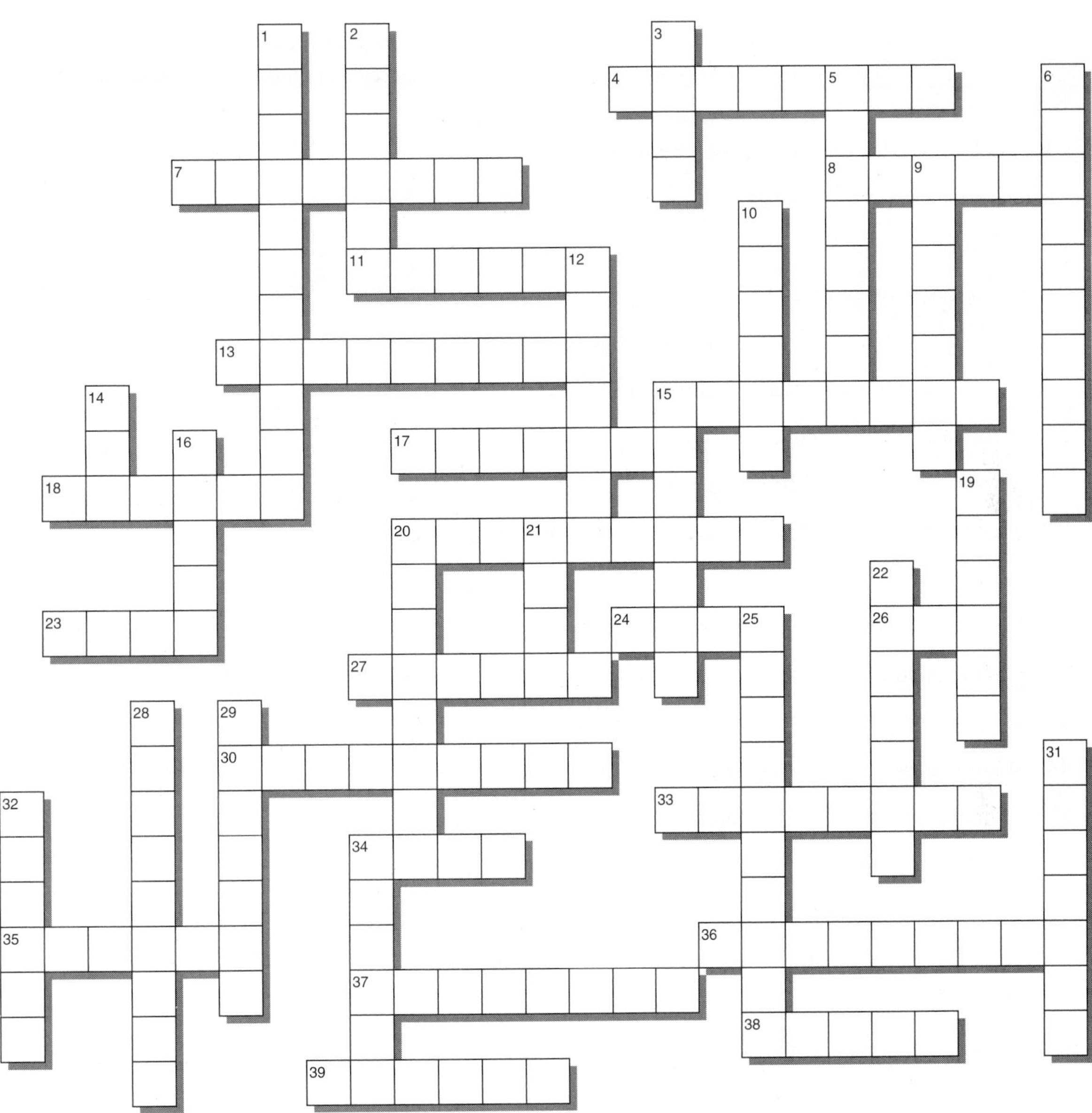

Nombre ______________________ **Sección** ____________ **Fecha** ____________

Práctica oral Listen to the following exercise on the audio program. The speaker will ask you some questions. Answer the questions, using the cues provided. The speaker will confirm the correct answer. Repeat the correct answer.

1. ¿Es Ud. de México? (no, de los Estados Unidos)
2. ¿De qué estado es Ud.? (de Colorado)
3. ¿Trabaja Ud. mucho? (sí)
4. ¿Cuántas horas trabaja Ud.? (cinco)
5. ¿Trabajan Ud. y los otros estudiantes en grupos? (no)
6. ¿Trabaja Ud. mejor independientemente? (sí)
7. ¿Qué necesita Ud. ahora? (el libro de español)
8. ¿Siempre trae Ud. el libro de español a la clase? (sí)
9. ¿Subraya Ud. las palabras con un lápiz rojo o amarillo? (rojo)
10. ¿Pinta Ud. con acuarela? (sí)
11. En la clase, ¿escribe Ud. con pluma o con lápiz? (con lápiz)
12. ¿Cómo es su letra? (muy clara)
13. ¿Dónde copia Ud. el vocabulario? (en el cuaderno de ejercicios)
14. ¿Con qué escribe Ud. en la pizarra? (con tiza)
15. ¿Cuántas pizarras tiene Ud. en la clase? (dos)
16. ¿Qué páginas debe leer Ud. hoy? (las páginas doce y trece)
17. ¿Busca Ud. muchas palabras en el diccionario? (sí)
18. ¿Cuándo es el examen de español? (la semana próxima)
19. ¿Tiene Ud. mapas en su clase? (sí, muchos)
20. ¿Dónde tiene Ud. las tijeras? (en el cajón)
21. ¿Dónde guarda Ud. sus papeles? (en el escritorio)
22. ¿Hoy tiene Ud. una práctica de incendios? (no, mañana)
23. ¿Come Ud. en la cafetería de la escuela? (no, en mi casa)
24. ¿Masca Ud. chicle en la clase? (no, nunca)
25. ¿Debe Ud. ir a la dirección? (sí, ahora mismo)

Lección 6

Un repaso de anatomía (I)

Objectives

Structures

- Stem-changing verbs **(o:ue)**
- Affirmative and negative expressions
- Direct object pronouns
- Pronouns as objects of prepositions

Communication

- Anatomy: talking about the human body; teaching students the names of different parts of the body

iLrn™

La semana próxima los alumnos van a tener varios exámenes. El lunes tienen uno de anatomía y ahora están repasando las lecciones.

Maestra —Hoy vamos a repasar anatomía. ¿Alguien recuerda cómo se llama la armazón que sostiene el cuerpo? ¿Mario?
Mario —Se llama esqueleto. El esqueleto está formado por los huesos.
Maestra —¡Muy bien! ¿Qué es una coyuntura?
Estela —Es la unión de dos o más huesos.
Maestra —Muy bien, pero tienes que levantar la mano antes de contestar.
José —¿La rodilla es una articulación?
Maestra —Sí, y también el codo. Bueno, ¿qué mueve los huesos? ¿Rosa?
Rosa —La sangre los mueve.
Maestra —No es la sangre, Rosa. La sangre lleva el oxígeno por todo el cuerpo. ¿Anita?
Anita —Los músculos mueven los huesos.
Maestra —Muy bien, Anita. ¿Y qué cubre todo nuestro cuerpo? ¿Gonzalo? ¿No recuerdas?
Gonzalo —La ropa.
Raquel —No, no... Es la piel.
Maestra —Muy bien. La piel protege nuestro cuerpo de los microbios.
Juan —Señorita, ¿por qué hay distintos colores de piel?

Maestra —Porque el color de la piel depende de la cantidad de pigmento. Si una persona tiene mucho pigmento, la piel es oscura. Si tiene poco, es muy clara. Bien, ¿con qué pensamos?
Paco —Con el cerebro. El cerebro está dentro de la cabeza, protegido por los huesos del cráneo.
Maestra —Muy bien. Cuando comemos, ¿adónde va la comida?
Rita —Primero masticamos y tragamos. Después la comida va al estómago y de allí a los intestinos, donde termina la digestión.
Paco —Cuando yo como mucho, siempre quiero dormir porque tengo sueño.
Rita —Porque tu cuerpo tiene que trabajar mucho para digerir toda la comida.
Maestra —Están contestando muy bien.

Suena el timbre para la salida.

Maestra —Mañana continuamos con la segunda parte. Gonzalo, ¿vas a repasar la primera parte de la lección conmigo?
Gonzalo —Sí, señorita, necesito repasarla, pero después tengo que ir a la biblioteca. ¿A qué hora la cierran?
Maestra —La cierran a las cinco. Bueno, podemos empezar.
Gonzalo —¿Puede esperarme un momento, señorita? Vuelvo enseguida.
Maestra —Está bien. Te espero.

¡Escuchemos! While listening to the dialogue, circle **V (verdadero)** if the statement is true and **F (falso)** if it is false.

1. Los alumnos tienen que repasar para los exámenes. V F
2. El esqueleto es la armazón que sostiene el cuerpo. V F
3. La sangre mueve los huesos. V F
4. La piel protege nuestro cuerpo. V F
5. El color de la piel depende de la cantidad de pigmento. V F
6. Si una persona tiene mucho pigmento, la piel es muy clara. V F
7. El cerebro protege los huesos del cráneo. V F
8. La digestión termina en los intestinos. V F
9. Gonzalo va a repasar la lección. V F
10. La maestra no puede esperar a Gonzalo. V F

Nombre ______________________ Sección ____________ Fecha ____________

VOCABULARIO

Cognados

la anatomía
la digestión
el intestino
el oxígeno
la persona
el pigmento

Nombres

la armazón *frame*
la biblioteca *library*
la cabeza *head*
la cantidad *quantity*
el cerebro *brain*
el codo *elbow*
la comida *food*
la coyuntura, la articulación *joint*
el cráneo *skull*
el cuerpo *body*
el esqueleto *skeleton*
el estómago *stomach*
el hueso *bone*
el microbio *germ*
el músculo *muscle*
la piel *skin*
la rodilla *knee*
la ropa *clothes*
la salida *dismissal*
la sangre *blood*
el timbre, la campana *bell*
la unión *joining together, union*

Verbos

contestar *to answer*
cubrir *to cover*
depender *to depend*
digerir (e:ie) *to digest*
dormir (o:ue) *to sleep*
mover (o:ue) *to move*
pensar (e:ie) *to think*
poder (o:ue) *to be able to, can, may*
proteger[1] *to protect*
recordar (o:ue) *to remember*
sonar (o:ue) *to ring*
sostener[2] *to support, to hold*
tragar *to swallow*
volver (o:ue) *to return, to go (come) back*

Adjetivos

distinto(a) *different*
oscuro(a) *dark*
poco(a) *little*
protegido(a) *protected*
segundo(a) *second*

Otras palabras y expresiones

alguien *someone, somebody*
antes (de) *before*
¿Cómo se llama...? *What is . . . called?*
conmigo *with me*
¿cuándo? *when?*
enseguida *right away*
está formado(a) *is made up; is formed*
levantar la mano *to raise one's hand*
nada *nothing*
para *in order to*
por todo *throughout*
se llama *it is called*
tener sueño *to be sleepy*
todo(a) *all, everything*
Vuelvo enseguida. *I'll be right back.*

---

[1]Orthographic change in the first person: **yo protejo**
[2]Conjugated like **tener**

Nombre ______________________ Sección ____________ Fecha ____________

VOCABULARIO ADICIONAL

Para hablar del cuerpo humano
(To talk about the human body)

la boca *mouth*
el brazo *arm*
la cara *face*
el cuello *neck*
el dedo *finger*
el dedo del pie *toe*
los dientes *teeth*
la espalda *back*
la lengua *tongue*
la mano *hand*
la nariz *nose*
el oído *inner ear*
el ojo *eye*
la oreja *ear*
el pecho *chest*
el pelo, el cabello *hair*
el pie *foot*
la pierna *leg*
el tobillo *ankle*

Notas Culturales

In Spanish-speaking countries, most families have meals together. After they finish eating, they often linger, seated around the table, conversing. This is called **hacer la sobremesa.**

Actividades

Dígame... Answer the following questions, basing your answers on the dialogue.

1. ¿Qué van a tener los niños la semana próxima?

   ____

2. ¿Qué día es el examen de anatomía?

   ____

3. ¿Qué están repasando los niños ahora?

   ____

4. ¿Qué tienen que hacer los niños antes de contestar?

   ____

Nombre ______________________ **Sección** ____________ **Fecha** ____________

5. ¿Qué protege el cuerpo?

____

6. ¿Qué depende de la cantidad de pigmento?

____

7. ¿Quiénes contestan bien?

____

8. ¿Quién va a repasar la lección con la maestra?

____

9. ¿Adónde tiene que ir Gonzalo? ¿A qué hora cierran la biblioteca?

____

10. ¿La maestra puede esperar a Gonzalo? ¿Cuándo vuelve él?

____

Hablemos

With a partner, take turns asking each other the following questions.

1. ¿Cuándo tiene Ud. exámenes?
2. Antes de los exámenes de español, ¿repasan Uds.? ¿Con quién?
3. ¿Qué es el esqueleto? ¿Qué hace?
4. ¿De qué está formado el esqueleto?
5. ¿Cómo se llama la unión de dos o más huesos?
6. ¿Qué son el codo y la rodilla?
7. ¿De qué protege la piel al cuerpo?
8. ¿Dónde está el cerebro?
9. ¿Qué protegen los huesos del cráneo?
10. Cuando comemos, ¿qué hacemos primero, masticamos o tragamos?
11. ¿Dónde termina la digestión?
12. ¿Mastica Ud. bien la comida antes de tragar?
13. ¿Digiere Ud. bien la comida?
14. Después de comer mucho, ¿Ud. siempre quiere dormir? ¿Por qué?
15. ¿A qué hora vuelve Ud. a su casa?

Nombre ______________________ Sección ____________ Fecha ____________

Vamos a practicar

Quiz

A Complete the following sentences, using the present indicative of the verbs given.

MODELO Ella no ___________ (poder) ir a la biblioteca.
Ella no **puede** ir a la biblioteca.

1. Yo no ___________ (recordar) cómo se llama él, pero tú sí ___________ (recordar) su nombre.
2. Ellos ___________ (mover) la cabeza y nosotros ___________ (mover) las manos.
3. El timbre ___________ (sonar) a las tres.
4. Ella ___________ (dormir) nueve horas y nosotros ___________ (dormir) ocho horas.
5. ¿A qué hora ___________ (volver) tú a tu casa? ¿Tú ___________ (poder) estudiar conmigo hoy?

B Answer the following questions, substituting direct object pronouns for the underlined words.

MODELO ¿Tú tienes los libros?
Sí, yo *los* tengo.

1. ¿Tú masticas bien la comida?

   ____

2. ¿El profesor contesta tus preguntas (*questions*)?

   ____

3. ¿La piel protege el cuerpo?

   ____

4. ¿A qué hora abren la biblioteca?

   ____

5. ¿Alguien te espera hoy?

   ____

6. ¿El profesor los llama a Uds.?

   ____

Nombre ______________________ Sección ____________ Fecha ____________

C Change the following sentences from the affirmative to the negative.

MODELO Hay alguien aquí.
***No* hay *nadie* aquí.**

1. Él siempre estudia por la noche.

____

2. Tú estudias anatomía y yo también.

____

3. Ellos necesitan algo.

____

4. El maestro habla con algunos estudiantes.

____

5. Tengo que estudiar anatomía o geografía.

____

D Complete the following exchanges with the correct form of the preposition and/or pronoun.

MODELO El libro es para ____________. (*her*)
El libro es para **ella.**

1. —Maestra, tengo algo para ____________. (*you, formal*)

   —¿Para ____________? (*me*) ¡Gracias! ¿Qué es?

   —Un libro.

2. —Mario, ¿puedes ir ____________ a la biblioteca? (*with me*)

   —No, Anita, no puedo ir ____________ ahora. (*with you, fam.*)

3. —¿Los lápices son para Rosa?

   —No, no son para ____________; son para ____________. (*her / you, fam.*)

Nombre ______________________ Sección ____________ Fecha ____________

Conversaciones breves

Complete the following dialogue, using your imagination and the vocabulary from this lesson.

En la clase de anatomía.

Julia —______________________________

Maestra —El examen de anatomía es el jueves.

Julia —______________________________

Maestra —Sí, hoy vamos a repasar. ¿Tienen algunas preguntas?

Teresa —______________________________

Maestra —Depende de la cantidad de pigmento de la piel.

Darío —______________________________

Maestra —No, no termina en el estómago; termina en el intestino.

Carmen —______________________________

Maestra —Los huesos del cráneo.

Ester —______________________________

Maestra —Se llama esqueleto.

Ángel —______________________________

Maestra —Sí, el codo es una articulación. Bueno, mañana continuamos con el repaso.

En estas situaciones

With two or more classmates, act out the following situations in Spanish.

1. You tell a colleague that you are reviewing anatomy because your students have a test next week, and describe the specific aspects of the human body on which your review focuses.
2. You ask your students the following questions, reminding them they must raise their hands before answering.
   a. What is a joint? What are two joints found in the body?
   b. What covers the body? From what does it protect the body?
   c. Where does food go when we eat?
   d. Why are there different colors of skin?
3. A student wants to review a lesson with you. You can study with him/her, but you need to go to the library, and it closes at five. Ask him/her if he/she can wait for you.

Casos

With you and a partner playing the roles, work through the following scenarios.

1. A teacher asks a student questions about anatomy.
2. A teacher and a new student discuss the opening and closing times of the library and the cafeteria.

Nombre ______________________ Sección ____________ Fecha ____________

Un paso más Review the **Vocabulario adicional** in this lesson and name the following parts of the body.

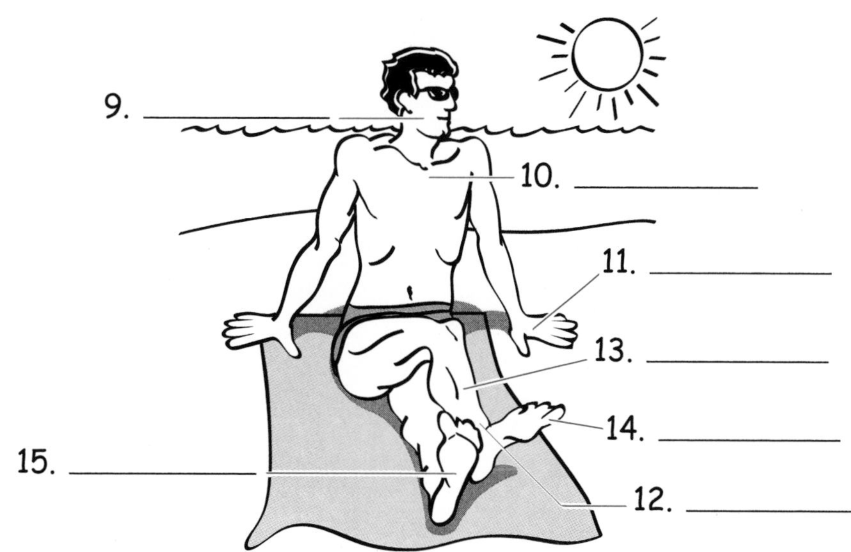

Nombre ______________________ Sección ____________ Fecha ____________

Actividad en grupo In groups of three or four, prepare a quiz on anatomy in which students have to complete sentences with the correct information.

____

____

____

____

____

Un repaso de anatomía (II)

Objectives

Structures

- Stem-changing verbs (**e:i**)
- Irregular first person forms
- Indirect object pronouns
- **Saber** contrasted with **conocer**

Communication

- Anatomy: talking about the respiratory system, the heart, and the blood

iLrn™

Hoy la maestra sigue hablándoles de anatomía a los niños.

Maestra —Uds. ya están casi listos para el examen. Cecilia, ¿puedes nombrar las partes del aparato respiratorio?
Cecilia —No sé cuáles son, señorita.
José —Yo lo sé... son la nariz, la tráquea, los bronquios y los pulmones.
Maestra —Muy bien. Como Uds. saben, necesitamos oxígeno para vivir. ¿Qué pasa cuando respiramos? ¿Alicia?
Alicia —Los pulmones toman el oxígeno para purificar la sangre.
Maestra —¿Quién puede decirme de qué aparato forma parte la sangre? Paco, ¿tú lo sabes?
Paco —Sí, la sangre forma parte del aparato circulatorio.
Maestra —Muy bien. También el corazón, las arterias, las venas y los vasos capilares, como pueden ver en esta lámina...
Anita —Yo no la veo bien, señorita...
Maestra —Puedes venir aquí, al frente. Carlos, ¿por qué es importante el corazón?
Carlos —Porque es el órgano que envía la sangre a todo el cuerpo.
Rita —Yo conozco a un hombre que padece del corazón y ahora van a operarlo.
Gerardo —¿Se puede vivir sin el corazón?
Maestra —No. Lo necesitamos para poder vivir... Margarita, ¿qué elementos forman la sangre?
Margarita —Los glóbulos rojos, los glóbulos blancos y las plaquetas.

Maestra	—Muy bien, Margarita. Gonzalo, ¿puedes decirles a tus compañeros para qué sirven las plaquetas?
Gonzalo	—Para coagular la sangre.
Maestra	—Correcto. Bueno, mañana traigo una lámina para estudiar el sistema nervioso. Ahora vamos a almorzar.
Gerado	—¿Qué sirven hoy en la cafetería, señorita?
Maestra	—No sé, Gerardo.
Alicia	—¿Dónde pongo las láminas, maestra?
Maestra	—En mi escritorio.

Los niños salen del aula y van a la cafetería.

¡Escuchemos!

While listening to the dialogue, circle **V (verdadero)** if the statement is true and **F (falso)** if it is false.

1.	La nariz, la tráquea, los bronquios y los pulmones son partes del aparato respiratorio.	V	F
2.	El oxígeno purifica la sangre.	V	F
3.	La sangre forma parte del aparato digestivo.	V	F
4.	El corazón envía la sangre a todo el cuerpo.	V	F
5.	Van a operar a Rita.	V	F
6.	Los glóbulos rojos, los glóbulos blancos y las plaquetas son los elementos que forman la sangre.	V	F
7.	Los glóbulos rojos sirven para coagular la sangre.	V	F
8.	Mañana los niños van a continuar estudiando el aparato circulatorio.	V	F
9.	Los niños almuerzan en la cafetería.	V	F
10.	Alicia tiene que poner las láminas en el escritorio de la maestra.	V	F

Nombre ______________________ **Sección** ____________ **Fecha** ____________

VOCABULARIO

Cognados

la arteria
el elemento
importante
el órgano
la vena

Nombres

el aparato circulatorio *circulatory system*
el aparato respiratorio *respiratory system*
los bronquios *bronchial tubes*
el corazón *heart*
los glóbulos blancos (rojos) *white (red) blood cells*
el hombre *man*
la nariz *nose*
la plaqueta *blood platelet*
los pulmones *lungs*
el sistema nervioso *nervous system*
la tráquea *windpipe, trachea*
los vasos capilares *capillaries*

Verbos

almorzar (o:ue) *to have lunch*
coagular *to coagulate*
conocer[1] *to know, to be acquainted with*
decir (e:i)[2] *to say, to tell*
enviar[3] *to send*
nombrar *to name*
operar *to operate*
padecer[4] **(de)** *to suffer (from)*
pasar *to happen*
purificar *to purify*
respirar *to breathe*
salir[5] *to go out, to get out*
seguir (e:i) *to continue*
servir (e:i) *to serve, to be good for*
tomar *to take*
ver[6] *to see*

Adjetivos

blanco(a) *white*
este(a) *this*

Otras palabras y expresiones

al frente (de) *to the front (of)*
como *as*
formar parte de *to be (a) part of*
padecer del corazón *to have heart trouble*
¿Para qué sirven...? *What are . . . good for?*
sin *without*
Vamos a almorzar. *Let's have lunch.*

---

[1]Irregular first person: **yo conozco**
[2]Irregular first person: **yo digo**
[3]Present indicative forms: **envío, envías, envía, enviamos, envían**
[4]Irregular first person: **yo padezco**
[5]Irregular first person: **yo salgo**
[6]Irregular first person: **yo veo**

Nombre ______________________ Sección ____________ Fecha ____________

VOCABULARIO ADICIONAL

El aparato digestivo
(*The digestive system*)

la boca *mouth*
el esófago *esophagus*
el estómago *stomach*
el intestino delgado *small intestine*
el intestino grueso *large intestine*

Las glándulas anexas
(*The annexed glands*)

las glándulas salivales *salivary glands*
el hígado *liver*
el páncreas *pancreas*

El sistema nervioso
(*The nervous system*)

el cerebelo *cerebellum*
el cerebro *brain*
la médula espinal *spinal cord*
el nervio *nerve*

Los sentidos (*The senses*)

el gusto *taste*
el oído *hearing*
el olfato *smell*
el tacto *touch*
la vista *taste*

Notas Culturales

With respect to interpersonal relations, Latino cultures tend to emphasize the importance of judging a person based on core personal qualities rather than economic or social status or visible achievements. Trust is based on familiarity and is built up over time. In a school setting, this cultural value might manifest itself in a greater willingness on the part of students or parents to devote extensive time to discussing personal matters as a means of getting to know someone, rather than "getting down to business" as the first step in solving a problem or accomplishing a task.

Actividades

Dígame... Answer the following questions, basing your answers on the dialogue.

1. ¿Qué repasan los alumnos hoy?

____

2. ¿Sabe Cecilia cuáles son las partes del aparato respiratorio?

____

3. ¿Cuáles son las partes del aparato circulatorio?

____

Nombre ______________________ Sección ____________ Fecha ____________

4. ¿Quién no ve bien la lámina?

____

5. ¿Cómo va la sangre a todo el cuerpo?

____

6. ¿A quién van a operar del corazón? ¿Por qué?

____

7. ¿Qué elementos forman la sangre?

____

8. ¿Para qué sirven las plaquetas?

____

9. ¿Qué va a traer la maestra mañana? ¿Para qué?

____

10. ¿Qué van a hacer los alumnos ahora?

____

11. ¿Dónde tiene que poner Alicia las láminas?

____

12. ¿De dónde salen los niños y adónde van?

____

Hablemos

With a partner, take turns asking each other the following questions.

1. ¿Repasa Ud. con sus alumnos antes de un examen?
2. ¿Sabe Ud. cuáles son las partes del aparato respiratorio?
3. ¿Podemos vivir sin oxígeno? ¿Para qué lo necesitamos?
4. ¿Por qué es importante dar sangre?
5. ¿Qué láminas de anatomía tiene Ud. para su clase?
6. ¿Ve Ud. bien?
7. ¿A qué hora almuerza Ud.? ¿Dónde almuerza?
8. ¿A qué hora sale Ud. de su casa por la mañana?
9. ¿Está Ud. listo(a) para el próximo examen de español?

Nombre ______________________ Sección ____________ Fecha ____________

Quiz

Vamos a practicar

A Rewrite the following sentences, using the element in parentheses to replace the underlined word(s). Make all necessary changes.

1. Yo visito a Carmen. (conocer)

   ____

2. ¿Para qué sirven las plaquetas? (el corazón)

   ____

3. Yo no necesito nada. (saber)

   ____

4. Uds. siguen estudiando. (nosotros)

   ____

5. Ella dice que va a almorzar ahora. (Yo)

   ____

6. Yo no llamo a Rosa. (ver)

   ____

7. Ellos traen las láminas y las ponen en el escritorio. (yo)

   ____

8. Nosotros salimos a las ocho. (yo)

   ____

B Complete the following sentences with the Spanish equivalent of the words in parentheses.

MODELO Ella __________ las láminas. (*gives him*)
Ella **le da** las láminas.

1. Yo __________ la ropa. (*bring them*)

   ____

2. La maestra __________ en español. (*speaks to us*)

   ____

3. Nosotros __________ la comida. (*serve her*)

   ____

Nombre ______________________ **Sección** __________ **Fecha** __________

4. Yo __________ que él sabe mucho. (*tell you, pl.*)

____

5. Ellos pueden __________ el examen, Anita. (*give you, fam.*)

____

C Complete the minidialogues with the correct form of **saber** or **conocer.**

1. —¿__________ Ud. al maestro nuevo?

   —No, no lo __________.

2. —¿Quién __________ la respuesta?

   —¡Maestra, yo la __________!

3. —¿__________ los estudiantes las partes del aparato respiratorio de memoria (*from memory*)?

   —Sí, ellos las __________.

4. —¿Tú __________ México?

   —No, pero __________ Guatemala y Costa Rica.

5. —¿__________ tú las novelas de García Márquez?

   —No, no las __________.

6. —¿__________ ellos dibujar?

   —Sí, ellos __________ dibujar muy bien.

Conversaciones breves

Complete the following dialogue, using your imagination and the vocabulary from this lesson.

La Srta. Vázquez continúa con el repaso de anatomía.

Maestra —Elsa, ¿puedes nombrar las partes del aparato circulatorio?

Elsa —____

Maestra —Muy bien. ¿Quién sabe cuáles son los elementos que forman la sangre?

Raúl —____

Maestra —¿Cuál es el órgano que envía la sangre a todo el cuerpo?

Ramiro —____

Nombre ______________________ Sección ____________ Fecha ____________

Maestra —¿Cuáles son las partes del aparato respiratorio?

Aurora —____

Maestra —No, el corazón no es parte del aparato respiratorio.

Carmela —____

Maestra —Los pulmones toman el oxígeno para purificar la sangre.

Rafael —____

Maestra —No, no podemos vivir sin él; es una parte importante del aparato circulatorio. Bueno, creo que están listos para el examen.

En estas situaciones

With two or more classmates, act out the following situations in Spanish.

1. You are summarizing a lesson on anatomy. You remind your students that:
   - a. The nose, the trachea, the bronchial tubes, and the lungs are part of the respiratory system.
   - b. When we breathe, the lungs take oxygen to purify the blood.
   - c. The blood, the heart, the arteries, the veins, and the capillaries are part of the circulatory system.
   - d. The elements that form the blood are: the red blood cells, the white blood cells, and the blood platelets, which serve to coagulate the blood.
2. Tell the students they need to review the lesson if they want to be ready for the test. Answer their questions about what specific areas they need to review.

Casos

With you and a partner playing the roles, work through the following scenarios.

1. Two students quiz each other before an anatomy exam.
2. One student instructs another on how to diagram the respiratory and circulatory systems.

Un paso más

Review the **Vocabulario adicional** in this lesson and complete the following sentences.

1. La comida va de la boca al ____________ y después al ____________.
2. Los cinco sentidos son la ____________, el ____________, el ____________, el ____________ y el ____________.
3. El estómago y el intestino son partes del ____________.
4. El intestino delgado es más largo que el intestino ____________.

Nombre ______________________ Sección ____________ Fecha ____________

5. El cerebro, el ____________, la médula ____________ y los nervios forman parte del sistema ____________.

6. Las glándulas ____________, el páncreas y el ____________ son glándulas ____________ al aparato digestivo.

Actividad en grupo In groups of three or four, prepare a chart in which you include all the parts of the circulatory and respiratory systems. Describe some of their functions.

Lección 8 Una clase de ciencias

Objectives

Structures

- Demonstrative adjectives and pronouns
- Special construction with **gustar, doler,** and **hacer falta**
- Direct and indirect object pronouns used together

Communication

- Science class: talking about animals
- Vertebrates and invertebrates

iLrn™

Hoy la maestra está explicándoles a los estudiantes las diferentes clases de animales que existen en el mundo.

Maestra —El reino animal está dividido en dos grupos: los vertebrados y los invertebrados.
Ángel —¿Los peces son invertebrados, señorita?
Maestra —No. Los invertebrados no tienen columna vertebral. Los insectos son invertebrados.
Inés —Los mamíferos son vertebrados, ¿verdad, señorita?
Maestra —¡Muy bien, Inés! Las aves, los reptiles, los anfibios y los peces también pertenecen a ese grupo.
María —¿Qué es un anfibio?
Maestra —Un animal que en la primera parte de su vida vive en el agua y respira como los peces, y después vive en la tierra y respira como los mamíferos.
Diego —¡Como los renacuajos, que después son ranas! A mí me gustan las ranas. Yo tengo dos. Le voy a preguntar a mi mamá si puedo traerlas a la clase para mostrárselas.
Maestra —Puedes traerlas mañana, si quieres. ¿Y los reptiles? ¿Cuáles son?
Anita —Las serpientes, las lagartijas, los cocodrilos y las tortugas.
Carmen —Las aves también son reptiles.
Luis —¡Eso no es verdad! Las aves pueden volar.
Maestra —Muy bien, Luis. ¿Cuáles son las características de las aves?

Nombre ______________________ Sección ____________ Fecha ____________

Olga	—¡Yo puedo decírselas! Tienen plumas y la boca en forma de pico.
Maestra	—¡Eso es! En esta lámina vemos fotografías de diferentes clases de aves.
Antonio	—¡Yo sé otra cosa! Las aves nacen de huevos.
Maestra	—Sí, y los mamíferos nacen vivos. ¿Qué otras características tienen los mamíferos?
Oscar	—Tienen sangre caliente y el cuerpo cubierto de pelo.
Maestra	—¿Y los peces?
Teresa	—Tienen sangre fría, el cuerpo cubierto de escamas y respiran por branquias.
Maestra	—¡Muy bien! Ahora debemos ir a la biblioteca de la escuela. Allí hay varios libros sobre animales. Se los pueden pedir a la bibliotecaria.
Inés	—Señorita, me duele la cabeza.
Maestra	—Puedes ir a hablar con la enfermera.

¡Escuchemos!

While listening to the dialogue, circle **V (verdadero)** if the statement is true and **F (falso)** if it is false.

1. Hoy la maestra habla del reino animal. V F
2. Los reptiles son invertebrados. V F
3. Un anfibio pasa toda su vida en el agua. V F
4. Las ranas son primero renacuajos. V F
5. Las lagartijas son reptiles. V F
6. Las aves también son reptiles. V F
7. Los mamíferos nacen de huevos. V F
8. El cuerpo de los mamíferos está cubierto de pelo. V F
9. Los peces respiran por branquias. V F
10. A la maestra le duele la cabeza. V F

Nombre ______________________ Sección ____________ Fecha ____________

VOCABULARIO

Cognados

el anfibio
el animal
la característica
la ciencia
el cocodrilo
dividido(a)
la fotografía
el insecto
el invertebrado
el reptil
el vertebrado

Nombres

el ave (*f.*) *bird, fowl*
la boca *mouth*
las branquias, agallas *branchiae, gills*
la clase *kind, type*
la columna vertebral *spine*
el (la) enfermero(a) *nurse*
la escama *scale*
el huevo *egg*
la lagartija *lizard*
la mamá, la madre *mom, mother*
el mamífero *mammal*
el pelo *hair*
el pez[1] *fish*
el pico *beak*
la pluma *feather*
la rana *frog*
el reino *kingdom*
el renacuajo *tadpole*
la serpiente *snake, serpent*
la tierra *soil, earth, land*
la tortuga *turtle*
la vida *life*

Verbos

doler (o:ue) *to hurt, to ache*
existir *to exist*
explicar *to explain*
gustar *to be pleasing to, to like*
mostrar (o:ue), enseñar *to show*
nacer *to be born*
pedir (e:i) *to ask (for), to request*
pertenecer[2] *to belong*
preguntar *to ask (a question)*
volar (o:ue) *to fly*

Adjetivos

caliente *hot (temperature)*
cubierto(a) (de) *covered (with)*
ese(a) *that*
frío(a) *cold*
vivo(a) *alive*

Otras palabras y expresiones

en forma de *in the shape of*
eso (*neuter pronoun*) *that*
otra cosa *something else*

---

[1]Refers to a fish still in the water. Once caught, the word for fish is **pescado.**
[2]Irregular first person: **yo pertenezco**

Nombre ______________________ Sección ____________ Fecha ____________

VOCABULARIO ADICIONAL

Animales de la finca (*Farm animals*)

el caballo *horse*
la cabra, el (la) chivo(a) *goat*
el cerdo, el cochino *pig*
la gallina *hen*
el gallo *rooster*
el (la) ganso(a) *gander, goose*
la oveja *sheep*
el pato *duck*
el pavo, el guajolote (*Méx.*), **el guanajo** (*Cuba*) *turkey*
el toro *bull*
la vaca *cow*
la yegua *mare*

Animales domésticos (*Pets*)

el conejo *rabbit*
el gato *cat*
el pájaro *bird*
el perro *dog*

Animales salvajes (*Wild animals*)

el camello *camel*
la cebra *zebra*
el elefante *elephant*
el hipopótamo *hippopotamus*
la jirafa *giraffe*
el león *lion*
el mono, el chango (*Méx.*) *monkey*
el tigre *tiger*

Insectos (*Insects*)

la abeja *bee*
la avispa *wasp*
la hormiga *ant*
la mariposa *butterfly*
la mosca *fly*
el mosquito, el zancudo (*Méx.*) *mosquito*

Otros animales invertebrados (*Other invertebrates*)

la araña *spider*
el camarón *shrimp*
el cangrejo *crab*
el caracol *snail*
la langosta *lobster*

Notas Culturales

The Galapagos Islands in the Pacific Ocean near the Ecuadorian coast are considered one of the best preserved ecological zones in the world. The islands are named after the giant tortoises called **galápagos.** These tortoises weigh about 600 pounds and live for about 250 years. The different species of plants and animals that are found on the islands have no similarity to those on the South American continent.

Nombre ______________________ Sección ______________ Fecha ______________

Actividades

Dígame... Answer the following questions, basing your answers on the dialogue.

1. ¿Qué les está explicando la maestra a los niños?

2. ¿Qué pregunta Inés?

3. ¿Qué tiene Diego? ¿A él le gustan las ranas?

4. ¿Qué le va a preguntar Diego a su mamá? ¿Para qué quiere traerlas?

5. ¿Por qué dice Luis que las aves no son reptiles?

6. ¿Qué puede decir Olga?

7. ¿Qué pueden ver los niños en la lámina que tiene la maestra?

8. ¿Qué dice la maestra que hay en la biblioteca? ¿A quién se los pueden pedir?

9. ¿Qué le duele a Inés?

10. ¿Con quién puede hablar la niña?

Hablemos With a partner, take turns asking each other the following questions.

1. ¿Sabe Ud. mucho de los animales?
2. ¿Cuál es su animal favorito?
3. ¿Es un animal vertebrado o invertebrado?
4. ¿Es el animal un reptil, un anfibio, un pez o un mamífero?

5. ¿Cómo lo sabe Ud.?
6. ¿Tiene Ud. un animal doméstico? ¿Cuál es?
7. ¿Tiene Ud. peces de colores en su casa?
8. Si yo necesito un libro sobre los animales, ¿a quién se lo puedo pedir?
9. Si yo necesito láminas de animales, ¿puede Ud. dármelas?
10. En la biblioteca de la escuela, ¿hay muchos libros con fotografías de animales?

Quiz

Vamos a practicar

A Write the corresponding demonstrative adjectives before each noun.

MODELO *that* __________ tortuga
esa tortuga

1. *this*
   a. ____________________ libro
   b. ____________________ lámina
2. *these*
   a. ____________________ ranas
   b. ____________________ renacuajos
3. *that*
   a. ____________________ pájaro
   b. ____________________ lagartija
4. *those*
   a. ____________________ mamíferos
   b. ____________________ serpientes

B Answer the questions in the affirmative, substituting the corresponding direct and indirect object pronouns for the underlined words.

MODELO ¿La profesora les explica <u>la lección</u> <u>a Uds.</u>?
Sí, la profesora *nos la* explica.

1. ¿Raúl les da <u>la fotografía</u> <u>a ellos</u>?

   ____

2. ¿Tú <u>nos</u> traes <u>los libros</u> mañana?

   ____

3. ¿Él <u>te</u> da <u>las láminas de las aves</u>?

   ____

4. ¿Puedes traer<u>me</u> <u>el lápiz</u>? (*Use the **tú** form.*)

   ____

5. ¿Les piden <u>a Uds.</u> <u>los cuadernos</u>?

   ____

Nombre ______________________ Sección ____________ Fecha ____________

C Write the following dialogues in Spanish.

1. "Do your feet hurt, Alicia?"
   "Yes, they hurt a lot."

   ____

   ____

2. "Are you going to ask the librarian (*f.*) for the books?"
   "Yes, and I'm going to ask her if she has some illustrations."

   ____

   ____

3. "Do you like this book, Miss Silva?"
   "No, I like that one better."

   ____

   ____

Conversaciones breves

Complete the following dialogue, using your imagination and the vocabulary from this lesson.

La Srta. Rivera les hace preguntas a los alumnos sobre los animales.

Maestra —____

Rosita —Tienen sangre caliente y el cuerpo cubierto de pelo.

Maestra —____

Aurora —No, señorita, no nacen de huevos. Nacen vivos.

Maestra —____

Pedro —Son los animales que tienen columna vertebral.

Maestra —____

Guadalupe —Tienen el cuerpo cubierto de plumas y la boca en forma de pico.

Maestra —____

Raúl —No, señorita, no es un pez. Es un anfibio.

Maestra —____

Carlos —No, tienen sangre fría, como los peces.

Nombre ______________________ Sección ____________ Fecha ____________

 **En estas situaciones** With two or more classmates, act out the following situations in Spanish.

1. Tell your students that you are going to discuss the different kinds of animals that exist in the world. Then ask them about the characteristics of mammals, fish, birds, and amphibians.
2. Ask your students where there are more books about animals. Then tell them when you will go there and explain that they can ask the librarian for books.

Casos With you and a partner playing the roles, work through the following scenarios.

1. A teacher and a student discuss different kinds of animals.
2. Two students quiz each other by describing characteristics of each group of animals for the other to identify.
3. Students give names of animals they have seen at the zoo.

Un paso más Review the **Vocabulario adicional** in this lesson, and write the names of the following animals in the spaces provided.

1. ______________

2. ______________

3. ______________

4. ______________

5. ______________

6. ______________

7. ______________

8. ______________

9. ______________

Nombre ______________________ Sección ______________ Fecha ______________

10. ______________

11. ______________

12. ______________

13. ______________

14. ______________

15. ______________

16. ______________

17. ______________

18. ______________

19. ______________

20. ______________

21. ______________

22. ______________

23. ______________

Nombre ______________________ Sección ____________ Fecha ____________

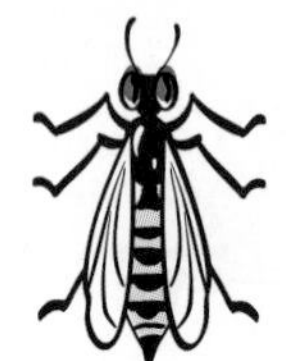

24. ______________

25. ______________

26. ______________

27. ______________

28. ______________

29. ______________

30. ______________

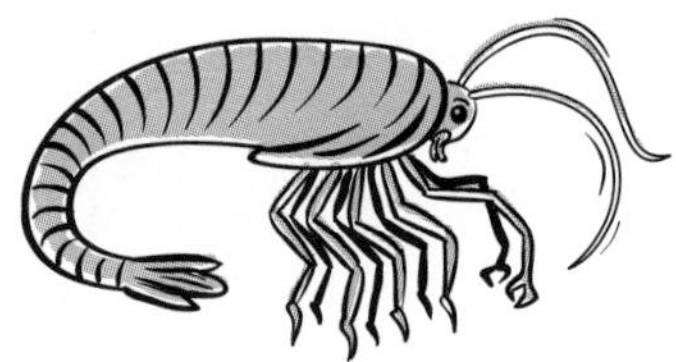

31. ______________

Actividad en grupo In groups of three or four, prepare a list of ten questions to ask your students about the animal kingdom.

______________________ ______________________

______________________ ______________________

______________________ ______________________

______________________ ______________________

______________________ ______________________

Lección 9 Una conferencia

Objectives

Structures

- Possessive pronouns
- Command forms: **Ud.** and **Uds.**
- Reflexive constructions
- Uses of object pronouns with command forms

Communication

- Parent–teacher conference: talking to parents about academic and social issues

iLrn™

La Sra. Silvia Gómez habla con el maestro de su hijo Antonio.

Maestro —Siéntese aquí, por favor, Sra. Gómez. Quiero hablar con Ud. sobre su hijo Antonio.
Señora —Sé que está atrasado en lectura...
Maestro —Bueno, todavía no lee al nivel del grado, pero está mejorando un poco.
Señora —¿Se porta mal en clase?
Maestro —No, pero muchas veces llega tarde, y eso es un problema. Además, a veces se pelea con los otros niños y les pega.
Señora —Yo no sé qué le pasa...
Maestro —Yo tampoco. No sé por qué no se lleva bien con sus compañeros de clase.
Señora —Castíguelo. Déjelo en la escuela después de clase...
Maestro —Ésa no es la solución. Trate de ayudarlo con la tarea y venga a observarlo en clase de vez en cuando.
Señora —Yo no puedo porque trabajo, pero como mi esposo no trabaja los lunes, puede venir él.
Maestro —Bueno... ¿El niño come bien? ¿Duerme bien? ¿Hay problemas en la casa?
Señora —A veces no come nada por la mañana.
Maestro —Dele un buen desayuno. Eso es muy importante.
Señora —Muy bien. Mire, Sr. Soto, aunque Antonio está en el grupo de lectura más bajo, yo creo que es inteligente...
Maestro —Sí, tiene habilidad, pero debe esforzarse más.

Señora —Yo creo que también tiene problemas con la vista. Quizás necesita anteojos... Yo necesito ir al oculista para cambiar los míos, así que puedo pedir turno para él también.

Maestro —Buena idea. Si estas medidas no son suficientes, podemos hablar de la posibilidad de hacerle una evaluación para determinar si sus dificultades se deben a un problema de aprendizaje, como la dislexia.

Señora —¿Quién hace esas evaluaciones?

Maestro —La psicóloga de la escuela, y son gratis.

Señora —Gracias, Sr. Soto.

Maestro —De nada, Sra. Gómez. Gracias por venir.[1] ¡Ah! Ésta es la libreta de calificaciones de Antonio. Fírmela antes de irse, por favor.

¡Escuchemos! While listening to the dialogue, circle **V (verdadero)** if the statement is true and **F (falso)** if it is false.

1.	Antonio está atrasado en lectura.	V	F
2.	El maestro les pega a los niños.	V	F
3.	Antonio se lleva muy bien con los otros niños.	V	F
4.	La mamá de Antonio dice que el maestro debe castigar al niño.	V	F
5.	El papá de Antonio va a venir a observar la clase.	V	F
6.	El maestro dice que el niño no necesita desayunar.	V	F
7.	La mamá de Antonio piensa que quizá el niño necesita anteojos.	V	F
8.	El maestro dice que el niño necesita una evaluación para ver si puede esforzarse.	V	F
9.	Las evaluaciones cuestan mucho dinero.	V	F
10.	La mamá tiene que firmar la libreta de calificaciones de Antonio.	V	F

[1] In Spanish, the infinitive is used after a preposition.

Nombre ______________________ Sección ____________ Fecha ____________

VOCABULARIO

Cognados

la conferencia
la dificultad
la dislexia
la evaluación
la habilidad
la medida
el (la) psicólogo(a)
la solución
suficiente

Nombres

los anteojos, los lentes, los espejuelos (*Cuba, Puerto Rico*), **las gafas** (*Spain*) *eyeglasses*
el (la) compañero(a) de clase *classmate*
el desayuno *breakfast*
el (la) esposo(a) *spouse, husband (wife)*
el (la) hijo(a) *child, son (daughter)*
el nivel *level*
el (la) oculista *eye doctor*
el problema de aprendizaje *learning disability*
la vista *sight, eyesight*

Verbos

cambiar *to change*
castigar *to punish*
creer *to think, to believe*
dejar *to leave (behind)*
esforzarse (o:ue) *to try, to make an effort*
irse *to leave, to go away*
mejorar(se) *to get better, to improve (oneself)*
mirar *to look (at)*
observar *to observe*
pegar *to hit*
pelearse *to fight*
portarse *to behave*
sentarse (e:ie) *to sit down*
tratar (de) *to try (to)*

Adjetivos

atrasado(a) *behind*
bajo(a) *low*
gratis *free (of charge)*

Otras palabras y expresiones

además *besides*
al nivel del grado *at grade level*
así que *so*
aunque *even though*
como *since*
de vez en cuando *once in a while*
llegar tarde *to be late*
llevarse bien *to get along*
muchas veces *many times*
pedir turno, hacer una cita *to make an appointment*
portarse mal *to misbehave*
que *who*
quizá(s) *maybe, perhaps*
se debe(n) a... *it is (they are) due to . . .*
tampoco *neither*
todavía no *not yet*
un poco *a little*

Nombre ______________________ Sección ____________ Fecha ____________

VOCABULARIO ADICIONAL

Para hablar con los padres (*To talk with parents*)

Su hijo(a)...

- **está adelantado(a).** *is ahead of the class.*
- **está enfermo(a).** *is sick.*
- **está progresando.** *is progressing.*
- **interrumpe la clase.** *disturbs the class.*
- **no devuelve los libros.** *doesn't return books.*
- **no se siente bien.** *isn't feeling well.*
- **tiene fiebre, tiene calentura.** *has a fever.*
- **vomitó.** *threw up.*

Es urgente. *It is urgent.*

No se preocupe. *Don't worry.*

¿Puede venir a buscar (recoger) a su hijo(a)? *Can you come to pick up your son (daughter)?*

Sea consistente. *Be consistent.*

Notas Culturales

- The form **vos** is used in several Central and South American countries. In conversation, the form **vos** is used in Argentina, Costa Rica, Paraguay, and Uruguay, in place of the informal **tú.** Instead of **tú vienes,** in these countries one says **vos venís.** This phenomenon is known as **voseo.**

Actividades

Dígame... Answer the following questions, basing your answers on the dialogue.

1. ¿Sobre quién quiere hablar el maestro con la Sra. Gómez?

   ____

2. ¿Cuál es uno de los problemas que tiene Antonio?

   ____

3. ¿Lee al nivel del grado? ¿Está mejorando?

   ____

4. ¿Antonio se porta mal en clase?

   ____

5. ¿Cómo se lleva Antonio con sus compañeros de clase? ¿Qué hace a veces?

____

6. ¿Sabe la Sra. Gómez lo que le pasa a Antonio? ¿Y el maestro?

____

7. ¿Qué cree el maestro que debe hacer la Sra. Gómez?

____

8. ¿Qué debe darle la Sra. Gómez a su hijo por la mañana?

____

9. ¿Adónde debe llevar la Sra. Gómez a su hijo? ¿Por qué?

____

10. ¿Qué pueden hacerle a Antonio?

____

11. ¿Qué pueden determinar esas evaluaciones?

____

12. ¿Quién las hace? ¿Son gratis?

____

Hablemos With a partner, take turns asking each other the following questions.

1. ¿Presta Ud. atención en la clase de español?
2. ¿Llega Ud. tarde a clase a veces?
3. ¿Habla Ud. español de vez en cuando?
4. ¿Alguien lo (la) ayuda a Ud. con la tarea?
5. ¿Qué hace Ud. para mejorar en la clase de español?
6. Yo tengo mi libro de español. ¿Dónde está el suyo?
7. ¿Observa Ud. a veces las clases de otros maestros?
8. ¿Castiga Ud. a sus estudiantes? ¿Cómo?
9. ¿Tiene Ud. problemas con la vista?
10. ¿Necesita Ud. anteojos para leer?

Nombre ______________________ Sección ____________ Fecha ____________

Quiz

Vamos a practicar

A Ask a parent to do (or not to do) the following things.

Modelo llevar a su hijo al oculista
***Lleve* a su hijo al oculista.**

1. ayudar a su hijo con la tarea y no castigarlo

____

2. observar la clase

____

3. darle un buen desayuno al niño

____

4. firmar la libreta de calificaciones

____

5. no sentarse allí

____

6. ir a hablar con el director y decirle que su hijo tiene problemas, pero no ir hoy

____

B Tell your students (as a group) to do (or not to do) the following things.

Modelo esforzarse más
***Esfuércense* más.**

1. no dejar los libros en casa, traerlos todos los días

____

2. no pelearse con los otros niños y no pegarles

____

3. portarse bien y prestar atención

____

4. no llegar tarde a clase

____

5. hacer la tarea

____

6. no portarse mal en clase

____

C Complete the following sentences with the Spanish equivalent of the words in parentheses.

1. Su hijo ______________ en la clase. (*behaves badly*)
2. Ellos ______________ en la escuela. (*fight*)
3. Yo ______________ ahora. (*go away*)
4. Nosotros ______________ aquí. (*sit down*)
5. Mi libro está aquí. ¿Dónde está ______________, Rosita? (*yours*)
6. Ellos tienen sus anteojos pero yo no tengo ______________. (*mine*)
7. Yo traigo mis lápices. ¿Trae Mario ______________? (*his*)
8. La libreta de calificaciones es ______________, pero el libro verde es ______________. (*hers/his*)

Conversaciones breves

Complete the following dialogue, using your imagination and the vocabulary from this lesson.

La Sra. Vargas viene a hablar con la maestra de su hija.

Maestra —Sra. Vargas, tengo muchos problemas en clase con Luisa.

Sra. Vargas —¿______________________________?

Maestra —Sí, se porta muy mal. Y no hace la tarea.

Sra. Vargas —______________________________

Maestra —Eso no es verdad. Ella tiene tarea todos los días.

Sra. Vargas —______________________________

Maestra —Castigarla no es la solución. Ud. debe ayudarla.

Sra. Vargas —______________________________

Maestra —Sí, yo también creo que los tiene. Quizás necesita lentes.

Sra. Vargas —______________________________

Maestra —Llévela, por favor.

Nombre ______________________ Sección ____________ Fecha ____________

Sra. Vargas —____

Maestra —Sí, señora, pero no se esfuerza en clase.

Sra. Vargas —____

Maestra —Sí, por favor, ayúdela con la tarea y dígale que debe estudiar más.

Sra. Vargas —____

Maestra —Sí, aquí está. Fírmela antes de irse, por favor.

En estas situaciones

With two or more classmates, act out the following situations in Spanish.

1. At a parent-teacher conference, you tell a parent to take his/her son to the eye doctor because you think the child has a vision problem and may need eyeglasses.
2. A child is misbehaving in your class; he fights with other children and hits them. He is also behind in reading. You call the child's parent to describe the child's problems in the classroom and to discuss the possibility of having the child evaluated by the school psychologist for learning disabilities or other problems.
3. A mother/father thinks he/she should punish his/her daughter for not studying. You don't think that is the solution; it would be better if the girl's parents helped her with her homework.

Casos

With you and a partner playing the roles, work through the following scenarios.

1. A parent and a teacher discuss a child's progress and discipline problems, and how the child's performance and behavior might be improved.
2. A student discusses his/her vision problems with his/her teacher. The teacher responds with an appropriate course of action for the student and his/her parents.

Un paso más

Review the **Vocabulario adicional** in this lesson and decide how to convey the following information to the parents of your students.

1. Your daughter's library books are always overdue.

   ____

2. Your son is making good progress.

   ____

3. Your daughter disturbs the class.

   ____

4. Your daughter has done more work than the other students in the class.

   ____

5. Your son isn't feeling well.

____

6. Your son is sick.

____

7. Your daughter threw up.

____

8. It is urgent.

____

9. Can you come to pick up your daughter?

____

10. There's nothing to worry about.

____

11. You need to be consistent with your son.

____

Actividad en grupo In groups of three or four, prepare a list of rules and regulations of student behavior for the parents.

____

____

____

____

____

Lección 10 Una excursión al jardín botánico

Objectives

Structures

- The preterit of regular verbs
- The preterit of **ser, ir,** and **dar**
- Uses of **por** and **para**

Communication

- Field trip: dealing with students outside the school setting
- Talking about plants

iLrn™

El Sr. Ochoa y la Sra. Pérez, maestros de una escuela primaria, llevan a sus alumnos de segundo y tercer grado de excursión al jardín botánico para enseñarles algo acerca de las plantas.

Sr. Ochoa —Por favor, bájense del autobús y pónganse en fila. No se separen de nosotros.
Sra. Pérez —Caminen de dos en dos y tómense de la mano.
Sr. Ochoa —Aquí vamos a ver plantas de distintos países y climas.
Paco —(*Lee un letrero.*) Aquí hay un árbol de Cuba. ¡Qué alto es!
Sra. Pérez —Los árboles son las plantas más grandes. ¿Quién recuerda cuáles son las partes de una planta?
Aurora —La raíz, el tallo y las hojas.
Carlos —¡Y las flores y los frutos! Yo tengo un naranjo en mi patio. Me lo dio mi tío.
Sra. Pérez —¡Muy bien, Aurora y Carlos! ¿Dónde está Raquel?
Eva —Fue al baño. Allí viene ya.
Sr. Ochoa —¿Por qué son importantes los árboles?
Ramón —Porque nos dan madera para hacer muebles y papel.
Sra. Pérez —Muy bien. ¡Y también producen oxígeno! ¿Cómo se alimentan las plantas? ¿Alguien lo sabe?
Raúl —¿Con agua?
Sra. Pérez —El agua ayuda, pero la planta toma parte de sus alimentos de la tierra...
Elena —¿Y eso sube por el tronco?
Sra. Pérez —Sí, y las hojas usan la luz del sol para transformarlo en alimento para la planta.

Nombre ______________________ **Sección** ____________ **Fecha** ____________

José	—Yo quiero ir a ver los cactos. El año pasado fuimos a Arizona y vi muchos allí.
Sr. Ochoa	—Eso es porque los cactos son plantas del desierto.
Teresa	—Yo encontré una semilla y alguien me la quitó. ¿Quién fue?
Sara	—¡Fue Jorge!
Sra. Pérez	—Nadie puede llevarse nada del jardín botánico.

Los niños pasaron toda la mañana en el jardín botánico y aprendieron mucho. Ahora tienen que volver a la escuela.

Sra. Pérez	—Apúrense porque hace viento y está empezando a llover.
Sr. Ochoa	—Vamos por aquí. Suban al autobús y siéntense.

¡Escuchemos!

While listening to the dialogue, circle **V (verdadero)** if the statement is true and **F (falso)** if it is false.

1.	Los niños de segundo y tercer grado no pueden ir al jardín botánico.	V	F
2.	Las plantas más grandes son los árboles.	V	F
3.	La raíz y el tallo son partes de una planta.	V	F
4.	Carlos tiene un árbol frutal en su patio.	V	F
5.	Las plantas solamente necesitan agua para alimentarse.	V	F
6.	La luz del sol no es importante para el alimento de las plantas.	V	F
7.	Los cactos son plantas del desierto.	V	F
8.	Teresa quiere saber quién le quitó la semilla.	V	F
9.	Los niños fueron del jardín botánico a su casa.	V	F
10.	Los niños tienen que subir al autobús y sentarse.	V	F

Nombre ______________________ Sección ____________ Fecha ____________

VOCABULARIO

Cognados

el cacto
el desierto
el jardín
la planta

Nombres

el alimento *nourishment, food, nutrient*
el año *year*
el autobús, el ómnibus, la guagua (*Cuba, Puerto Rico*), **el camión** (*Méx.*) *bus*
la escuela primaria, la escuela elemental *grade school*
la excursión *field trip*
la fila *line*
la flor *flower*
el fruto *fruit*
la hoja *leaf*
la luz del sol *sunlight*
la madera *wood*
los muebles *furniture*
el naranjo *orange tree*
el patio *backyard*
la raíz *root*
la semilla *seed*
el sol *sun*
el tallo *stem*
el tronco (*tree*) *trunk*

Verbos

alimentar(se) *to feed, to nourish, to take nourishment*
apurarse, darse prisa *to hurry up*
bajar(se) *to get off*
caminar *to walk*
encontrar (o:ue) *to find*
enseñar *to teach*
llevarse *to take away, to carry out*
llover (o:ue) *to rain*
pasar *to spend (time)*
quitar(se) *to take away, to remove*
separar(se) *to separate, to get separated*
subir(se) *to get on, to rise*
transformar *to turn into, to transform*

Otras palabras y expresiones

acerca de *about*
allí viene ya *she's/he's coming now*
de dos en dos *two by two, in twos, in pairs*
ponerse en fila *to stand in line, to get in line*
por aquí *this way*
tómense de la mano *hold hands*

Nombre ______________________ Sección ____________ Fecha ____________

VOCABULARIO ADICIONAL

Algunas flores (*Some flowers*)

la camelia *camellia*
el clavel *carnation*
la margarita *daisy*
la orquídea *orchid*
el pensamiento *pansy*
la rosa *rose*
la violeta *violet*

Algunas frutas (*Some fruit*)

la cereza *cherry*
la fresa *strawberry*
el limón *lemon*
la manzana *apple*
la naranja, la china (*Puerto Rico*) *orange*
la pera *pear*
el plátano, la banana, el guineo (*Puerto Rico*) *banana*
la toronja *grapefruit*
la uva *grape*

Algunos vegetales (*Some vegetables*)

el ají, el chile verde (*Méx.*) *bell pepper*
el ajo *garlic*
el apio *celery*
la cebolla *onion*
la lechuga *lettuce*
la papa, la patata (*Spain*) *potato*
la zanahoria *carrot*

Las estaciones del año (*The seasons of the year*)

la primavera *spring*
el verano *summer*
el otoño *fall, autumn*
el invierno *winter*

Notas Culturales

In the Southern Hemisphere the seasons are reversed: when it is winter in the United States, it is summer in Argentina and Chile. Thus, the school year begins in March and ends in December. During the month of June, there is a winter break or *vacaciones de invierno.*

ACTIVIDADES

Dígame... Answer the following questions, basing your answers on the dialogue.

1. ¿Adónde va el grupo de estudiantes?

____

2. ¿Para qué los llevan allí?

____

Nombre ______________________ Sección ____________ Fecha ____________

3. ¿Cómo deben caminar los niños?

____

4. ¿Quiénes saben las partes de una planta?

____

5. ¿Qué tipo de árbol tiene Carlos? ¿Quién se lo dio?

____

6. ¿Para qué sirven los árboles?

____

7. ¿Adónde fue José el año pasado y qué plantas vio?

____

8. ¿Quién encontró una semilla? ¿Quién se la quitó?

____

9. ¿Qué pueden llevarse los niños del jardín botánico?

____

10. ¿Por qué deben apurarse los niños?

____

 **Hablemos** With a partner, take turns asking each other the following questions.

1. ¿Llevó Ud. a sus alumnos al jardín botánico alguna vez (*ever*)?
2. ¿Sus alumnos se ponen en fila antes de entrar en la clase?
3. ¿Qué se hace con la madera?
4. ¿Tiene Ud. árboles en su patio? ¿Cómo son?
5. ¿Tiene Ud. muchas flores en su jardín?
6. ¿Fue Ud. al desierto alguna vez?
7. ¿Qué grado enseñó Ud. el año pasado?
8. ¿Qué saben sus alumnos acerca de las plantas?
9. ¿Llueve mucho donde Ud. vive?

Nombre ______________________ Sección ____________ Fecha ____________

Vamos a practicar

Quiz

A Rewrite the following sentences in the preterit tense.

Modelo Hablas con ellos.
***Hablaste* con ellos.**

1. Los niños van de excursión.

____

2. Llevan a Marta al jardín botánico.

____

3. Allí ve muchas plantas.

____

4. Le damos plantas para el patio.

____

5. No te separas de nosotros.

____

6. Aprende mucho acerca de las plantas.

____

7. Tú me escribes.

____

8. Ellos son mis alumnos.

____

B Complete the following sentences with **por** or **para,** as appropriate.

Modelo Vamos a estar allí ______________ dos horas.
Vamos a estar allí **por** dos horas.

1. Los llevan al jardín botánico ______________ ver las plantas.
2. Necesitamos las semillas ______________ mañana ______________ la tarde.
3. Tiene que estar aquí ______________ cuatro horas.
4. Las plantas son ______________ el director.
5. ¿Cuánto pagó (*paid*) Ud. ______________ las semillas?

Nombre ______________________ Sección ____________ Fecha ____________

Conversaciones breves

Complete the following dialogue, using your imagination and the vocabulary from this lesson.

La Srta. Soto y sus alumnos están en el jardín botánico.

Maestra —______________________

Jorge —La raíz, el tallo, las hojas, las flores y los frutos.

Maestra —______________________

María —Porque nos dan oxígeno y también madera.

Maestra —______________________

Carlos —Toma parte de sus alimentos de la tierra.

Maestra —______________________

Jorge —Hay muchos cactos en el desierto.

Maestra —______________________

Eva —Ahora queremos ir a ver las flores.

Susana —¡Srta. Soto! ¡Está empezando a llover!

Maestra —______________________

En estas situaciones

With two or more classmates, act out the following situations in Spanish.

1. You are explaining how a tree gets its nourishment. Tell your students that a tree takes part of its food from the soil, and that goes up the trunk. Add that the leaves use the sunlight to turn it into food.
2. Your students are on a field trip. Tell them to get off the bus, walk in pairs, and hold hands.
3. Comment that it is beginning to rain. Tell your students to hurry up and get on the bus.
4. Another teacher asks you where Antonio is. Tell her that he went to the bathroom and that he's coming now.

Casos

With you and a partner playing the roles, work through the following scenarios.

1. A teacher and a student talk about plants.
2. Two teachers give instructions to students during a field trip.
3. Two adults discuss the flora in their backyards.

Nombre ______________________ Sección ____________ Fecha ____________

Un paso más Review the **Vocabulario adicional** in this lesson and write the names of the flowers, vegetables, or fruit in the spaces provided.

1. ______________________
2. ______________________
3. ______________________
4. ______________________
5. ______________________

6. ______________________
7. ______________________
8. ______________________

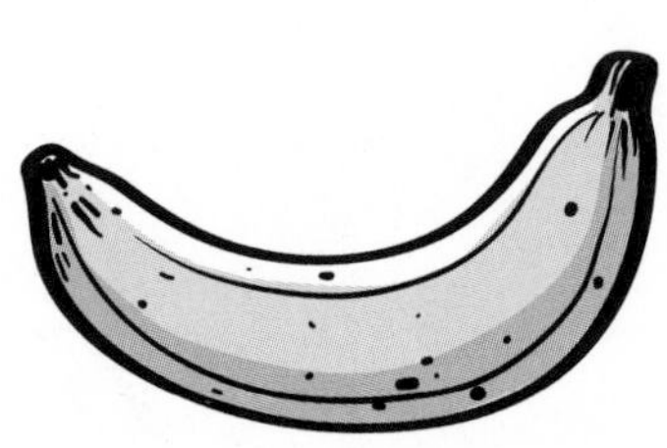

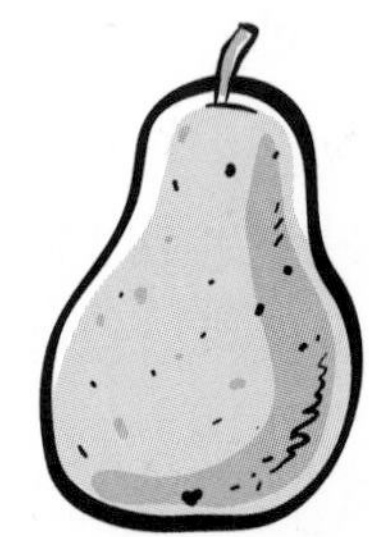

9. ______________________
10. ______________________
11. ______________________

Nombre ____________ Sección ____________ Fecha ____________

12. ____________

13. ____________

14. ____________

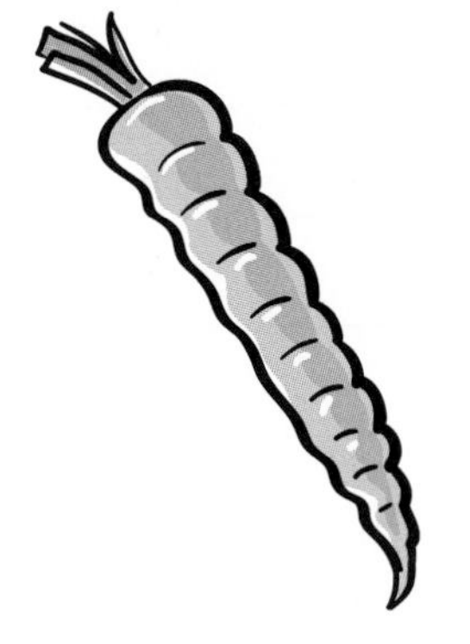

15. ____________

16. ____________

17. ____________

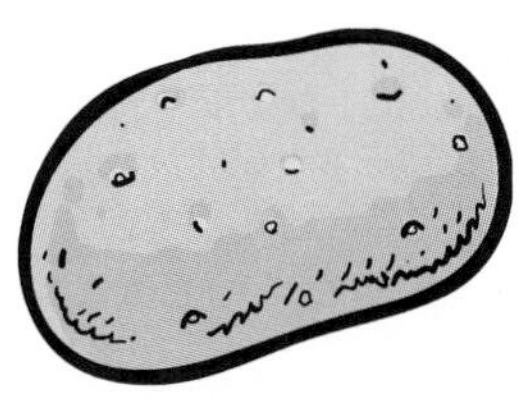

18. ____________

19. ____________

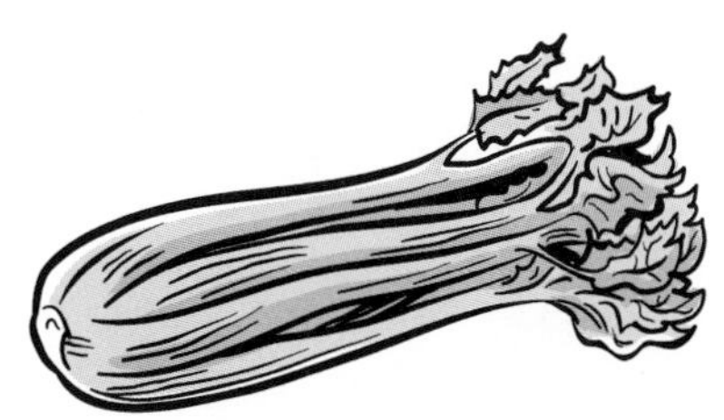

20. ____________

21. ____________

Nombre ______________________ Sección ____________ Fecha ____________

Actividad en grupo In groups of three or four, prepare eight or ten questions for students to ascertain their knowledge of plants.

____

____

____

____

____

____

____

____

Lectura 2 Reglas de la escuela

Read the following information from a handout about school rules. Try to guess the meaning of all cognates.

REGLAS DE LA ESCUELA

EN EL PATIO, DURANTE EL RECREO[1]

1. No se peleen, no empujen y no tiren piedras ni arena.
2. Obedezcan[2] las instrucciones de los maestros.
3. Jueguen solamente en los lugares designados para jugar.
4. A la hora del almuerzo, pónganse en fila[3] inmediatamente.
5. Antes de comenzar las clases, y a la hora del recreo, párense[4] inmediatamente cuando suene el timbre y luego vayan al lugar donde tienen que hacer fila.
6. No jueguen ni en los baños ni cerca de los baños.
7. No digan malas palabras.[5]
8. No se paren ni en los bancos[6] ni en las mesas.

EN LA CAFETERÍA

1. No griten.[7]
2. Quédense sentados[8] mientras[9] comen.
3. No salgan de la cafetería sin permiso.
4. Pongan la basura[10] en el basurero[11] antes de salir.
5. No se tiren[12] comida ni otros objetos.

EN LA CLASE

Obedezcan las reglas de sus maestros. Al comenzar el año escolar, cada maestro les enviará a los padres una copia de las reglas de la clase.

[1] **recreo** *recess*
[2] **Obedezcan** *Obey*
[3] **pónganse en fila** *stand in line*
[4] **párense** *stand up*
[5] **malas palabras** *swearwords*
[6] **bancos** *benches*
[7] **griten** *shout*
[8] **Quédense sentados** *Remain seated*
[9] **mientras** *while*
[10] **basura** *trash*
[11] **basurero** *trash container*
[12] **tiren** *throw*

Nombre ______________________ Sección ____________ Fecha ____________

Dígame... Based on the handout, circle **V** for **verdadero** or **F** for **falso.**

1.	Los niños pueden pelearse, si quieren.	V	F
2.	Los niños no deben tirar piedras.	V	F
3.	Los maestros no les dan instrucciones a los niños.	V	F
4.	A la hora del almuerzo, los niños deben ponerse en fila enseguida.	V	F
5.	Cuando suena el timbre, los niños deben comer.	V	F
6.	Los baños son para jugar.	V	F
7.	Los niños no deben decir malas palabras.	V	F
8.	Los niños tienen que pararse en las mesas.	V	F
9.	Los niños no pueden hablar en la cafetería.	V	F
10.	Los niños necesitan el permiso de los maestros para salir de la cafetería.	V	F
11.	Los niños tienen que llevar la basura a la clase.	V	F
12.	Los padres van a recibir una copia de las reglas de la clase.	V	F

Nombre ____________________ Sección ____________ Fecha ____________

REPASO

Práctica de vocabulario

A Circle the word or phrase that does not belong in each group.

1. articulación coyuntura animal
2. cráneo cerebro planta
3. hueso desierto esqueleto
4. hoja sangre glóbulos rojos
5. timbre rodilla codo
6. bronquios pulmones vena
7. flor fruto pulmones
8. estómago digestión tierra
9. anteojos jardín espejuelos
10. piel pigmento sol
11. músculo tronco tallo
12. enseñar padecer operar
13. rana renacuajo plaqueta
14. caliente grande frío
15. pelo cactos desierto
16. vena nivel arteria
17. reptil tráquea cocodrilo
18. invertebrado insecto vida
19. ayudar pelearse pegar
20. pedir turno portarse mal hacer una cita
21. bibliotecario camarón enfermero
22. primavera verano yegua
23. cerdo toro cochino
24. yegua rana otoño
25. gustar salir volver

Nombre ______________________ Sección ____________ Fecha ____________

B Circle the word or phrase that best completes each sentence.

1. Caminen de dos en dos y tómense (del pelo / de la cabeza / de la mano).
2. El corazón es el órgano que (opera / envía / nombra) la sangre a todo el cuerpo.
3. Se porta muy mal. Voy a (pensarlo / castigarlo / sostenerlo).
4. Las plantas toman su alimento de (la tierra / la clase / la unión).
5. Vamos a comer. Es la hora (de llegar tarde / de levantar la mano / de almorzar).
6. La lagartija, el cocodrilo y la tortuga pertenecen al grupo de los (peces / mamíferos / reptiles).
7. La piel protege el cuerpo de (la raíz / la hoja / los microbios).
8. No mejora porque no (pelea / se esfuerza / deja).
9. Las aves (existen / explican / nacen) de huevos.
10. Una lagartija pertenece al reino (elemental / animal / vertebral).
11. Voy a pegar esta (fotografía / persona / ropa) en mi cuaderno.
12. Si no ve bien, tiene que (ir / ayudar / transformar) al frente de la clase.
13. No trabaja al nivel del grado, así que está (oscuro / protegido / atrasado).
14. Las plantas necesitan la luz del (sol / elemento / pico).
15. Las aves tienen el cuerpo cubierto de (escamas / pelo / plumas).
16. Mi hijo está en segundo grado. Va a la escuela (baja / elemental / distinta).
17. No podemos ir al jardín botánico porque va a (llegar / volar / llover).
18. En la clase de ciencias, la maestra nos (movió / encontró / enseñó) las características de varios tipos de animales.
19. Éste es el problema. La (solución / semilla / habilidad) depende de Ud.
20. Solamente lo veo de vez en (como / cuando / otro).
21. Son mis (agallas / compañeras / gansas) de clase.
22. Alberto (se porta / puede / pone) mal en clase.
23. Me (duelo / muestro / llevo) bien con mis amigos.
24. No termina el trabajo. (Además / Enseguida / Aunque), necesita estudiar más.
25. Voy a la biblioteca. Vuelvo (enseguida / dividido / invierno).

Nombre ______________________ Sección ______________ Fecha ______________

C Match the questions in column **A** with the answers in column **B**.

A

_____ 1. ¿Las aves nacen vivas?
_____ 2. ¿A qué hora se cierra?
_____ 3. ¿De qué padece?
_____ 4. ¿Qué cantidad necesitas?
_____ 5. ¿De qué trata la lección?
_____ 6. ¿De qué se alimentan los árboles?
_____ 7. ¿Cómo se llama la unión de dos huesos?
_____ 8. ¿En cuántas partes se divide?
_____ 9. ¿Qué animales tienen la boca en forma de pico?
_____ 10. ¿Cuál es uno de los elementos que forman la sangre?
_____ 11. ¿Cuánto tiempo va a pasar aquí?
_____ 12. ¿Cómo se llama la armazón del cuerpo?
_____ 13. ¿Qué hacen antes de comer?
_____ 14. ¿Por dónde vamos?
_____ 15. ¿Qué pasa aquí?
_____ 16. ¿De qué está formado el esqueleto?
_____ 17. ¿Quieres cambiarlo?
_____ 18. ¿Les enseñaste algo?
_____ 19. ¿Dónde están los libros?
_____ 20. ¿Es verde oscuro?

B

a. De la tierra.
b. Los glóbulos blancos.
c. En la biblioteca.
d. Quizás estudian.
e. Coyuntura.
f. Los niños se están peleando.
g. Dos días.
h. A las cinco.
i. De huesos.
j. Trata de los mamíferos.
k. Por aquí.
l. Necesito treinta.
m. Las aves.
n. No, nacen de huevos.
o. No, claro.
p. Del corazón.
q. Sí, aprendieron mucho acerca de las plantas.
r. No, me gusta mucho así.
s. En tres partes.
t. Esqueleto.

Nombre ______________________________ Sección ____________ Fecha ____________

D Crucigrama

Horizontales

1. No es igual (*same*). Es ___________.
6. La ___________ cubre todo nuestro cuerpo.
8. Las plaquetas sirven para ___________ la sangre.
13. Los pulmones toman oxígeno para ___________ la sangre.
14. El ___________ animal se divide en dos grupos.
15. El esqueleto es la ___________ del cuerpo.
20. El corazón es parte del aparato ___________.
22. Estudiamos el sistema nervioso en la clase de ___________.
23. Esta planta da flores y ___________.
24. Los insectos son animales ___________.
25. El opuesto (*opposite*) de bajarse es ___________.
27. Tengo problemas con la vista. Voy a pedirle turno al ___________.
29. Necesitamos ___________ para purificar la sangre.
30. Los vertebrados tienen columna ___________.
31. Vamos de excursión al jardín ___________.

Verticales

1. primera comida del día
2. La ___________ es un reptil.
3. Ellos no pueden ___________ nada del jardín botánico.
4. Los pulmones forman parte del aparato ___________.
5. Las aves pueden ___________ porque tienen alas (*wings*).
7. Hay muchas ___________ en el jardín botánico.
9. La tortuga es un ___________.
10. Es la ___________ de salida.
11. Suena el ___________ para la salida.
12. La rana es un ___________.
16. Los peces tienen el cuerpo cubierto de ___________.
17. Los peces respiran por ___________.
18. La naranja es el fruto del ___________.
19. lentes
21. El ___________ tiene 365 días.
26. Ella no lee bien. Está en un grupo de lectura más ___________.
28. No tiene mucho; tiene ___________.

Nombre _______________ Sección _______ Fecha _______

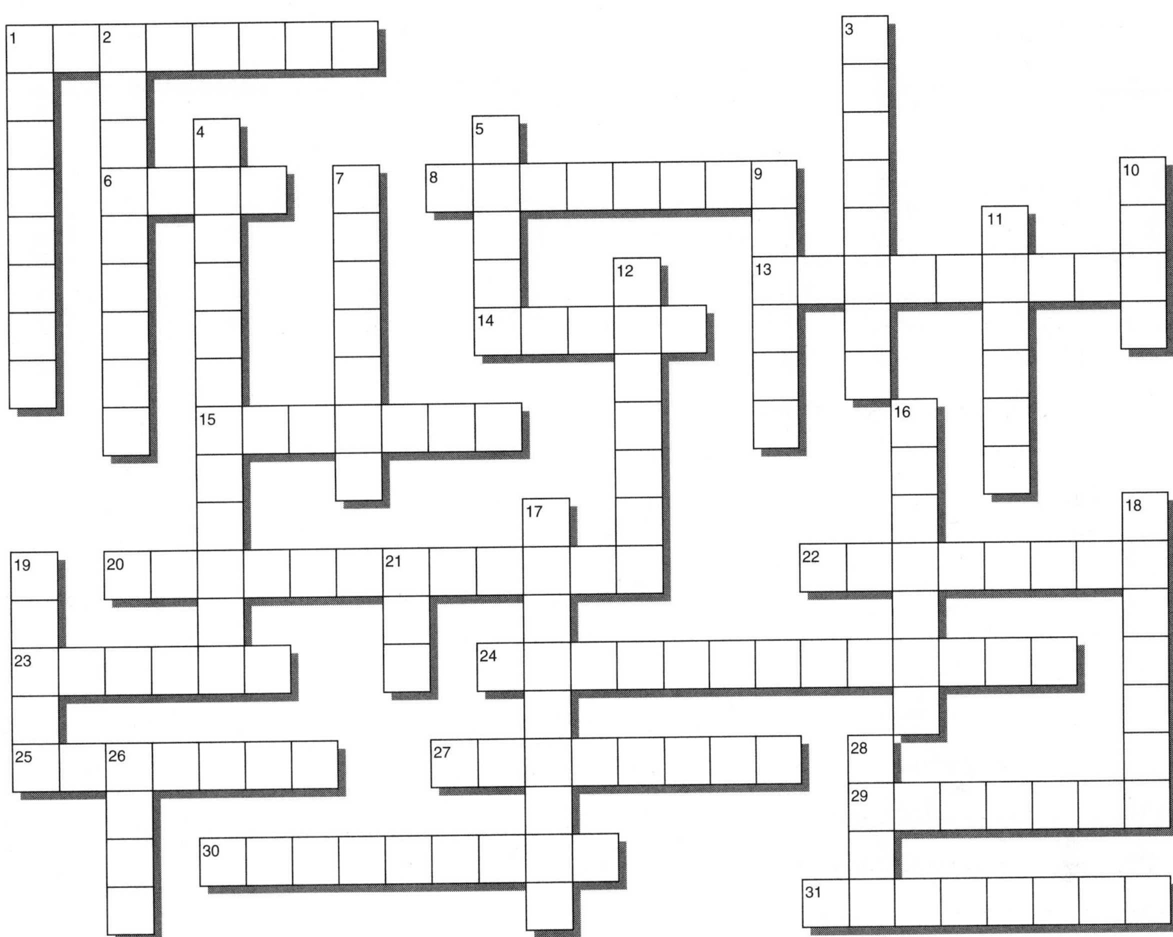

Nombre ______________________ Sección ____________ Fecha ____________

Práctica oral

Listen to the following exercise on the audio program. The speaker will ask you some questions. Answer the questions, using the cues provided. The speaker will confirm the correct answer. Repeat the correct answer.

1. ¿A qué hora almuerza Ud.? (a las doce)
2. ¿Tiene Ud. sueño después de comer? (sí, a veces)
3. ¿Digiere Ud. bien la comida? (sí)
4. ¿Lo van a operar a Ud. de algo? (no)
5. ¿Padece Ud. del corazón? (no)
6. ¿Tiene Ud. problemas respiratorios? (no)
7. ¿Ve Ud. bien o usa lentes? (veo bien)
8. ¿Cuántas horas duerme Ud.? (ocho horas)
9. ¿Sabe Ud. mucho de los animales? (sí)
10. ¿Tiene Ud. láminas de animales en su clase? (sí, muchas)
11. ¿Qué animales cree Ud. que son bonitos? (las aves)
12. ¿Cuáles son sus animales favoritos? (los perros y los gatos)
13. ¿Tiene Ud. algún animal doméstico? (sí, dos perros)
14. ¿Tiene Ud. peces de colores en su casa? (no)
15. ¿Qué insectos cree Ud. que son bonitos? (las mariposas)
16. ¿Puede Ud. prestarme algunos libros sobre animales? (sí)
17. ¿Tiene Ud. un jardín en su casa? (sí)
18. ¿Qué flores prefiere Ud.? (las rosas)
19. ¿Tiene Ud. árboles en su casa? (sí, un naranjo)
20. ¿Qué frutas prefiere Ud.? (las naranjas y las uvas)
21. ¿En qué grado dio Ud. clases el año pasado? (en segundo grado)
22. ¿Cuántas clases dio Ud. cada día? (cinco)
23. ¿Llevó Ud. a sus alumnos de excursión la semana pasada? (sí)
24. ¿Adónde los llevó? (al jardín botánico)
25. ¿Qué vieron allí? (plantas de distintos países)

Lección 11 Algunas reglas de ortografía

Objectives

Structures

- Time expressions with **hacer**
- Irregular preterits
- The preterit of stem-changing verbs (**e:i** and **o:u**)
- Command forms: **tú**

Communication

- Spelling bee: teaching Spanish spelling and pronunciation rules
- Talking about spelling

iLrn™

Hace dos semanas que los alumnos de la Srta. Suárez se preparan para un concurso de ortografía. Hoy siguen practicando las reglas. Muchos alumnos vinieron muy bien preparados a la clase.

Maestra —Ramón, dime las reglas que debemos recordar sobre el sonido de la letra *ce* antes de las vocales *i* o *e.*
Ramón —Antes de la *i* o de la *e,* la *ce* suena como la *ese.*
Dora —Sí, como en la palabra *cero.*
Maestra —Muy bien, Ramón y Dora. Y, ¿qué sonido tiene la *ce* antes de la *a,* la *o* o la *u*?
Miguel —Suena como la *ka.* Yo sé una palabra que tiene la *ce* así... *¡Carro!*
Maestra —¡Muy bien, Miguel! Y, ¿cómo se escribe la palabra *quizás*? Hilda, ve a la pizarra y escríbela.
Hilda —*Ce–i–zeta–a–ese.*
Maestra —No... ¿Quién recuerda las reglas de la letra *ce*?
Diego —Maestra, yo las sé. La *ce* antes de la *i* o de la *e* suena como *ese.* Deletreamos *quizás* con la letra *cu.*
Maestra —¡Muy bien, Diego! ¿Quién sabe cómo se escribe *que*?
Hilda —*Cu–u–e,* ¿verdad, señorita?
Maestra —¡Sí! A ver... ¿quién puede decirnos algo sobre la consonante *ge*?
Mónica —¿Como en la palabra *goma*? Tiene el mismo sonido en la palabra *gusto,* por ejemplo.
Maestra —¿Es la única manera de pronunciarla?

Mónica —Yo creo que sí.
Silvia —¡No! Hay excepciones. Hace una semana que las estudiamos. Se pronuncia como la letra *jota* cuando está antes de la *e* o de la *i*.
Maestra —¡Excelente! A ver, ¿quién puede deletrear *geografía*? (*Varios estudiantes contestan a la vez.*) Solamente una persona. Mónica, deletréala.
Mónica —Eso es fácil. *¡Ge–e–o–ge–ere–a–efe–i–a!*
Maestra —¡Muy bien! Aprendiste la regla, Mónica. Otra pregunta. ¿Qué lleva la *i* de *geografía*? ¿Sandra?
Sandra —Lleva acento, ¿verdad?
Maestra —Sí, *geografía* lleva acento en la penúltima sílaba. Todavía deben repasar cómo se forman los adverbios, y el pasado de los verbos irregulares.
Sandra —Maestra, yo hice los ejercicios de los verbos regulares ayer. ¿Ud. los corrigió?
Maestra —No, voy a corregirlos mañana. No todos los trajeron ayer.

La maestra repitió algunas de las reglas; les pidió las tareas a los niños, las puso en su escritorio y se despidió de ellos hasta el día siguiente.

¡Escuchemos!

While listening to the dialogue, circle **V (verdadero)** if the statement is true and **F (falso)** if it is false.

1.	Los alumnos de la Srta. Suárez van a tener un concurso de geografía.	V	F
2.	Pocos alumnos están bien preparados para el concurso.	V	F
3.	En español, la letra *ce* suena como *ese* antes de la *e* y de la *i*.	V	F
4.	En la palabra *cocos* la *ce* suena como *ka*.	V	F
5.	En español, la letra *ge* siempre tiene el mismo sonido.	V	F
6.	La palabra *geografía* lleva acento en la *i*.	V	F
7.	La palabra *quizás* lleva el acento en la última sílaba.	V	F
8.	Los estudiantes de la Srta. Suárez deben estudiar los verbos regulares.	V	F
9.	La maestra ya corrigió todos los ejercicios.	V	F
10.	La maestra les pidió las tareas a los niños.	V	F

Nombre ______________________ Sección ____________ Fecha ____________

VOCABULARIO

Cognados

el acento
el adverbio
la consonante
la excepción
irregular
preparado(a)
regular
la sílaba

Nombres

el concurso *contest*
el concurso de ortografía *spelling bee*
la manera *manner, way*
el pasado *past*
la pregunta *question*
la regla *rule*
el sonido *sound*
la vocal *vowel*

Verbos

corregir (e:i)[1] *to correct*
deletrear *to spell*
despedirse (e:i) (de) *to say good-bye to*
formar *to form*
ocurrir *to happen*
practicar *to practice*
preparar(se) *to prepare (oneself), to get ready*
pronunciar *to pronounce*
repetir (e:i) *to repeat*
sonar (o:ue) *to sound*

Adjetivos

mismo(a) *same*
penúltimo(a) *next to last, penultimate*
último(a) *last*
único(a) *only*

Otras palabras y expresiones

a la vez *at the same time, simultaneously*
a ver... *let's see . . .*
ayer *yesterday*
como *like*
Creo que sí. *I think so.*
entonces *then, in that case*
excelente *excellent*
Llevan dos semanas preparándose. *They have been preparing for two weeks.*
por ejemplo *for example*
siguiente *following*
solamente *only*
todavía *still*
Ud. iba a... *You were going to . . .*

---

[1]Orthographic change in the first person: **yo corrijo**

Nombre ______________________ Sección ______________ Fecha ______________

VOCABULARIO ADICIONAL

Los signos de puntuación (*Punctuation marks*)

’ **apóstrofe**
// **barras**
, **coma**
“ ” **comillas**
[ ] **corchetes**
: **dos puntos**
- **guión**
— **raya**
( ) **paréntesis**
. **punto**
; **punto y coma**
¡ ! **signos de admiración**
¿ ? **signos de interrogación**

Otras palabras y frases relacionadas con la ortografía (*Other words and phrases related to spelling*)

agregar, añadir *to add*
el alfabeto, el abecedario *alphabet*
la contracción *contraction*
el dictado *dictation*
mudo(a), sin sonido *silent*
el prefijo *prefix*
la raíz *root*
singular *singular*
el sufijo *suffix*

Notas Culturales

- There are about 330 million people in the world whose native language is Spanish, the fourth most widely spoken language. It is the official language of Spain and of most Latin American countries.
- Spanish (**español,** also called **castellano**) derives from Latin. Since its origins, however, the Spanish language has been enriched by other languages. For almost eight hundred years (711 C.E.–1492 C.E.), parts of Spain were under Muslim rule. During that time, Spanish was heavily influenced by the Arabic language. After the Spaniards came to the New World in 1492, the Spanish language came in contact with the languages spoken by Native Americans. Words such as **chocolate, maíz** (*corn*), **tomate,** and **aguacate** (*avocado*) are examples of Native American words. Nowadays, like most other languages around the world, Spanish is heavily influenced by English, especially in the fields of sports, entertainment, and technology.

Nombre ______________________ Sección ____________ Fecha ____________

Actividades

Dígame... Answer the following questions, basing your answers on the dialogue.

1. ¿Cuánto tiempo hace que[1] los alumnos se preparan para el concurso de ortografía?

2. ¿Los alumnos vinieron preparados?

3. ¿Qué sonido tiene la letra *ce* antes de la *i* o de la *e*?

4. ¿Quién repite la regla de la letra *ce*? ¿Por qué?

5. ¿Cuándo se pronuncia la letra *ge* como *jota*?

6. ¿Aprendió Mónica la regla? ¿Cómo lo sabe Ud.?

7. ¿Qué deben estudiar todavía los niños?

8. ¿Quién hizo ya el ejercicio de los verbos irregulares? ¿Cuándo lo trajo?

9. ¿Corrigió la maestra los ejercicios? ¿Cuándo los va a corregir?

10. ¿Qué repitió la maestra y qué les pidió a los niños?

11. ¿Dónde puso las tareas?

12. ¿Qué hizo después?

[1]To ask how long something has been going on, ask: **¿Cuánto tiempo hace que...?**

Nombre ______________________ **Sección** ____________ **Fecha** ____________

Hablemos

With a partner, take turns asking each other the following questions.

1. ¿Cómo se escribe su nombre?
2. ¿Es fácil o difícil pronunciar su apellido (*surname*)?
3. ¿Participan sus alumnos en los concursos de ortografía de vez en cuando?
4. ¿Cuánto tiempo hace que Ud. estudia español?
5. ¿Siempre viene Ud. preparado(a) a la clase?
6. Para aprender a hablar bien el español, ¿es suficiente saber las reglas de gramática (*grammar*)?
7. ¿Cuánto tiempo hace que Ud. enseña?
8. ¿Corrigió Ud. la tarea de sus alumnos ayer?

Quiz

Vamos a practicar

A Tell for how long each action has been going on. Use the expression **hace... que** in your response.

Modelo Roberto empezó a estudiar a las seis. (Son las ocho.)
Hace dos horas que Roberto estudia.

1. Ellos empezaron a prepararse para el concurso el lunes. (Hoy es jueves.)

   ____

2. Empecé a corregir los exámenes a las doce. (Ahora son las cinco.)

   ____

3. Empezaste a revisar los ejercicios a las once. (Son las seis y media.)

   ____

B Rewrite the following sentences in the preterit.

Modelo Él no quiere ir.
Él no *quiso* ir.

1. Él no tiene clases en esta aula.

   ____

2. Yo pongo los libros en el escritorio.

   ____

3. No podemos ir con ellos.

   ____

Nombre ______________________ Sección ____________ Fecha ____________

4. Él no hace la tarea.

____

5. Los alumnos no traen los libros.

____

6. Ellos vienen a la escuela.

____

7. ¿Dónde está Silvia?

____

8. ¿Qué dicen Uds.?

____

C Answer the following questions first with affirmative familiar commands, and then with negative familiar commands. Use the corresponding object pronoun when necessary.

MODELO ¿Hago *la tarea*?
Sí, hazla.
No, no la hagas.

1. ¿Voy a la biblioteca?

____

____

2. ¿Traigo *los libros*?

____

____

3. ¿*Los* pongo en la mesa?

____

____

4. ¿Escribo *las palabras*?

____

____

Nombre ______________________ Sección ____________ Fecha ____________

5. ¿Salgo de la clase ahora?

____

____

6. ¿Vengo mañana?

____

____

Conversaciones breves

Complete the following dialogue, using your imagination and the vocabulary from this lesson.

El maestro habla con sus estudiantes en la clase.

Diego —Señor, ¿dónde lleva el acento la palabra *árbol*?

Maestro —____

Carlota —¿Qué sonido tiene la *ge* cuando está antes de la *i* o de la *e*?

Maestro —____

Rita —¿Tenemos que estudiar cómo se forman los adverbios?

Maestro —____

Raúl —¿Tenemos que estudiar el pasado de los verbos irregulares también?

Maestro —____

Carmen —Yo todavía no entiendo lo que Ud. explicó ayer...

Maestro —____

Carmen —Yo estudio... pero es muy difícil.

Maestro —____

Teresa —¿Necesitamos traer el diccionario mañana?

Maestro —____

En estas situaciones

With two or more classmates, act out the following situations in Spanish.

1. You are speaking to your students about spelling rules. Explain the following:
   a. There are some rules we must remember about the consonants *c* and *g* before the vowels *i* and *e*.
   b. The syllables *que* and *qui* must be spelled with a *cu* because of that rule.
2. Tell a student to come to class tomorrow with his/her homework and a dictionary.
3. Ask a student to spell words for you that have an accent on the next-to-last syllable.

Nombre ______________________ Sección ____________ Fecha ____________

Casos With you and a partner playing the roles, work through the following scenarios.

1. A teacher tries to explain some spelling rules to a student after class.
2. Two students practice some spelling words to prepare for tomorrow's spelling bee.

Un paso más

A Review the **Vocabulario adicional** in this lesson and write the names of the following punctuation marks.

1. - ______________________
2. ; ______________________
3. // ______________________
4. , ______________________
5. ¿ ? ______________________
6. ’ ______________________
7. : ______________________
8. ( ) ______________________
9. . ______________________
10. ¡ ! ______________________
11. [ ] ______________________
12. “ ” ______________________

B Complete the following sentences with words or phrases related to spelling.

1. El ____________ tiene veintiséis letras.
2. La palabra *del* es una ____________.
3. En la palabra *hola,* la letra *h* es ____________.
4. No es plural; es ____________.
5. Para formar el plural de *letra,* es necesario ____________ una *-s.*
6. En la palabra *desconocer,* la sílaba *des-* es un ____________.
7. En la palabra *hablamos,* la ____________ es *habl-.*
8. En un ____________, Uds. escriben lo que yo digo.
9. En la palabra *naturalmente, -mente* es un ____________.

Actividad en grupo In groups of three or four, prepare five to eight rules about English spelling and pronunciation to help Spanish-speaking people learn English.

Lección 12

Una clase de historia

Objectives

Structures

- The imperfect tense
- The past progressive
- The preterit contrasted with the imperfect
- **En** and **a** as equivalents of ***at***

Communication

- History class: talking about U.S. history
- Talking about events that happened in the past

iLrn™

Los estudiantes de la Sra. López estaban haciendo unos ejercicios de matemáticas cuando la maestra los interrumpió para decirles que tenían que repasar la lección de historia. Ahora están hablando de los acontecimientos más importantes en la historia de los Estados Unidos.

Maestra	—¿Quién descubrió América?
José	—La descubrió Cristóbal Colón en el año 1492.
Silvia	—Pero Colón nunca vino a los Estados Unidos, ¿verdad?
Maestra	—No, los que colonizaron este país fueron principalmente los ingleses, pero hubo gente de otras nacionalidades.
José	—¿De qué países eran?
Maestra	—De España, Francia, Holanda...
Carlos	—Pero los peregrinos que llegaron en el Mayflower eran ingleses, ¿no?
Maestra	—Sí, mucha gente vino de Inglaterra para librarse de la persecución religiosa.
Carlos	—¿Pero cuándo se formaron los Estados Unidos?
Maestra	—En el siglo XVII y a principios del XVIII, de un grupo de colonias inglesas que estaban establecidas en la costa este.
Eduardo	—¿Por qué vino la gente a América?
Maestra	—Porque sabía que había mucha tierra cultivable y barata. ¿Qué pasó en el año 1776?
Luisa	—Se declaró la independencia de los Estados Unidos.
Maestra	—¿Quién fue el primer presidente y en qué año lo eligieron?

Mario —Jorge Washington. Lo eligieron en 1778. Ésas fueron las primeras elecciones bajo la constitución.
Maestra —Muy bien. ¿Cuándo comenzó la Guerra Civil y cuánto tiempo duró?
Antonio —Comenzó en 1861 y duró cuatro años.
Maestra —¿Quién era el presidente en esa época?
Eva —Abraham Lincoln. Él abolió la esclavitud.
Maestra —¡Correcto! (*Suena el timbre.*) Para mañana, lean la página 231 del libro de historia.

Ésta es parte de la información que aparece en la página 231 del libro de historia.

A fines del siglo XIX y principios del XX, los Estados Unidos eran ya una potencia mundial.

En 1914 estalló la Primera Guerra Mundial. Los Estados Unidos trataron de mantenerse neutrales, pero entraron en la guerra en 1917.

Durante la década de los años veinte hubo prosperidad en los Estados Unidos, pero en 1929 comenzó la depresión.

En 1939 comenzó la Segunda Guerra Mundial. Los Estados Unidos se mantuvieron neutrales hasta el año 1941, cuando los japoneses bombardearon Pearl Harbor y el Congreso declaró la guerra contra el Japón. La guerra terminó en 1945.

¡Escuchemos!

While listening to the dialogue, circle **V (verdadero)** if the statement is true and **F (falso)** if it is false.

1. Cristóbal Colón descubrió América en 1495. V F
2. Personas de España, Inglaterra y Holanda colonizaron los Estados Unidos. V F
3. Los peregrinos del Mayflower vinieron a los Estados Unidos por razones económicas. V F
4. En América había mucha tierra cultivable barata. V F
5. En 1778 eligieron al primer presidente de los Estados Unidos. V F
6. La Guerra Civil de los Estados Unidos duró seis años. V F
7. Abraham Lincoln abolió la esclavitud. V F
8. La depresión en los Estados Unidos empezó en 1920. V F
9. Estados Unidos entró en la Primera Guerra Mundial en 1917. V F
10. En 1941 Estados Unidos le declaró la guerra a Japón. V F

Nombre ______________________ Sección ____________ Fecha ____________

VOCABULARIO

Cognados

América
civil
el congreso
la constitución
la década
la depresión
la elección
establecido(a)
Francia
la historia
Holanda
la independencia
la información
Japón
el (la) japonés(esa)
las matemáticas
la nacionalidad
neutral
el (la) norteamericano(a)
la persecución
la prosperidad
religioso(a)

Nombres

el acontecimiento *event*
la costa *coast*
Cristóbal Colón *Christopher Columbus*
la esclavitud *slavery*
España *Spain*
la gente *people*
la guerra *war*
Inglaterra *England*
el (la) peregrino(a) *pilgrim*
la potencia *power*
el siglo *century*
el tiempo *time*

Verbos

abolir *to abolish*
aparecer[1] *to appear*
bombardear *to bomb*
colonizar *to colonize*
declarar *to declare*
descubrir *to discover*
durar *to last*
elegir[2] **(e:i)** *to elect, to choose*
interrumpir *to interrupt*
librarse (de) *to be (become) free (from)*
llegar *to arrive*
mantener(se)[3] *to keep (oneself), to maintain (oneself)*

Adjetivos

barato(a) *inexpensive, cheap*
mundial *world, worldwide*

Otras palabras y expresiones

a fines de *at the end of*
a principios de *at the beginning of*
bajo *under*
contra *against, versus*
durante *during*
en esa época *at that time*
estalló la guerra *the war started*
había *there was, there were (imperfect)*
hubo *there was, there were (preterit)*
los (las) que *the ones who*
principalmente *mainly*
tierra cultivable *land suitable for farming*

---

[1]Irregular first person: **yo aparezco**
[2]Orthographic change in the first person: **yo elijo**
[3]Conjugated like **tener**

VOCABULARIO ADICIONAL

Algunas palabras relacionadas con la historia o con el gobierno (*Some useful words related to history or government*)

el alcalde, la alcaldesa *mayor*
los aliados *allies*
la batalla *battle*
el capitalismo *capitalism*
la ciudad *city*
el comunismo *communism*
conquistar *to conquer*
la democracia *democracy*
los esclavos *slaves*
fundar *to found*
el (la) gobernador(a) *governor*
el gobierno *government*
los indios *Indians*
la ley *law*
liberar *to liberate*
libre *free*
luchar *to fight*
la monarquía *monarchy*
la paz *peace*
los pioneros *pioneers*
los puritanos *Puritans*
los representantes *congressional delegates*
los senadores *senators*
el territorio *territory*
vencer, derrotar *to defeat*
votar *to vote*

Notas Culturales

- The term **Latinoamérica** (*Latin America*) includes Brazil (colonized by Portugal), Haiti, and other countries colonized by France. **Hispanoamérica** (*Hispanic America*) only includes the countries colonized by Spain.
- The word *Hispanic* refers to someone of Spanish or Hispanic American descent, that is, someone whose language and culture, or those of his or her ancestors, derive from Spain or a Hispanic American country. In Latin American countries, however, this designation is rarely used, as people in these countries are identified according to their national origin. The term *Hispanic* does not refer to race; a Hispanic person can be black, Caucasian, Native American, or multiethnic, such as **mestizo(a)** or **mulato(a).**

ACTIVIDADES

Dígame... Answer the following questions, basing your answers on the dialogue.

1. ¿Qué estaban haciendo los estudiantes de la Srta. López?

   ____

2. ¿Qué hizo la maestra? ¿Por qué?

   ____

Nombre ______________________ Sección ____________ Fecha ____________

3. ¿Quién descubrió América? ¿En qué año?

____

4. ¿Quiénes colonizaron este país?

____

5. ¿Por qué salió mucha gente de Inglaterra?

____

6. ¿Qué formaron las colonias? ¿Cuándo?

____

7. ¿En qué año se declaró la independencia de los Estados Unidos?

____

8. ¿En qué año eligieron presidente a Jorge Washington?

____

9. ¿Cuándo comenzó la Guerra Civil y cuánto tiempo duró?

____

10. ¿En qué año estalló la Primera Guerra Mundial?

____

11. ¿Qué pasó en los años veinte?

____

12. ¿Qué hizo el Congreso de los Estados Unidos en 1941? ¿Por qué?

____

Hablemos With a partner, take turns asking each other the following questions.

1. ¿Vive Ud. cerca de alguna de las trece colonias originales?
2. ¿Sabe Ud. quién era el presidente de los Estados Unidos cuando Ud. nació? Y ahora, ¿quién es?
3. ¿Qué estaba haciendo Ud. durante la década de los noventa?
4. ¿Participa Ud. en todas las elecciones?
5. ¿Fue Ud. a Europa alguna vez? ¿Cuándo?
6. ¿Sabe Ud. quién era el presidente de los Estados Unidos durante la Guerra del Golfo en 1990?
7. ¿Sabe Ud. en qué año terminó la Guerra de Vietnam?

Nombre ______________________________ Sección ____________ Fecha ____________

8. ¿Qué páginas tienen que estudiar Uds. para la próxima clase de español?
9. ¿Qué parte de la historia de los Estados Unidos prefiere estudiar Ud.?
10. ¿Qué sabe Ud. de la Guerra Civil de los Estados Unidos?

Quiz

Vamos a practicar

A Complete the following sentences, using the preterit or the imperfect of the verbs given.

Modelo Ayer ellos me __________ (decir) que Eva __________ (estar) en Lima.
Ayer ellos me **dijeron** que Eva **estaba** en Lima.

1. ¿Dónde __________ (vivir) tú cuando __________ (ser) niño?
2. Lincoln __________ (abolir) la esclavitud en el siglo XIX.
3. Ayer, cuando él __________ (ir) a la bibiloteca, él __________ (ver) a nuestra maestra.
4. En esa época la gente __________ (querer) venir a América porque __________ (haber) mucha tierra barata.
5. Nosotros __________ (estar) enfermos (*sick*) todo el día.
6. La clase siempre __________ (durar) dos horas.
7. __________ (ser) las diez cuando la clase __________ (terminar) ayer.
8. Anoche Eva me __________ (decir) que ella __________ (necesitar) estudiar matemáticas.

B Complete the following sentences, using the past progressive of the verbs given.

Modelo Ana __________ (dormir).
Ana **estaba durmiendo.**

1. Ellos __________ (estudiar) la constitución.
2. ¿Tú __________ (hablar) de la depresión?
3. Nosotros __________ (leer) la información sobre el presidente.
4. Rafael __________ (pedir) un libro de historia.
5. Yo __________ (escribir) sobre la Guerra Civil.

Nombre ______________________________ Sección ______________ Fecha ______________

C Complete the following telephone conversation between a business traveler and her husband using **en** or **a.**

—¿Y __________ qué hora llegaste, Isabel?

—Llegué __________ las cinco de la mañana.

—¡Ay, no! ¿Dónde desayunaste?

—Desayuné __________ el restaurante del hotel. ¿Qué hicieron tú y los niños ayer?

—Estuvimos __________ casa todo el día. ¡Ah, no! __________ las seis fuimos __________ comer.

—¿Dónde están los niños ahora?

—__________ la biblioteca.

Conversaciones breves

Complete the following dialogue, using your imagination and the vocabulary from this lesson.

Hoy los estudiantes tienen un repaso de historia.

Maestra —¿De qué países eran los que colonizaron los Estados Unidos?

Rosa —______________________________

Maestra —¿Dónde estaban establecidas las colonias inglesas de las que se formaron los Estados Unidos?

Ana —______________________________

Maestra —¿A quién eligieron presidente en las primeras elecciones?

Carlos —______________________________

Maestra —¿Cuántos años duró la Primera Guerra Mundial?

Raúl —______________________________

Maestra —¿Se mantuvieron neutrales los Estados Unidos durante la Primera Guerra Mundial?

Eva —______________________________

Maestra —¿Contra qué país declaró guerra el Congreso en 1941?

Estela —______________________________

Maestra —¿En qué año entraron los Estados Unidos en la Segunda Guerra Mundial?

René —______________________________

Maestra —¿En qué década hubo prosperidad en los Estados Unidos?

Cristina —______________________________

Maestra —Muy bien. Para mañana estudien la lección que aparece en las páginas 315, 317 y 320 del libro de historia.

Nombre ________________ Sección ________ Fecha ________

En estas situaciones

With two or more classmates, act out the following situations in Spanish.

1. In honor of President's Day, your students had to do outside reading about George Washington and Abraham Lincoln. Today in class, they are reporting on some achievements of these presidents and on the times in which they lived.
2. You and your students are spending part of a class reviewing for a major test on World War II. You want them to name two events that preceded the war, to identify the years in which the war began and ended, and to state how long the war lasted.

Casos

With you and a partner playing the roles, work through the following scenarios.

1. Two students prepare for an exam on important events in the history of the United States that occurred from 1985 to 2005.
2. A guest speaker discusses with a teacher his/her upcoming talk on the discovery of America and the American Revolution.

Un paso más

Review the **Vocabulario adicional** in this lesson and complete the following sentences with the correct form of the appropriate word.

1. Nelson ___________ a Napoleón en la ___________ de Waterloo.
2. El comunismo es lo opuesto del ___________.
3. El sistema de gobierno de los Estados Unidos no es una monarquía; es una ___________.
4. Los ___________ y los ___________ forman el Congreso y son los que hacen las ___________.
5. Lincoln liberó a los ___________.
6. Hernán Cortés ___________ México.
7. En la Segunda Guerra Mundial, Inglaterra y Francia eran ___________ de los Estados Unidos.
8. Terminó la guerra. Ahora tenemos ___________.
9. Los primeros habitantes de América eran ___________.
10. No son esclavos. Son hombres ___________.
11. Antes de ser presidente, Ronald Reagan fue ___________ de California.
12. Los ___________ mormones colonizaron Utah, que primero fue un ___________ y después fue un estado.
13. Los españoles ___________ muchas ciudades en Latinoamérica.

Nombre ______________________________ **Sección** ____________ **Fecha** ____________

14. Él es el nuevo __________ de la ciudad.

15. Los __________ vinieron a este país para librarse de la persecución religiosa.

16. Siempre debe __________ en las elecciones.

Actividad en grupo In groups of three or four, prepare a presentation on the American Thanksgiving celebration and what it commemorates. This information is to be given to Spanish-speaking children who do not know about this custom.

____

____

____

____

____

En la clase de matemáticas

Objectives

Structures

- **Hace** meaning ***ago***
- **¿Qué?** and **¿cuál?** used with **ser**
- Changes in meaning with the imperfect and preterit of **conocer, saber,** and **querer**

Communication

- Math class: teaching math (addition, subtraction, multiplication, division)
- Talking about digits
- Roman and Arabic numerals

iLrn™

Los alumnos acaban de llegar al aula y la maestra empieza la clase de matemáticas.

Maestra —Ahora, para repasar lo que ya sabemos, vamos a resolver un problema. El Sr. Pérez nació en 1915 y murió en 1982. ¿Qué edad tenía cuando murió? Esteban, ¿cuál es la operación que tenemos que hacer para resolver el problema? ¿Es una suma o una resta?

Esteban —Tenemos que restar 1915 de 1982, ¿verdad?

Maestra —Muy bien. ¿Es el 5 mayor (>) o menor que (<) el 2?

Guadalupe —Es mayor que el 2. ¡Yo sé lo que tenemos que hacer! Tenemos que pedirle prestada una decena al 8 y sumarle las dos unidades.

Maestra —¡Perfecto! Ahora, ¿cuántas unidades hay?

Roberto —Ahora hay 12 porque una decena tiene diez unidades. Ya podemos quitarle 5 al 12. Y la respuesta es 67 años.

Maestra —Muy bien. A ti te gusta mucho resolver problemas, ¿no?

Roberto —Sí, maestra, pero no me gusta estudiar las tablas.

Maestra —¡Necesitas estudiarlas! Bien, pero ahora vamos a mirar la respuesta. Carlos, ¿cuántos dígitos tiene el número 67?

Carlos —Tiene dos dígitos, señorita. El 6 está en el lugar de las decenas y el 7 está en el lugar de las unidades.

Maestra —Muy bien, Carlos. ¿Está escrita la respuesta en números romanos o en números arábigos?

Nombre ______________________ **Sección** __________ **Fecha** __________

Carmen —En números arábigos. Los números romanos se escriben con letras.
Laura —Yo no sabía que se escribían con letras...
Aurora —Sí, se usan siete letras para escribirlos. La *I* vale uno, la *V* vale cinco, la *X* vale diez, la *L* vale cincuenta, la *C* vale cien, la *D* vale quinientos y la *M* vale mil.
Maestra —Muy bien, Aurora y Carmen. Ahora... ¿el 67 es un número par o impar?
Estela —Es impar porque no es múltiplo de dos. También se puede decir que no es divisible por dos.
Esteban —Maestra, ¿cuándo vamos a estudiar los quebrados?
Maestra —Pronto, Esteban. Primero tenemos que estudiar los números primos y las medidas lineales; luego podemos estudiar los quebrados y los decimales.
Carlos —Mi primo va a otra escuela y ya hace dos semanas que empezó a estudiar los quebrados.
Maestra —Nosotros tuvimos vacaciones... ¡Ah! ¿Alguien sabe por qué no vino José hoy?
Roberto —No quiso venir. Se quedó en su casa porque le dolía la cabeza.

¡Escuchemos!

While listening to the dialogue, circle **V (verdadero)** if the statement is true and **F (falso)** if it is false.

1.	Para resolver el problema de la edad del Sr. Pérez es necesario restar.	V	F
2.	Roberto dice que una decena tiene diez unidades.	V	F
3.	En el número 84 hay tres dígitos.	V	F
4.	En el número 76 el 7 está en el lugar de las unidades.	V	F
5.	Los números pueden ser arábigos y romanos.	V	F
6.	Los números romanos se escriben con letras.	V	F
7.	En los números romanos la *C* vale quinientos.	V	F
8.	El 28 es un número par.	V	F
9.	Los números impares son divisibles por 2.	V	F
10.	En la clase de matemáticas no van a estudiar los quebrados.	V	F

Nombre ______________________ Sección ____________ Fecha ____________

VOCABULARIO

Cognados

arábigo(a)
decimal
el dígito
divisible
lineal
el múltiplo
la operación
perfecto(a)
primo(a)
romano(a)
la tabla
las vacaciones[1]

Nombres

la casa *house, home*
la decena *ten*
la edad *age*
el lugar *place*
la medida *measurement*
el (la) primo(a) *cousin*
los quebrados, las fracciones *fractions*
la resta *subtraction*
la suma *addition*
la unidad *unit*

Verbos

contar (o:ue) *to count*
morir (o:ue) *to die*
prestar *to lend*
quedarse *to stay, to remain*
resolver (o:ue) *to solve, to resolve*
valer[2] *to be worth*

Adjetivos

impar *odd (number)*
mayor *bigger, larger, greater*
menor *smaller, less*
par *even (number)*

Otras palabras y expresiones

acabar de (+ inf.) *to have just (done something)*
está escrito(a) *is written*
luego *then, later*
pedir (e:i) prestado *to borrow*
pronto *soon*

---

[1]**Vacaciones** is always used in the plural form in Spanish.
[2]Irregular first person: **yo valgo**

Nombre ______________________ Sección ____________ Fecha ____________

VOCABULARIO ADICIONAL

Más palabras relacionadas con las matemáticas (*More words related to math*)

5, 324, 572

- unidad
- decena
- centena
- unidad de millar
- decena de millar
- centena de millar
- unidad de millón

$$\begin{array}{r} 3 \\ +2 \\ \hline 5 \end{array}$$

sumandos addends

suma o total total

$$\begin{array}{r} 8 \\ -4 \\ \hline 4 \end{array}$$

minuendo minuend

sustraendo subtrahend

resto o diferencia difference

$$\begin{array}{r} 9 \\ \times 8 \\ \hline 72 \end{array}$$

multiplicando multiplicand

multiplicador multiplier

factores factors

producto product

23 — **cociente** quotient

divisor 4 ⟌ 95 — **dividendo** dividend

8
15
12
3 — **residuo** remainder

signos signs

- (+) **más**
- (−) **menos**
- (×) **por**
- (÷) **entre**

Notas Culturales

- In Spanish-speaking countries, division is done differently: the dividend is placed on the left, the divisor is placed on the right, and the quotient is placed beneath the divisor.

dividendo → 95 |4 ← divisor
15 23 ← (cociente)
(3) ← residuo

Nombre ____________________ Sección ____________ Fecha ____________

- One billion in the United States is equal to one thousand million or **mil millones,** but **un billón,** in Spanish, is equivalent to a trillion in the United States.

one billion:	1,000,000,000
un billón:	1.000.000.000.000

Actividades

Dígame... Answer the following questions, basing your answers on the dialogue.

1. ¿Qué tiene que hacer Guadalupe antes de restar 15 de 82?

2. ¿Qué le gusta hacer a Roberto y qué no le gusta hacer?

3. ¿Los números romanos se escriben con números o con letras?

4. ¿Cuánto vale la *V* en números romanos? ¿Y la *X*?

5. ¿Cómo se llaman los números que son múltiplos de dos?

6. ¿Qué van a hacer los chicos muy pronto?

7. ¿Qué tienen que estudiar antes?

8. ¿Cuánto tiempo hace que el primo de Carlos empezó a estudiar los quebrados?

9. ¿Por qué no quiso José venir a clase hoy?

Nombre ______________________ Sección ____________ Fecha ____________

Hablemos With a partner, take turns asking each other the following questions.

1. ¿En qué año nació su compañero(a) (*partner*)? ¿Sabe Ud. cuántos años tiene? ¿Cómo puede averiguarlo (*find it out*)?
2. ¿Le gusta a Ud. resolver problemas?
3. ¿Les gusta a sus alumnos resolver problemas? ¿Cuáles?
4. ¿Les enseña Ud. a sus alumnos los números romanos o solamente los números arábigos?
5. ¿Cómo se escribe su edad en números romanos?
6. ¿Es su edad un número par o impar? ¿Tiene mitad o no?
7. ¿Quieren sus estudiantes estudiar los quebrados?
8. ¿En qué grado estaba Ud. cuando estudió los quebrados? ¿Y los decimales?

Quiz VAMOS A PRACTICAR

A Complete the following sentences, using the preterit or the imperfect of the verbs given.

MODELO Yo no __________ (saber) que ella era tu prima.
Yo no **sabía** que ella era tu prima.

1. Nosotros no __________ (conocer) al primo de Octavia. Lo __________ (conocer) anoche.
2. Olga no __________ (querer) venir a clase, pero tuvo que venir porque tenía un examen.
3. Ellos no __________ (saber) que Silvia estaba aquí. Lo __________ (saber) ayer.
4. Rafael no __________ (querer) ir al jardín botánico. Se quedó en su casa.

B Complete the following questions using **qué** or **cuál(es).**

1. ¿__________ son los problemas que tenemos que hacer?
2. ¿__________ son las medidas lineales?
3. ¿__________ es su fecha de nacimiento (*birth*)?
4. ¿__________ es una fracción?
5. ¿__________ es un número par? ¿El número que tiene mitad?
6. ¿__________ son los números romanos?

Nombre ______________________ Sección ______________ Fecha ______________

C Write the following dialogues in Spanish.

1. "How long ago did your cousin arrive, Anita?"

   "He arrived two days ago."

   ____

   ____

2. "What time does the library open?"

   "It opens at eight."

   "What time does it close?"

   "It closes at nine in the evening."

   ____

   ____

   ____

   ____

Conversaciones breves Complete the following dialogue, using your imagination and the vocabulary from this lesson.

Los alumnos de la Sra. Álvarez se preparan para el examen de matemáticas.

Maestra —Rafael, ¿cuántas decenas hay en el número 200?

Rafael —____

Maestra —¿Por qué no es par el número 25?

Carlos —____

Maestra —¿Qué clase de número es?

Teresa —____

Raúl —Señorita, no puedo resolver el problema 72 – 24 porque el cuatro es mayor que el dos.

Maestra —____

Carlos —Señorita, ya es la hora del recreo.

Nombre ______________________ Sección __________ Fecha __________

En estas situaciones

With two or more classmates, act out the following situations in Spanish.

1. Explain Roman numerals to your students.
2. Given the numbers 25 and 19, ask your students which one is larger, if they are even or uneven, and how many digits each number has.
3. Tell a student who is not very fond of multiplication tables that you know that he/she doesn't like to study but that he/she has to know them in order to work out many math problems.

Casos

With you and a partner playing the roles, work through the following scenarios.

1. Two students who are studying for a math exam quiz each other.
2. A student explains Roman numerals to a younger sibling.
3. A teacher tutors a student about how to solve a subtraction problem.

Un paso más

Review the **Vocabulario adicional** in this lesson and give the names for the following items.

1. 13 ______________
5)68 ______________
5
18
15
(3) ______________
____

2. 92 ______________
× 3 ______________
276 ______________

3. 24 ______________
−18 ______________
6

4. 72 ______________
+ 24 ______________
96 ______________

Nombre ______________________ Sección ____________ Fecha ____________

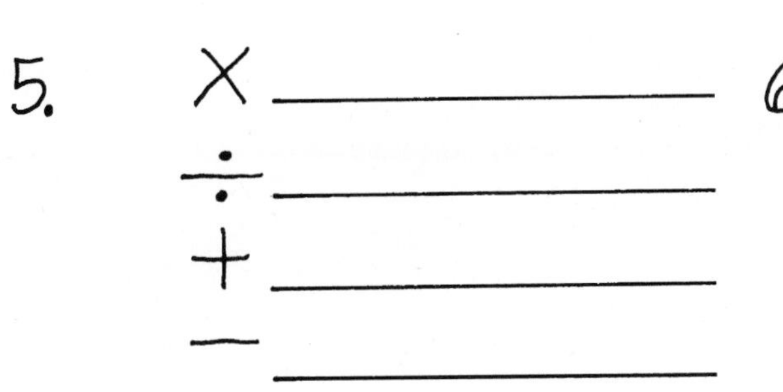

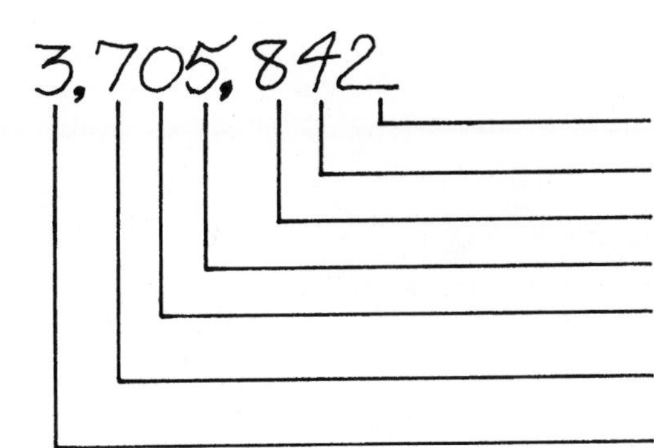

Actividad en grupo In groups of three or four, write some mathematical word problems to give to your students.

____

____

____

____

____

Un repaso de matemáticas

Objectives

Structures

- The past participle
- The present perfect tense
- The past perfect (pluperfect) tense
- **Hace** meaning ***ago***

Communication

- Math class: reviewing math terms
- Talking about fractions
- Measurements and the metric system

iLrn™

La Sra. Martínez les había dicho a los alumnos que hoy iba a darles un examen, pero ellos le han pedido un repaso antes del examen.

Maestra —¿Cómo se llaman los términos de las fracciones?
Rafael —Numerador y denominador.
Maestra —¿Qué son números mixtos?
Carmen —Los que están formados por un entero y un quebrado.
Maestra —¿Cómo se simplifica un quebrado?
Ana —Se dividen el numerador y el denominador entre el mismo número.
Maestra —¿Qué se hace para sumar o restar quebrados de distinto denominador?
Teresa —Se reducen a un común denominador y se suman o restan los numeradores.
Maestra —¿Cuál es el recíproco de $\frac{4}{5}$ (cuatro quintos)?
Carlos —$\frac{5}{4}$ (cinco cuartos).
Maestra —¿Es ésa una fracción propia o impropia?
Eduardo —Es una fracción impropia porque el numerador es mayor que el denominador.
Maestra —Bueno, veo que han estudiado muy bien los quebrados, pero, ¿qué otro tipo de fracciones hay?
Rita —Las fracciones decimales.
Maestra —¿Qué usamos para separar los enteros de los decimales?
Raúl —Usamos el punto decimal.
Maestra —¿Cómo se llama el primer lugar después del punto decimal?

Elvira —Décima.
Maestra —¿Cuál es la equivalencia de $\frac{1}{2}$ (un medio) en decimales?
Carmen —Es 0.50 (cincuenta centésimas) ó[1] 0.5 (cinco décimas).
Maestra —¿Y en tanto por ciento?
Carmen —Yo lo sé. Es el 50% (cincuenta por ciento).
Maestra —¿Cuánto por ciento de 8 es 2?
Estela —Es el 25% (veinticinco por ciento).
Carmen —Señorita, Ud. nos había dicho que no teníamos que estudiar el tanto por ciento para este examen, ¿verdad?
Maestra —No, el tanto por ciento también va a estar en el examen porque ya hace una semana que terminamos esa lección.
Manuel —Señorita, ¿cuáles son las medidas de longitud que debemos estudiar?
Maestra —La pulgada, el pie, la yarda y la milla. También deben saber las medidas del sistema métrico.
Ricardo —¿Todas?
Maestra —No, solamente las medidas de peso.
María —¿La libra, la onza y la tonelada?
Maestra —No, el gramo y el kilogramo.

La clase ha terminado y los niños se han ido, pero la maestra se ha quedado en el aula, trabajando.

¡Escuchemos!

While listening to the dialogue, circle **V (verdadero)** if the statement is true and **F (falso)** if it is false.

1.	El denominador es uno de los términos de un quebrado.	V	F
2.	Un entero y un quebrado forman un número mixto.	V	F
3.	Para simplificar un quebrado se suman el numerador y el denominador.	V	F
4.	$\frac{7}{3}$ es una fracción propia.	V	F
5.	Los decimales y los quebrados son fracciones.	V	F
6.	Las centésimas ocupan el primer lugar después del punto decimal.	V	F
7.	El 50% es igual a $\frac{1}{2}$.	V	F
8.	La pulgada es una medida de latitud.	V	F
9.	El galón es una medida de capacidad.	V	F
10.	En los Estados Unidos se usa el sistema métrico decimal.	V	F

[1]The word *or,* when used with numerals, gains an accent (**ó**) to distinguish it from the numeral zero (*0*).

Nombre ______________________ Sección ____________ Fecha ____________

VOCABULARIO

Cognados

el denominador
la equivalencia
el gramo
el kilogramo
el numerador
el recíproco
la yarda

Nombres

la centésima *hundredth*
la décima *tenth*
el entero *whole*
la libra *pound*
la longitud *length*
la onza *ounce*
el peso *weight*
el pie *foot*
la pulgada *inch*
el punto *point*
el sistema métrico *metric system*
el término *term*
la tonelada *ton*

Verbos

reducir *to reduce*
simplificar *to simplify*

Adjetivos

impropio(a) *improper*
mixto(a) *mixed*

Otras palabras y expresiones

entre, por *by*
por ciento *percent*
el tanto por ciento *percentage*
un cuarto *one-fourth*
un medio *one-half*
un quinto *one-fifth*

VOCABULARIO ADICIONAL

Medidas cuadradas o de superficie (*Square or surface area measurements*)

acre *acre*
pie (cuadrado) *(square) foot*
pulgada (cuadrada) *(square) inch*

Medidas cúbicas o de volumen (*Cubic or volume measurements*)

pie (cúbico) *(cubic) foot*
pulgada (cúbica) *(cubic) inch*

Medidas de capacidad (*Liquid measurements*)

el cuarto, el cuarto de galón *quart*
el galón *gallon*
el litro *liter*
la pinta *pint*
la taza *cup*

Medidas del sistema métrico (*Metric system measurements*)

el centímetro *centimeter*
el decímetro *decimeter*
el kilómetro *kilometer*
el metro *meter*
el milímetro *millimeter*

Nombre ______________________ Sección ____________ Fecha ____________

Lugares decimales (*Decimal places*)

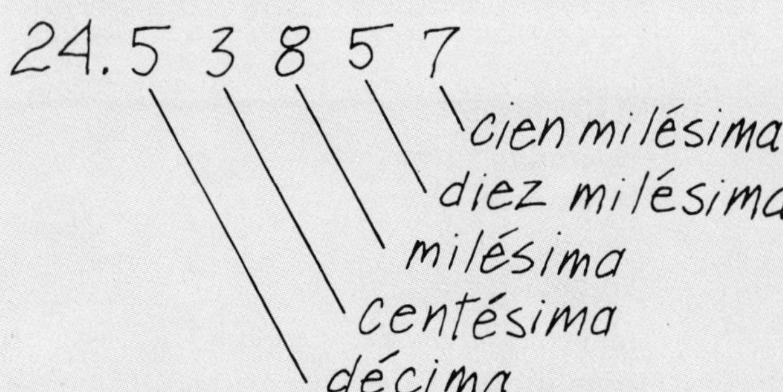

Quebrados (*Fractions*)

$\frac{1}{2}$ (medio) $\frac{2}{3}$ (tercios) $\frac{5}{6}$ (sextos) $\frac{2}{7}$ (séptimos)

$\frac{7}{8}$ (octavos) $\frac{8}{9}$ (novenos) $\frac{6}{10}$ (décimos) $\frac{7}{11}$ (onceavos)

Notas Culturales

- In most Spanish-speaking countries a comma is used instead of a period to separate whole numbers from decimals: United States 17.93; Spanish-speaking countries 17,93.
- The metric system is used in all Spanish-speaking countries. The basic unit of this system is the meter, which is equivalent to 3.28 feet.

Actividades

Dígame... Answer the following questions, basing your answers on the dialogue.

1. ¿Qué les había dicho la Sra. Martínez a los alumnos?

   ____

2. ¿Qué le han pedido los alumnos a la Sra. Martínez?

   ____

Nombre ______________________ Sección ____________ Fecha ____________

3. ¿Qué han estudiado muy bien los alumnos?

____

4. ¿Les había dicho la maestra a los niños que no tenían que estudiar el tanto por ciento?

____

5. ¿Cuánto tiempo hace que los alumnos terminaron la lección del tanto por ciento?

____

6. ¿Qué medidas de longitud tienen que estudiar los niños?

____

7. ¿Tienen los niños que estudiar todas las medidas del sistema métrico?

____

8. ¿Sabe María cuáles son las medidas de peso del sistema métrico?

____

9. Los niños se han ido. ¿La maestra se ha ido también?

____

10. ¿Qué se ha quedado haciendo ella?

____

 **Hablemos** With a partner, take turns asking each other the following questions.

1. ¿Cuántos exámenes les ha dado Ud. a sus alumnos este año?
2. ¿Le han pedido sus estudiantes a Ud. un repaso últimamente (*lately*)?
3. ¿Han estudiado sus estudiantes los quebrados? ¿Y los decimales?
4. ¿Saben sus alumnos cómo se simplifica un quebrado?
5. En su clase, ¿han estudiado las medidas?
6. ¿Qué tipo de medidas han estudiado?
7. ¿Usan Uds. el sistema métrico en su clase?
8. ¿A sus alumnos les gusta estudiar matemáticas?
9. ¿Cuántas pulgadas hay en un pie? ¿Y en una yarda?
10. ¿Cuántas libras hay en un kilogramo?

Nombre ______________________________ Sección ______________ Fecha ______________

Vamos a practicar

Quiz

A Rewrite the following sentences, putting the italicized verbs first in the present perfect and then in the pluperfect.

Modelo Ellos *hacen* la tarea.
Ellos *han hecho* la tarea.
Ellos *habían hecho* la tarea.

1. Ella no *dice* nada.

____

____

2. *Escriben* todas las medidas de longitud.

____

____

3. *Hago* la tarea de matemáticas.

____

____

4. *Simplificamos* todas las fracciones.

____

____

5. ¿Tú les *hablas* del tanto por ciento y de los decimales?

____

____

6. ¿Ud. lo *divide* por el mismo número?

____

____

B Write the past participles that correspond to the verbs in parentheses in the following sentences. Be sure to make them agree with the nouns they modify.

Modelo La niña está ____________ (dormir).

La niña está **dormida.**

1. Los libros están ____________ (abrir).

2. La puerta está ____________ (cerrar).

Nombre ______________________ **Sección** ____________ **Fecha** ____________

3. El árbol no está ____________ (morir).
4. El trabajo no está bien ____________ (hacer).
5. Las ventanas están ____________ (romper).

C Complete the following sentences with the Spanish equivalent of the words in parentheses.

1. ¿______________________ empezaron Uds. a estudiar los quebrados? (*How long ago*)
2. ______________________ que empezamos. (*Two weeks ago*)
3. ¿______________________ estudiaste las medidas de peso? (*How long ago*)
4. Las estudié ______________________. (*three days ago*)
5. ______________________ que compré el libro de matemáticas. (*Four weeks ago*)
6. Él lo compró ______________________. (*one week ago*)
7. ¡Y Susana lo compró ______________________! (*three days ago*)

Conversaciones breves

Complete the following dialogue, using your imagination and the vocabulary from this lesson.

Teresa y Ana estudian juntas para el examen de matemáticas.

Teresa —Ana, ¿cuáles son las medidas de peso del sistema métrico?

Ana —______________________

Teresa —Muy bien.

Ana —______________________

Teresa —Hay mil gramos en un kilogramo. ¿Cuántas libras hay en una tonelada?

Ana —______________________

Teresa —¿Para qué usamos el punto decimal?

Ana —______________________

Teresa —¿Qué tipo de número es $3\frac{2}{5}$?

Ana —______________________

Teresa —¿Tenemos que estudiar el tanto por ciento para este examen?

Ana —______________________

Nombre ______________________ Sección ____________ Fecha ____________

En estas situaciones

With two or more classmates, act out the following situations in Spanish.

1. You need to tell your students the following things about fractions:

a. To simplify a fraction, the numerator and the denominator are divided by the same number.

b. To add or subtract fractions of different denominators, they are reduced to a common denominator and the numerators are added or subtracted.

c. If the numerator is bigger than the denominator, we have an improper fraction.

2. You are reading the following fractions for your students: $\frac{2}{5}$; $\frac{1}{2}$; $\frac{3}{4}$.

3. You tell your students that fractions are going to be included in the exam but that decimals and percentages are not.

4. You tell your students what the standard measurements of length are in the American system, and, for clarity, you explain how they are related. For example, there are twelve inches in a foot.

Casos

With you and a partner playing the roles, work through the following scenarios.

1. Two students quiz each other about fractions before a math exam.

2. A teacher explains how fractions, decimals, and percentages are related.

Un paso más

A Review the **Vocabulario adicional** in this lesson and write the following in Spanish.

1. 23"² ______________________

2. 72'³ ______________________

3. 2/3 ______________________

4. 3/7 ______________________

5. 7/10 ______________________

6. 8/15 ______________________

Nombre ______________________ Sección ____________ Fecha ____________

7. 5/6 ____

8. 8/9 ____

9. 4/8 ____

B Complete the following sentences with words from the **Vocabulario adicional.**

1. Hay cuatro __________ en un galón.
2. La pulgada cuadrada es una medida de __________ y el pie cúbico es una medida de __________.
3. Hay dos __________ en un cuarto y hay dos __________ en una pinta.
4. Un __________ tiene mil metros y un metro tiene cien __________.
5. Un decímetro tiene 10 __________ y un centímetro tiene 10 __________.

C Write the names of the following decimal places.

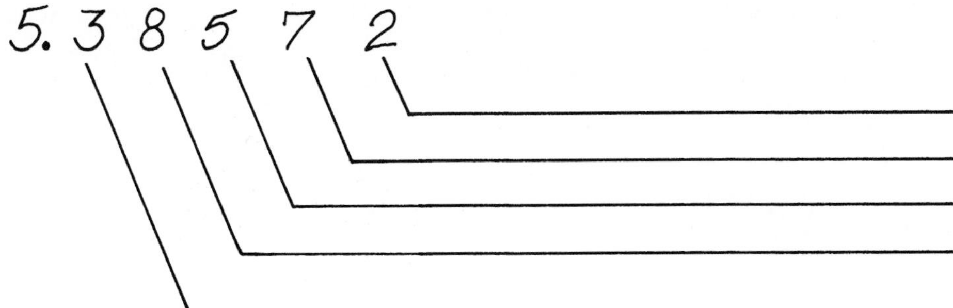

Actividad en grupo In groups of three or four, prepare a quiz for your students on fractions and decimals.

____

____

____

____

____

Lección 15 En la clase de ciencias

Objectives

Structures

- The future tense
- The conditional tense
- Some uses of the prepositions **a, de,** and **en**

Communication

- Science class: talking about astronomy, physics, and chemistry

iLrn™

Hace una semana que comenzaron las clases y la maestra quiere comprobar cuánto recuerdan los alumnos sobre las ciencias. Ahora va a hacerles unas preguntas sobre algunos conocimientos básicos.

Astronomía:

Maestra —¿Qué es la Tierra?
Ángel —La Tierra es el planeta donde vivimos.
Maestra —Bien. ¿De qué sistema forma parte la Tierra?
Raúl —Del sistema solar.
Maestra —¿Qué es la luna?
Carmen —Es el satélite de nuestro planeta.
Diego —¡A mí me gustaría hacer un viaje a la luna!
Maestra —Supongo que algún día todos podremos viajar en el espacio... Sonia, ¿qué es el sol?
Sonia —Es una estrella que nos da energía, luz y calor.
Maestra —Muy bien. ¿A qué galaxia pertenece el sistema solar?
Rosa —A la Vía Láctea.

Física:

Maestra —¿Cuáles son los estados en que aparece la materia en la naturaleza?
Rafael —Son tres, maestra: sólido, líquido y gaseoso.

Maestra —¡Excelente, Rafael! Raúl, ¿puedes darme un ejemplo de algo en estado líquido?
Raúl —El agua, señorita.
Maestra —¿Cómo se llama el cambio del estado líquido al estado gaseoso?
Carmen —Se llama evaporación.
Maestra —Bien. ¿Qué tipos de máquinas simples conocen Uds.?
Gustavo —La palanca, la polea, el plano inclinado y el torno.
Maestra —Muy bien, Gustavo.

Química:

Maestra —¿La sal de cocina es un cuerpo simple o compuesto?
Eduardo —Es un cuerpo compuesto.
Maestra —Pedro, ¿podrías decirme qué elementos componen la sal?
Pedro —El cloro y el sodio.
Maestra —Muy bien. ¿Cuál es el nombre científico de la sal de cocina?
Carlos —Cloruro de sodio.
Maestra —Bien, Carlos. ¿Cuál es la fórmula del agua?
Ester —H_2O.
Teresa —¿Qué significa eso?
Maestra —Que en cada molécula de agua hay dos átomos de hidrógeno y un átomo de oxígeno.
Rita —Señorita, ¿cómo están formados los átomos?
Maestra —¿Quién podría contestarle a Rita?
Mario —Yo lo sé. Están formados por protones, electrones y neutrones.
Maestra —Muy bien, Mario. Recuerdan mucho sobre las ciencias. ¡Estoy orgullosa de Uds.! Ya no tenemos más tiempo, pero mañana haremos varios experimentos con la electricidad.

Son las tres y media de la tarde. La maestra empieza a recoger las cosas para guardarlas en el armario.

¡Escuchemos!

While listening to the dialogue, circle **V (verdadero)** if the statement is true and **F (falso)** if it is false.

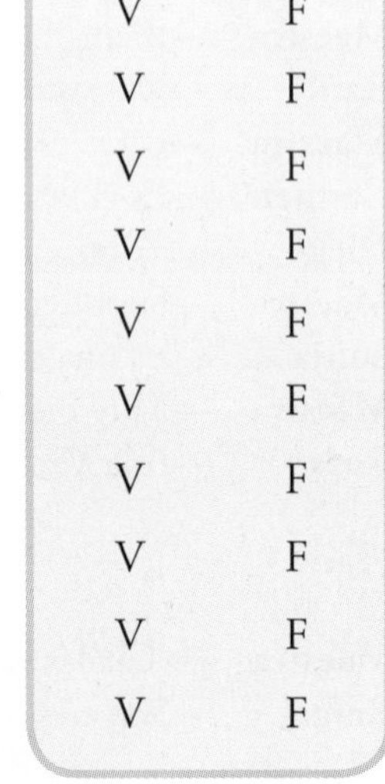

1. La Tierra forma parte del sistema solar. V F
2. La Tierra tiene dos satélites. V F
3. La luna nos da luz y calor. V F
4. La Vía Láctea es una galaxia. V F
5. La evaporación es el cambio del estado sólido al estado líquido. V F
6. La sal es un cuerpo simple. V F
7. Los electrones forman parte del átomo. V F
8. El nombre científico de la sal es cloruro de sodio. V F
9. La materia puede estar en tres estados. V F
10. La fórmula de la sal es H_2O. V F

Nombre ______________________ Sección ____________ Fecha ____________

VOCABULARIO

Cognados

la astronomía
el átomo
básico(a)
científico(a)
la electricidad
el electrón
la energía
la evaporación
el experimento
la física
la fórmula
la galaxia
gaseoso(a)
el hidrógeno
líquido
la materia
la molécula
el neutrón
el planeta
el protón
la sal
el satélite
simple
el sodio
solar
sólido

Nombres

el calor *heat*
el cambio *change*
el cloro *chlorine*
la cocina *kitchen*
el conocimiento *knowledge*
el ejemplo *example*
el espacio *space*
el plano inclinado *inclined plane*
la estrella *star*
la luna *moon*
la máquina *machine*
la naturaleza *nature*
la palanca *lever*
la polea *pulley*
la química *chemistry*
la Tierra *Earth*
el torno *lathe*
la Vía Láctea *Milky Way*
el viaje *trip*

Verbos

componer[1] *to compose, to be found in*
comprobar (o:ue) *to verify*
sentirse (e:ie) *to feel*
suponer[1] *to suppose*
viajar *to travel*

Adjetivos

compuesto(a) *compound*
orgulloso(a) *proud*

Otras palabras y expresiones

cloruro de sodio *sodium chloride*
hacer un viaje *to take a trip*

---

[1]Conjugated like **poner**

Nombre ________________ Sección ________ Fecha ________

VOCABULARIO ADICIONAL

Otras palabras relacionadas con las ciencias
(Other words related to science)

el año luz *light-year*
la condensación *condensation*
disolver (o:ue) *to dissolve*
filtrar *to filter*
inorgánico(a) *inorganic*
medir (e:i) *to measure*
la mezcla *mixture*
la onda corta *short wave*
la onda larga *long wave*
orgánico(a) *organic*
la pila, la batería *battery*
las propiedades *properties*
el símbolo *symbol*
la solidificación *solidification*
la velocidad *speed, velocity*

Notas Culturales

In most Spanish-speaking countries, the school dress code is very strict, and students wear uniforms. This erases the differences between the "haves" and the "have-nots" and emphasizes an atmosphere of learning and discipline. Nowadays, many schools in the United States either are embracing this concept or are seriously considering it.

Actividades

Dígame... Answer the following questions, basing your answers on the dialogue.

1. ¿Cuánto tiempo hace que comenzaron las clases?

   ____

2. ¿Qué hace la maestra para comprobar cuánto recuerdan sus alumnos?

   ____

3. ¿Qué le gustaría hacer a Diego? ¿Cree la maestra que podrá hacerlo?

   ____

4. ¿Cuántas máquinas simples conoce Gustavo? ¿Cuáles son?

   ____

5. ¿Cuál dice Carlos que es el nombre científico de la sal de cocina?

____

6. ¿Qué le pregunta Rita a la maestra?

____

7. ¿Quién le contesta a Rita?

____

8. ¿Qué harán los niños mañana?

____

9. ¿Qué hora es? ¿De la mañana o de la tarde?

____

10. ¿Qué empieza a hacer la maestra?

____

Hablemos With a partner, take turns asking each other the following questions.

1. ¿Tienen sus estudiantes algunos conocimientos básicos de física?
2. ¿Recuerdan sus estudiantes mucho después de las vacaciones?
3. ¿Cómo comprueba Ud. cuánto recuerdan? ¿Les da un examen?
4. ¿Qué tipo de ciencias enseña Ud. en clase, física, química o anatomía?
5. ¿Hacen sus estudiantes experimentos en la clase de ciencias? ¿De qué tipo?
6. ¿Qué máquinas simples saben usar sus alumnos?
7. ¿Qué saben sus alumnos sobre nuestro sistema solar?
8. ¿Le gustaría a Ud. viajar en el espacio? ¿Podrá hacerlo algún día?
9. ¿Hace Ud. muchos experimentos en su clase?
10. ¿Qué hará Ud. en su próxima clase de ciencias?

Nombre ______________________ Sección ____________ Fecha ____________

Quiz

Vamos a practicar

A Rewrite the following sentences, using the future tense in place of the italicized words.

MODELO Ana *va a viajar* en el verano.
Ana *viajará* en el verano.

1. *Vamos a hacer* un experimento con la electricidad.

____

2. *Van a estudiar* la polea y el plano inclinado.

____

3. ¿Dónde *vas a poner* la máquina?

____

4. Le *voy a decir* que va a hacer un viaje a la luna.

____

5. Él no *va a venir* a la clase de física.

____

B Fill in the blanks in the following sentences, using the conditional tense of the verbs in the list.

MODELO Nosotros lo __________ aquí.
Nosotros lo **pondríamos** aquí.

venir   gustar   escribir   saber   salir

1. Él no __________ contestar esas preguntas.
2. Ellos __________ las fórmulas en la pizarra.
3. ¿Tú __________ a la conferencia sobre astronomía?
4. A nosotros nos __________ viajar en el espacio.
5. Yo __________ de mi casa a las ocho.

C Complete the following sentences with the prepositions **a, de,** or **en** as necessary.

1. Él dijo que venía __________ verme __________ las cinco __________ la tarde.
2. Vamos __________ empezar __________ estudiar los planetas mañana.
3. Esperamos __________ la maestra. Ella va __________ llegar tarde __________ la clase.

Nombre ______________________ **Sección** ____________ **Fecha** ____________

4. Los libros que están __________ la mesa son __________ Rosaura.

5. Ellos hablaban __________ hacer un viaje __________ San Francisco. Van __________ ir __________ autobús.

Conversaciones breves

Complete the following dialogue, using your imagination and the vocabulary from this lesson.

Teresa y Anita estudian para el examen de ciencias que tendrán la semana próxima.

Teresa —______________________________

Anita —Los elementos que componen la sal son el cloro y el sodio.

Teresa —______________________________

Anita —La fórmula del agua es H_2O.

Teresa —______________________________

Anita —Están formados por protones, electrones y neutrones.

Teresa —______________________________

Anita —En tres estados: sólido, líquido y gaseoso.

Teresa —______________________________

Anita —El cambio de un líquido a gas se llama evaporación.

Teresa —______________________________

Anita —Muy bien. Bueno, ya no tenemos más tiempo. Mañana continuaremos.

En estas situaciones

With two or more classmates, act out the following situations in Spanish.

1. The topic of today's class is astronomy. You want to make sure that your students know what the Earth, sun, moon, and Milky Way are, and you want them to tell you how many planets there are in the solar system.
2. You and a colleague are examining two new science texts to decide which one would be best for use with your classes. You need to be sure that the texts include simple machines, evaporation, and the three states of matter.
3. You ask your students the following questions about chemistry in preparation for a science competition.
   - a. What is the formula for water?
   - b. What is the scientific name for kitchen salt?
   - c. How are atoms formed?
   - d. Are water and salt simple or compound materials (bodies)?

Nombre ______________________ Sección ______________ Fecha ______________

Casos With you and a partner playing the roles, work through the following scenarios.

1. Two students quiz each other before a science test.
2. A student explains some features of the solar system to his/her classmates.
3. A teacher gives examples of each state of matter.

Un paso más Review the **Vocabulario adicional** in this lesson and complete the following sentences.

1. Si disolvemos sal en el agua, tenemos una combinación, no una ___________.
2. El ___________ del oxígeno es O.
3. La ___________ es el cambio de un líquido a sólido, y la ___________ es el cambio de un gas a un líquido.
4. La ___________ de la luz es 300.000 kilómetros por segundo.
5. Necesito una ___________ nueva para mi radio.
6. No es una radio de ___________ corta, es de ___________ larga.
7. ¿Cuáles son los ___________ de la materia?
8. Este año estudiamos química inorgánica y el próximo año vamos a estudiar química ___________.
9. El agua tiene tierra. La tenemos que ___________.
10. La distancia de la Tierra a las estrellas se mide en ___________.

Actividad en grupo In groups of three or four, prepare ten definitions related to astronomy, physics, and chemistry for your students.

_____________________________ _____________________________

_____________________________ _____________________________

_____________________________ _____________________________

_____________________________ _____________________________

_____________________________ _____________________________

Lectura 3 Una carta

Read the following information from a letter about required vaccinations for students. Try to guess the meaning of all cognates.

SERVICIOS DE SALUD

4 de agosto de 2011

Estimados padres:

Queremos informarles que los niños que van a empezar en el jardín de infantes[1] o en el primer grado este año deben tener las siguientes vacunas:[2]

La segunda dosis contra el sarampión,[3] las paperas[4] y la rubéola.[5]

La serie de vacunas contra la hepatitis B. No es necesario completar la serie antes de comenzar las clases, pero es necesario haber comenzado[6] la vacunación.

La ley[7] prohíbe que los niños asistan[8] a la escuela sin tener estas vacunas.

Después de que su hijo(a) reciba las vacunas necesarias, traiga el certificado de vacunación. El certificado debe incluir el nombre del niño, la fecha de su nacimiento,[9] la fecha de la vacunación y el nombre del médico.

Sinceramente,

Inés Castro

Inés Castro
Coordinadora del Departamento de Salud

[1]**jardín de infantes** *kindergarten*
[2]**vacuna** *immunization, vaccination*
[3]**sarampión** *measles*
[4]**paperas** *mumps*
[5]**rubéola** *rubella*
[6]**haber comenzado** *to have started*
[7]**ley** *law*
[8]**asistan** *attend*
[9]**fecha de nacimiento** *date of birth*

Nombre ______________________ Sección ______________ Fecha ______________

Actividades

Dígame... Answer the following questions about the letter.

1. ¿Quiénes van a necesitar vacunas?

____

2. ¿Contra qué enfermedades (*diseases*) van a necesitar la segunda dosis?

____

3. ¿Es necesario completar la serie contra la hepatitis B antes de comenzar las clases? ¿Qué es necesario hacer?

____

4. ¿Qué prohíbe la ley?

____

5. ¿Qué debe traer el niño a la escuela después de recibir las vacunas?

____

6. Dé una lista de lo que debe estar incluido en el certificado.

   a. ____

   b. ____

   c. ____

   d. ____

7. ¿Quién firma la carta?

____

8. ¿Qué posición tiene ella?

____

Nombre ______________________ Sección ____________ Fecha ____________

REPASO

Práctica de vocabulario

A Circle the word or phrase that does not belong in each group.

1. pulgada onza libra
2. España Japón Francia
3. equivalencia numerador denominador
4. entero décima centésima
5. durar descubrir colonizar
6. diez años década siglo
7. palanca tierra polea
8. estrella luna máquina
9. protones espacio electrones
10. cloruro de sodio azúcar sal
11. par mayor impar
12. divisor múltiplo primo
13. única todavía solamente
14. arábigo decena romano
15. Vía Láctea torno galaxia
16. entero quinto medio
17. durante bajo en esa época
18. entonces luego solamente
19. astronomía física sociología
20. deletrea ortografía colonia
21. despedirse quedarse decir adiós
22. casa suma resta

Nombre ______________________ **Sección** ____________ **Fecha** ____________

B Circle the word or phrase that best completes each sentence.

1. La letra *ce* (suena / cuenta / repite) como la *ese* antes de la *i* o la *e*.
2. En la Segunda Guerra Mundial, los Estados Unidos trataron de (liberarse / mantenerse / prepararse) neutrales, pero más tarde entraron en la guerra.
3. Japón (comprobó / bombardeó / colonizó) Pearl Harbor.
4. Le presté el libro a Olga y nunca me lo (corrigió / contestó / devolvió).
5. La Primera Guerra Mundial estalló (a principios / a fines / antes) del siglo XX.
6. No me gusta la aritmética porque hay que resolver muchos (dígitos / problemas / acentos).
7. A ver... el átomo está formado por electrones, neutrones y (cloro / protones / conocimientos).
8. ¿Es la única (manera / costa / energía) de pronunciarla?
9. La palabra *geografía* lleva (líquido / acento / acontecimiento) en la *i*.
10. *Árbol* lleva acento en la penúltima (consonante / vocal / sílaba).
11. Aunque es una gran (constitución / naturaleza / potencia) mundial, Estados Unidos también tiene problemas económicos.
12. El congreso declaró la guerra (contra / como / entre) Japón.
13. Pronto los niños van a poder (interrumpir / contar / descubrir) de diez en diez.
14. Ayer no (hay / va a haber / hubo) tiempo para enseñarles el tanto por ciento.
15. Diciembre es el (primer / último / cuarto) mes (*month*) del año.
16. Las colonias estaban (establecidas / aparecidas / liberadas) en la costa este.
17. La historia estudia (los acontecimientos / las operaciones / las evaporaciones) más importantes.
18. Los chicos no tienen ningún conocimiento (lineal / mixto / científico).
19. En esa (época / naturaleza / palanca) había muchos problemas sociales.
20. El número tres es (par / impar / sólido).

Nombre ______________________ Sección ____________ Fecha ____________

C Match the questions in column **A** with the answers in column **B**.

A

_____ 1. ¿Cuál es el satélite de la Tierra?
_____ 2. ¿Qué ciencia estudia los planetas?
_____ 3. ¿Qué elementos forman el agua?
_____ 4. ¿Cuántas unidades hay en una decena?
_____ 5. ¿Cuáles son los estados de la materia?
_____ 6. ¿A qué sistema pertenece la Tierra?
_____ 7. ¿Qué otro nombre tiene el cloruro de sodio?
_____ 8. ¿Cuál es la fórmula del agua?
_____ 9. ¿De qué están formadas las moléculas?
_____ 10. ¿Quién era presidente durante la Guerra Civil?
_____ 11. ¿En qué año empezó la depresión?
_____ 12. ¿Qué vas a hacer con esos quebrados?
_____ 13. ¿Qué clase de número es $3\frac{4}{5}$?
_____ 14. ¿Quién pudo resolver el problema?
_____ 15. ¿En qué sílaba está el acento en la palabra *nació?*
_____ 16. ¿Está en el presente?
_____ 17. ¿Suena la *ce* como la *ese*?
_____ 18. ¿Es necesario saber todas las reglas?
_____ 19. ¿Qué vamos a estudiar mañana en la clase de matemáticas?
_____ 20. ¿Qué estrella nos da calor y energía?
_____ 21. ¿Cómo se escriben los números romanos?
_____ 22. ¿Cuándo vas de vacaciones?

B

a. Diez.
b. En 1929.
c. Mixto.
d. Sal de cocina.
e. Yo tengo la respuesta.
f. Lincoln.
g. La astronomía.
h. En la última.
i. Al sistema solar.
j. No, en el pasado.
k. En el verano.
l. La luna.
m. De átomos.
n. Sólido, líquido y gaseoso.
o. Voy a simplificarlos.
p. Hidrógeno y oxígeno.
q. No, solamente las que les di ayer.
r. Con letras.
s. Sí, antes de la *i* o de la *e*.
t. Los números primos.
u. El sol.
v. H_2O.

Nombre ______________________ Sección ____________ Fecha ____________

D Crucigrama

Horizontales

1. medidas lineales: medidas de ___________
4. La Guerra ___________ comenzó en 1861.
11. personas
13. Estudiamos la electricidad en la clase de ___________.
15. Declaró guerra ___________ Japón.
16. Hay dos mil libras en una ___________.
18. Vinieron a América buscando principalmente ___________ cultivable.
19. acerca de
21. La Primera ___________ Mundial comenzó en 1914.
22. El plano ___________ es una máquina simple.
23. Hay tres pies en una ___________.
24. Jorge Washington fue el primer ___________.
27. Otra manera de decir **quebrados** es ___________.
29. Lincoln abolió la ___________.
31. No es regular; es ___________.
32. verbo: prosperar; nombre: ___________
33. Va a haber una ___________. Van a elegir un nuevo presidente.

Verticales

2. No es una fracción propia; es una fracción ___________.
3. Hay mil gramos en un ___________.
5. Aprendemos cómo se escriben las palabras en la clase de ___________.
6. Los peregrinos vinieron de ___________.
7. No es simple; es ___________.
8. Los ___________ vinieron en el Mayflower para librarse de la persecución religiosa.
9. Los números pares son ___________ por dos.
10. No cuesta mucho. Es muy ___________.
12. La letra **a** es una ___________.
14. El 4 de julio celebramos el día de la ___________.
17. El punto ___________ separa los enteros de los decimales.
20. Es de Tokio; es ___________.
25. Vamos a tener un ___________ de ortografía.
26. $\frac{5}{4}$ es el ___________ de $\frac{4}{5}$.
28. opuesto de *singular*
30. Quiero hacer un ___________ a México.

Nombre ______________________ **Sección** __________ **Fecha** __________

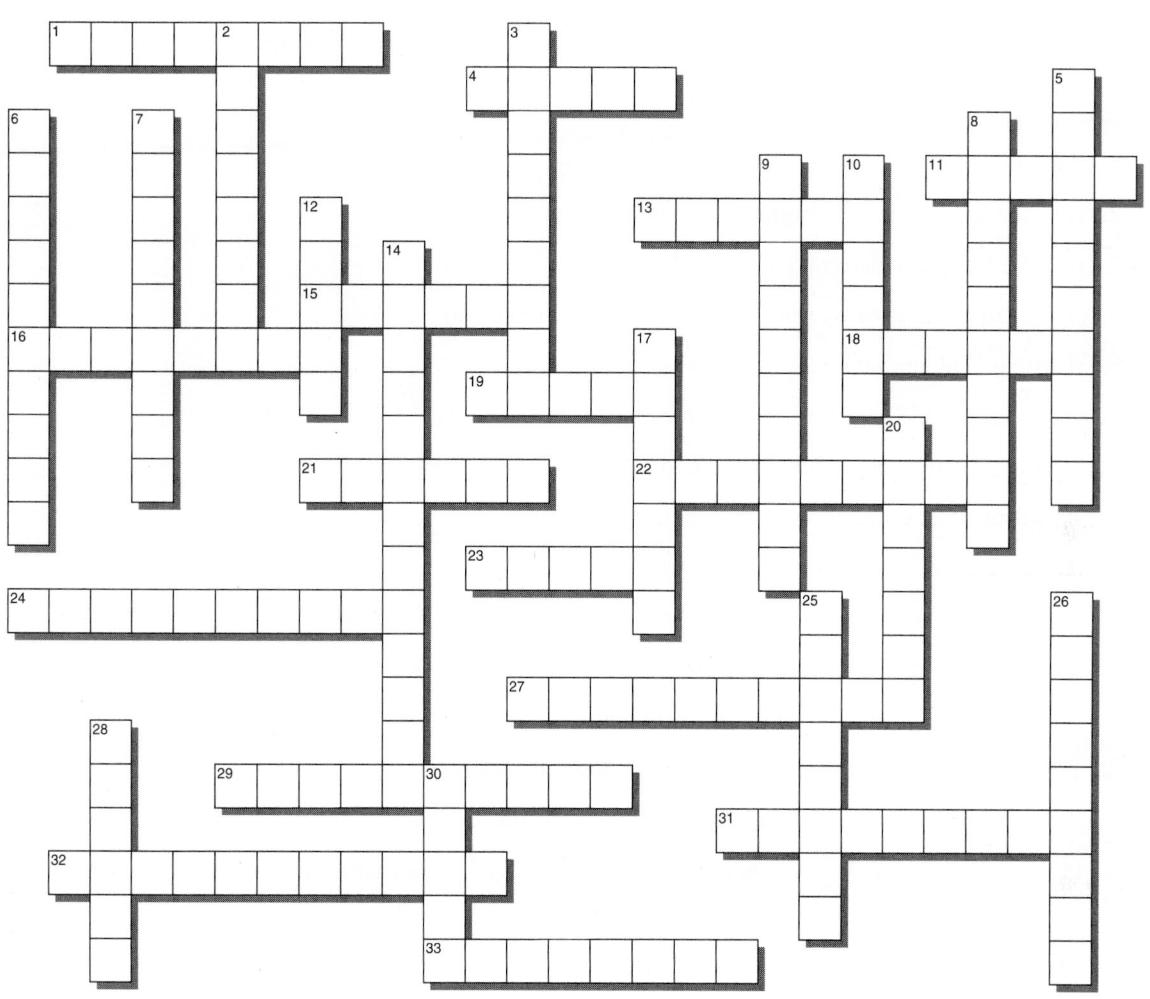

Nombre ______________________ Sección ______________ Fecha ______________

Práctica oral Listen to the following exercise in the audio program. The speaker will ask you some questions. Answer the questions, using the cues provided. The speaker will confirm the correct answer. Repeat the correct answer.

1. ¿Le gustaría a Ud. vivir en otro siglo? (sí, en el siglo XIII)
2. ¿De qué nacionalidad es su mamá? (inglesa)
3. ¿Estuvo Ud. en Inglaterra? (sí)
4. ¿Ha estado Ud. en otros países? (sí, en España y en Francia)
5. ¿Participa Ud. en todas las elecciones? (sí)
6. ¿Le gustaría a Ud. viajar por el espacio? (no)
7. ¿Haría Ud. un viaje a la luna? (no, tendría miedo)
8. ¿Le gusta a Ud. estudiar matemáticas? (sí)
9. ¿Le gusta a Ud. resolver problemas? (sí)
10. ¿Sabía Ud. todas las reglas de ortografía cuando estaba en la escuela primaria? (no)
11. ¿Cuántas sílabas tiene su nombre? (tres)
12. ¿Pronuncia Ud. bien el español? (sí, muy bien)
13. ¿Sabe Ud. todas las reglas de gramática del español? (no)
14. ¿Sabe Ud. todos los verbos irregulares del español? (no, solamente algunos)
15. Para aprender español, ¿a Ud. le basta con venir a clase? (no, necesito estudiar)
16. ¿Saben sus estudiantes reducir las fracciones? (todavía no)
17. ¿Cuánto tiempo hace que Ud. enseña historia? (cinco años)
18. ¿Qué números saben sus estudiantes? (los números arábigos y los números romanos)
19. ¿Les enseña Ud. los números decimales a sus alumnos? (sí)
20. ¿Sus estudiantes ya saben sumar y restar quebrados? (todavía no)
21. ¿Ya les enseñó Ud. a sus alumnos el sistema métrico? (sí, la semana pasada)
22. ¿Cuántos exámenes de química les ha dado Ud. a sus estudiantes este año? (uno)
23. ¿Cuándo corrige Ud. los exámenes? (los sábados)
24. ¿Qué le gusta más a Ud., enseñar física o matemáticas? (física)
25. ¿Hacen Uds. muchos experimentos en su clase de ciencias? (sí)

Lección 16: Con los niños del jardín de infantes

Objectives

Structures

- The present subjunctive
- The subjunctive with verbs of volition
- The absolute superlative

Communication

- Kindergarten: teaching smaller children
- Dealing with behavioral issues
- Playing educational games
- Singing a song

iLrn™

Los niños entran en la clase corriendo y la maestra se enoja un poco.

Maestra —¡Niños! ¡Niños! Siempre les digo que no entren corriendo.
Susana —¿Nos sentamos en la alfombra, señorita?
Maestra —Sí, pero primero quiero que cuelguen los abrigos.
Rosa —Señorita, yo quiero que se siente al lado mío. ¿Nos va a contar un cuento?
Maestra —Sí, si se portan bien. Pero necesito que me ayuden y usen la imaginación.
Mirta —(*A Carlos, uno de sus compañeros de clase*) ¡Carlos! La señorita quiere que nos sentemos en un círculo...

La maestra les cuenta un cuento, usando unos títeres muy graciosos. Luego saca una caja donde guarda muchas cosas.

Maestra —Ahora vamos a ver si Uds. pueden adivinar lo que tengo en esta caja.
Antonio —¡Yo quiero empezar!
Maestra —No, Antonio. Tú vas a empezar mañana. Hoy va a empezar María. María, quiero que te pares aquí y que saques una cosa de esta caja.
Alberto —¡Dígale que cierre los ojos! ¡Está mirando, señorita! ¿No le va a vendar los ojos?
Maestra —No, no es necesario. (*La niña saca una muñeca.*) Quiero que me digas qué es.
María —¡Es una muñeca!

Nombre ______________________ Sección ____________ Fecha ____________

Maestra —Muy bien, María! (*A los otros niños*) ¡Niños! ¡Están haciendo demasiado ruido! Quiero que estén callados y presten atención. Hay muchas otras cosas en la caja además de la muñeca.

Los niños sacan muchísimas cosas de la caja: una pelota de tenis, un teléfono, un bloque, una taza para té, etc.

Maestra —Ahora vamos a cantar. A ver... Hoy le toca elegir a Dora. Dora, ¿qué quieres que cantemos?

Dora sugiere una canción. Los niños la cantan y luego cantan varias canciones más. Después arman unos rompecabezas. Cuando suena el timbre para la salida, algunos saltan y corren hacia la puerta.

Maestra —¡Niños! Guarden los rompecabezas en el armario. No se olviden de ponerse el abrigo.
Estela —Señorita, no encuentro mi chaqueta.
Maestra —¿Es ésta? ¿Quieres que te ayude a abrocharla?
Estela —Sí... gracias. ¡Hasta mañana, señorita!
Maestra —¡Hasta mañana, Estela!

Los niños se van y la maestra se queda sola, recogiendo algunas cosas del suelo. Luego apaga la luz y cierra la puerta.

¡Escuchemos!

While listening to the dialogue, circle **V (verdadero)** if the statement is true and **F (falso)** if it is false.

1.	Los niños de diez años no estudian en el jardín de infantes.	V	F
2.	La maestra va a colgar los abrigos de los niños.	V	F
3.	Los niños no quieren escuchar un cuento.	V	F
4.	La maestra usa títeres para contarles cuentos a los niños.	V	F
5.	Los niños tienen que adivinar lo que hay en la caja que tiene la maestra.	V	F
6.	Lo único que hay en la caja es una muñeca.	V	F
7.	Los niños están muy callados.	V	F
8.	Los niños nunca cantan en la clase.	V	F
9.	Hoy hace frío.	V	F
10.	La maestra se va de la clase con los niños.	V	F

Nombre ______________________ Sección ____________ Fecha ____________

VOCABULARIO

Cognados

el bloque
el círculo
la imaginación
necesario(a)
el tenis

Nombres

el abrigo *coat*
la alfombra *carpet, rug*
la caja *box*
la canción *song*
el cuento *story, short story*
la chaqueta, la chamarra (*Méx.*) *jacket*
el jardín de infantes (de niños) (*Méx.*)**, el kindergarten** *kindergarten*
la muñeca *doll*
el ojo *eye*
la pelota *ball*
el rompecabezas *puzzle*
el ruido *noise*
el suelo, el piso *floor*
la taza *cup*
el té *tea*
el títere *puppet*

Verbos

abrochar *to fasten, to button*
adivinar *to guess*
apagar *to turn off*
armar *to put together, to assemble*
cantar *to sing*
colgar (o:ue) *to hang up*
contar (o:ue) *to tell*
correr *to run*
enojarse *to get angry*
olvidar(se) (de) *to forget (to)*
pararse *to stand, to stand up*
ponerse *to put on*
sacar *to take out*
saltar *to jump*
sugerir (e:ie) *to suggest*
vendar *to blindfold*

Adjetivos

callado(a)[1] *quiet, silent*
demasiado(a) *too, too much*
gracioso(a), cómico(a) *funny, comical*
solo(a) *alone*

Otras palabras y expresiones

además de *in addition to*
al lado *beside, next to*
al lado mío *next to me*
hacia *toward*
tocarle a uno(a) *to be one's turn*

[1]The diminutive **calladito(a)** may also be used. It is a bit less harsh and is appropriate for younger students.

Nombre ______________________ Sección ____________ Fecha ____________

VOCABULARIO ADICIONAL

Algunos artículos de ropa
(*Some articles of clothing*)

la blusa *blouse*
la bufanda *scarf*
los calcetines, las medias (de hombre) (*Puerto Rico*), **las tobilleras** *socks*
la camisa *shirt*
la camiseta *T-shirt*
el cinto, el cinturón *belt*
la falda *skirt*
los guantes *gloves*
el impermeable, la capa de agua (*Puerto Rico*) *raincoat*
las medias *stockings*
los pantalones *pants*
las pantimedias *pantyhose*
el vestido *dress*

Otras palabras y frases útiles
(*Other useful words and phrases*)

¿Cuáles son diferentes? *Which ones are different?*
¿Cuáles son iguales? *Which ones are the same?*
el disco compacto *compact disc* (*CD*)
el reproductor de DVD *DVD player*
encender (e:ie), prender *to turn on*
el reproductor de MP3 *MP3 player*
la película *movie, film*
¡Qué bien cantan! *How nicely you* (*pl.*) *sing!*
¿Qué palabra rima con...? *What word rhymes with . . . ?*
saludar la bandera *to salute the flag*
el televisor *TV set*
el vídeo *video*
la videograbadora *VCR*

Notas Culturales

As part of their efforts to instill respect for authority, some parents in some Spanish-speaking countries teach their children to avoid making direct eye contact when they are being addressed by their teachers, considering it to be a sign of defiance or provocation. This behavior may lead to misinterpretations in the United States, where direct eye contact is more likely to be regarded as a sign of honesty and directness. Likewise, a Latino child who is quiet in the classroom may be mistakenly assumed to be unprepared or lacking in ideas when he or she has simply been taught to show respect by speaking up in class only when called upon by the teacher.

Actividades

Dígame... Answer the following questions, basing your answers on the dialogue.

1. ¿Por qué se enoja un poco la maestra?

____

Nombre ______________________ Sección ____________ Fecha ____________

2. ¿Qué les dice siempre la maestra a los niños?

___

3. ¿Qué quiere Rosa que haga la maestra?

___

4. ¿Qué va a hacer la maestra si se portan bien los niños?

___

5. ¿Cómo quiere la maestra que se sienten los niños?

___

6. ¿Qué quiere Alberto que haga la maestra?

___

7. ¿Sabe María lo que sacó? ¿Qué es?

___

8. Además de un bloque y una taza, ¿qué otras cosas sacan los niños de la caja?

___

9. ¿A quién le toca elegir hoy lo que van a cantar?

___

10. ¿Qué hacen varios niños cuando suena el timbre para la hora de salida?

___

11. ¿Qué deben hacer los niños antes de salir?

___

12. ¿Qué hace la maestra cuando se queda sola?

___

 **Hablemos** With a partner, take turns asking each other the following questions.

1. ¿Tuvo Ud. alguna vez alumnos del jardín de infantes?
2. ¿Le gusta sentarse al lado de la ventana?
3. ¿Les cuenta Ud. cuentos a sus alumnos?
4. Generalmente, ¿cómo se portan sus alumnos en la clase?
5. ¿Cree Ud. que un(a) maestro(a) necesita tener mucha imaginación?

Nombre ______________________ Sección ____________ Fecha ____________

6. ¿Cuántos compañeros tiene Ud. en esta clase?
7. ¿Usa Ud. a veces títeres para enseñar?
8. ¿Se enoja Ud. cuando sus alumnos hacen ruido? ¿Qué les dice Ud.?
9. ¿Les enseña Ud. a sus alumnos a cantar algunas canciones? ¿Cuáles?
10. Cuando su clase termina, ¿salen corriendo sus alumnos?
11. ¿Qué hace Ud. cuando se queda solo(a) en la clase?
12. ¿Apaga Ud. siempre todas las luces antes de salir de la clase?

Quiz

Vamos a practicar

A Write the subjunctive form of the following verbs.

Modelo dar... que Uds... **den**

1. apagar ...que yo... ____________
2. contar ...que ellos... ____________
3. pararse ...que tú... ____________
4. quedarse ...que nosotros... ____________
5. estar ...que Ud... ____________
6. empezar ...que Ernesto... ____________
7. poner ...que Uds... ____________
8. ir ...que Carmen y yo... ____________

B Rewrite the following, using the new beginnings and making all the necessary changes. Follow the model.

Modelo Los niños arman los rompecabezas.
Yo quiero que **los niños armen los rompecabezas.**

1. La maestra nos cuenta un cuento.

   Queremos que ______________________________.

2. Ellas se sientan en la alfombra.

   La mamá no quiere que ______________________________.

Nombre ______________________ Sección ____________ Fecha ____________

3. Yo voy con mis compañeros de clase.

   Ella me sugiere que ____.

4. Tú traes las pelotas de tenis.

   Necesitamos que ____.

5. Nosotros nos enojamos.

   Ellos no quieren que ____.

6. Uds. cuelgan los abrigos.

   Les sugiero que ____.

7. Tú te olvidas de guardar los títeres en la caja.

   No quiero que ____.

8. Los niños se quedan callados.

   La maestra quiere que ____.

C Complete the following sentences with the absolute superlative of the word in parentheses.

Modelo Ellas son ____________ (graciosas).
Ellas son **graciosísimas.**

1. La muñeca de Susana es ______________________ (grande).
2. El títere es ______________________ (cómico).
3. Las canciones son ______________________ (largas).
4. La maestra es ______________________ (alta).
5. Él está ______________________ (atrasado).

Conversaciones breves

Complete the following dialogues, using your imagination and the vocabulary from this lesson.

La Srta. Estévez habla con sus alumnos del jardín de infantes.

Anita —Señorita, ¿puedo sacar las muñecas del armario?

Maestra —____

Carlos —¿Dónde vamos a sentarnos ahora?

Nombre ______________________ **Sección** ____________ **Fecha** ____________

Maestra —______________________________

Teresa —¿Puedo sentarme al lado suyo, señorita?

Maestra —______________________________

Daniel —Señorita, ¿me toca a mí elegir una canción hoy?

Maestra —______________________________

Daniel —La canción que aprendimos ayer.

Después de cantar varias canciones, la maestra les dice a los niños que cierren los ojos y traten de adivinar qué cosas les da.

Maestra —¿Qué es esto, Carlos?

Carlos —______________________________

Maestra —Muy bien, Carlos, pero no debes tratar de mirar.

Raúl —______________________________

Maestra —No, hoy no vamos a armar rompecabezas. Marta, ¿dónde está tu chaqueta?

Marta —______________________________

Maestra —Bueno, ya es la hora de salida. Hasta mañana.

En estas situaciones

With two or more classmates, act out the following situations in Spanish.

1. Tell a student that you want him/her to learn to button up his/her coat.
2. Your students are feeling very energetic today. You tell them that they are making too much noise and that you don't want them to sit on the floor. You prefer that they sit in chairs in a circle.
3. A parent arrives to pick up one of your students who has been exhibiting rambunctious behavior. You suggest to the parent that he/she tell his/her child not to jump in the classroom and not to run to the door when the bell rings.
4. You tell a student that you want him/her to stand next to you, to remain quiet, and to pay attention.
5. You tell your students that they are going to sing a song. One student wants to choose the song, but you tell him/her that it's another student's turn to do so.

Casos

With you and a partner playing the roles, work through the following scenarios.

1. Two kindergarten teachers share ideas about classroom activities and materials, and discuss the good behavior of their students, as well as some behavioral problems they have with the children.
2. A kindergarten student tells a classmate where the teacher wants them to sit, how to behave, and what they will be doing in class that day.

Nombre ______________________ Sección ______________ Fecha ______________

Un paso más

A Review the **Vocabulario adicional** in this lesson and name the following articles of clothing.

1. ______________

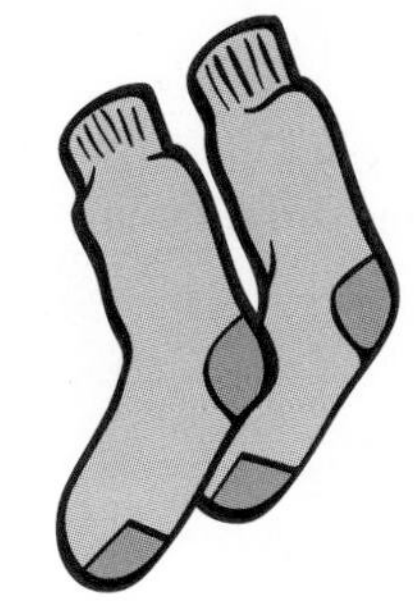

5. ______________

6. ______________

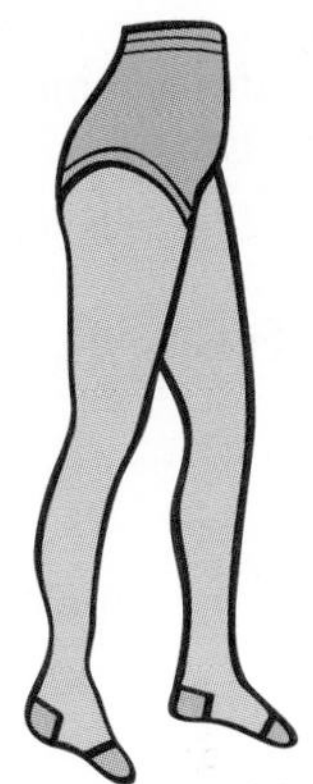

7. ______________

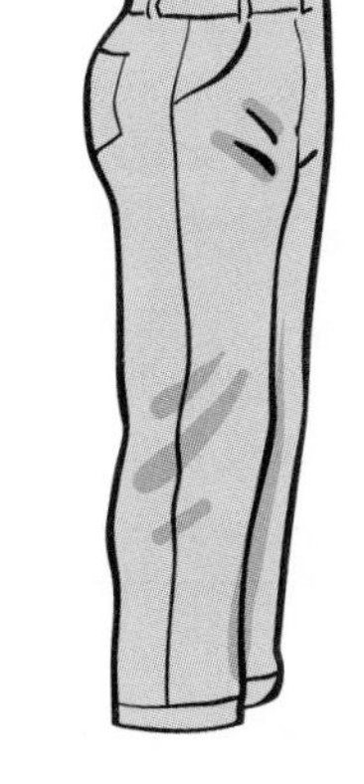

2. ______________

8. ______________

9. ______________

3. ______________

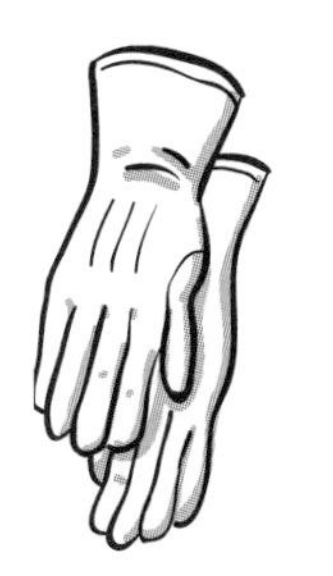

4. ______________

10. ______________

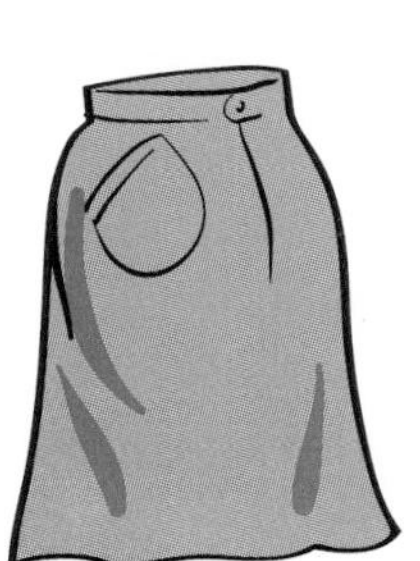

11. ______________

12. ______________

Nombre ______________________ **Sección** ____________ **Fecha** ____________

B Complete the following sentences appropriately with words from the **Vocabulario adicional.**

1. La palabra *canción* ___________ con *lección.*
2. ¿Por qué apagaron el televisor? Quiero que lo ___________ otra vez.
3. Ahora vamos a ___________ la bandera.
4. Estas palabras son ___________, pero estas palabras son diferentes.
5. Fui al cine y vi una ___________ interesantísima.
6. Uds. ya saben todas las canciones. ¡Y qué bien ___________!
7. Tengo muchísimas DVDs, pero no podemos escucharlas porque aquí no hay ___________.
8. Por favor, pon el vídeo en la ___________ porque vamos a verlo ahora.

Actividad en grupo In groups of three or four, prepare a list of 12 to 15 "do's and don'ts" for kindergarten children.

___________________________ ___________________________

___________________________ ___________________________

___________________________ ___________________________

___________________________ ___________________________

___________________________ ___________________________

___________________________ ___________________________

Lección 17

Una clase de geometría

Objectives

Structures

- The subjunctive to express emotion
- The subjunctive with some impersonal expressions
- Formation of adverbs

Communication

- Geometry class: talking about angles, shapes, and three-dimensional figures

iLrn™

Hoy la Sra. Álvarez va a comenzar el estudio de algunas figuras geométricas, pero antes es necesario que repase algunos conceptos básicos. Generalmente, ella les hace muchas preguntas a los niños.

Maestra —Rosa, ¿qué es un ángulo?
Rosa —Es la abertura que forman dos líneas o dos planos que se encuentran en un punto.
Maestra —Bien. ¿Cómo se llama el punto donde se unen las líneas que forman el ángulo?
Marta —Se llama vértice.
Maestra —Bien, Marta. ¿Qué es un ángulo recto?
Raúl —Es el ángulo formado por dos líneas perpendiculares.
Maestra —Muy bien. ¿Cuánto mide un ángulo recto?
Teresa —Mide noventa grados.
Maestra —¡Correcto, Teresa! ¿Qué ángulo forman dos líneas paralelas?
Ricardo —No forman ningún ángulo, señorita. Las paralelas nunca se encuentran.
Maestra —Muy bien. Me alegro de que sepas tanto. Pedro, ¿cómo se llama la línea que divide el círculo en dos partes iguales?
Pedro —Radio, maestra.
Teresa —No, Pedro. Es el diámetro.
Maestra —¿Cómo encontramos el área de un rectángulo?
Aurora —Multiplicando el largo por el ancho.
Maestra —¿Y el área de un triángulo?

Nombre ______________________________ Sección ____________ Fecha ____________

Carlos —Multiplicando la mitad de la base por la altura.
Maestra —¿Cómo encontramos el perímetro de un triángulo?
Diego —Sumando la longitud de sus lados.
Maestra —Bien, Diego. ¿Qué es una circunferencia?
Carmen —¡Qué fácil! Es el perímetro del círculo.
Maestra —Muy bien, Carmen, pero es necesario que esperes hasta que te pregunte.
Raúl —Señorita, ¿qué es un segmento?
Maestra —Es la parte de una línea entre dos puntos.
María —Los segmentos pueden ser rectos o curvos, ¿verdad?
Maestra —Muy bien. Raúl, ¿cómo pueden ser las líneas según su posición?
Raúl —Yo no sé, señorita. Falté a clase la semana pasada.
Maestra —Lo sé, Raúl, y quiero hablar de eso contigo después de la clase. Eres un buen alumno, pero es difícil que adelantes si no vienes a clase. Bueno, ¿quién sabe la respuesta?
Ana —Yo, señorita. Pueden ser verticales, horizontales o inclinadas.
Maestra —Muy bien. Desgraciadamente, no tenemos más tiempo hoy. Continuaremos mañana. Espero que terminen todos los ejercicios.
Aurora —(*A Carmen*) Ojalá que Eva me preste su libro, porque yo no encuentro el mío.

¡Escuchemos! While listening to the dialogue, circle **V (verdadero)** if the statement is true and **F (falso)** if it is false.

1. Un triángulo es la abertura que forman dos líneas. V F
2. Un ángulo recto está formado por dos líneas perpendiculares. V F
3. Un ángulo recto mide más de 90 grados. V F
4. Dos líneas paralelas forman un ángulo recto. V F
5. El diámetro divide el círculo en dos partes. V F
6. El perímetro de un triángulo es igual a la suma de sus lados. V F
7. Por su posición, las líneas sólo pueden ser horizontales o verticales. V F
8. La circunferencia es el perímetro del círculo. V F
9. La maestra les hace muchas preguntas a los niños. V F
10. Si un niño falta mucho a clase, no puede adelantar. V F

Nombre ______________________ Sección ____________ Fecha ____________

VOCABULARIO

Cognados

la base
el centro
la circunferencia
el concepto
el diámetro
el estudio
la figura
generalmente
la geometría
geométrico(a)
horizontal
igual
inclinado(a)
paralelo(a)
el perímetro
perpendicular
el plano
la posición
el radio
el segmento
vertical
el vértice

Nombres

la abertura *opening*
la altura *height*
el ancho *width*
el ángulo *angle*
el ángulo recto *right angle*
el grado *degree*
el lado *side*
el largo *length*

Verbos

adelantar *to progress*
alegrarse (de) *to be glad, to rejoice (at)*
encontrarse (o:ue) *to meet (each other)*
esperar *to hope*
faltar *to be missing*
medir (e:i) *to measure*
unir *to unite, to join*

Adjetivos

curvo(a) *curved*
mismo(a) *self*
ninguno(a)[1] *not any, none*
recto(a) *straight*

Otras palabras y expresiones

desgraciadamente *unfortunately*
entre *between, among*
hacer una pregunta *to ask a question*
Ojalá *I hope . . . , If only . . .*
¡Qué fácil! *How easy!*
según *according to*
tanto (*adv.*) *so much*

---

[1]The final **o** in **ninguno** is dropped when used before a masculine noun (i.e., **ningún ángulo**).

Nombre ______________________ Sección ____________ Fecha ____________

VOCABULARIO ADICIONAL

Más palabras relacionadas con la geometría (*More words related to geometry*)

Ángulos

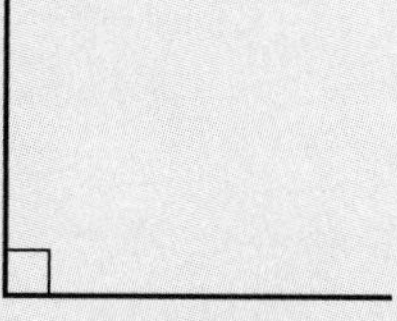

recto (90 grados)

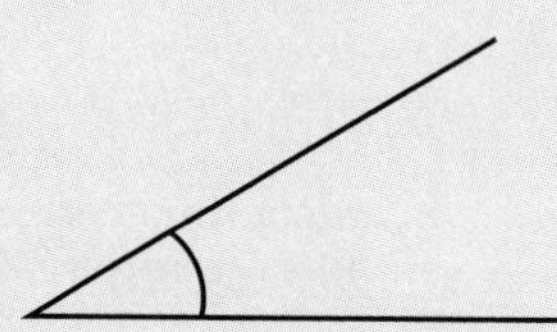

agudo (menos de 90 grados)

obtuso (más de 90 grados)

Triángulos

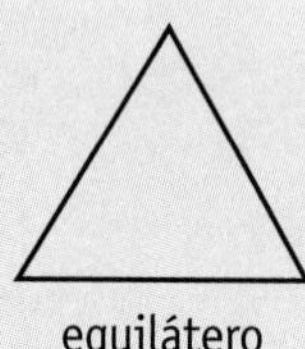

equilátero

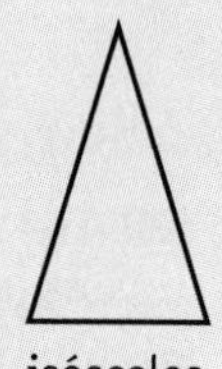

isósceles

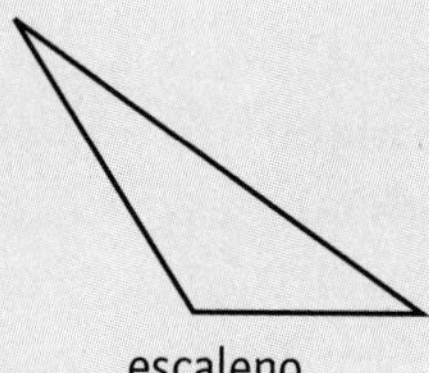

escaleno

Paralelogramos (*Parallelograms*)

cuadrado

rectángulo

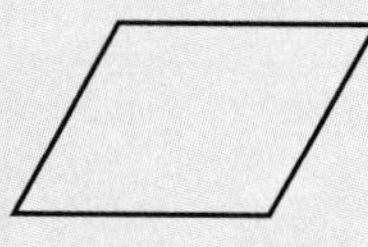

rombo

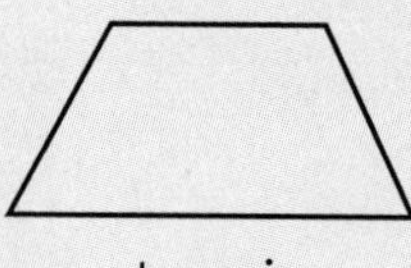

trapecio

Otros polígonos (*Other polygons*)

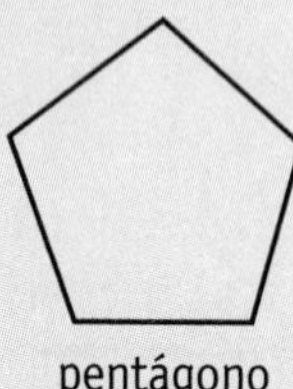

pentágono

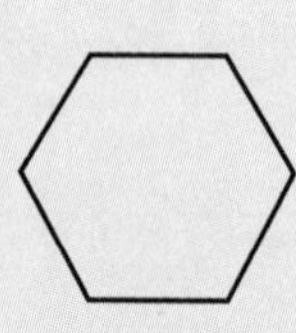

hexágono

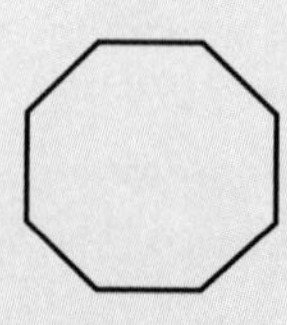

octógono

Figuras de tres dimensiones (*Three-dimensional figures*)

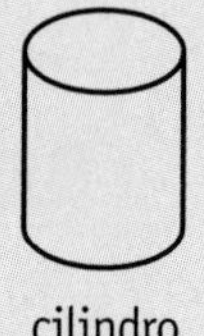

cilindro

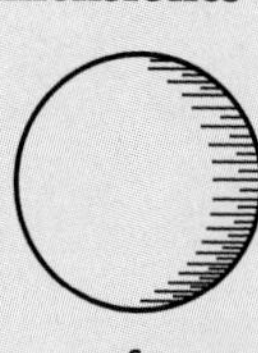

esfera

cono

pirámide

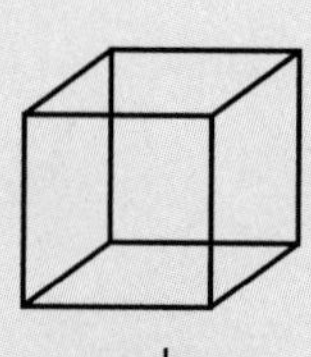

cubo

Nombre ______________________ Sección ______________ Fecha ______________

Notas Culturales

- In Spanish-speaking countries, it is a custom for students to study and do their homework in groups. The term **compañero(a) de estudios** is heard quite often to refer to students' study partners. Thus, the concept of "collaborative learning" has existed in these countries for a long time.
- In Spain and Latin America, the grading system uses numbers instead of letters. Generally, numbers from 1 to 5 or from 1 to 10 are assigned.

Actividades

Dígame... Answer the following questions, basing your answers on the dialogue.

1. ¿Qué va a enseñar la maestra hoy?

   ____

2. ¿Qué necesita hacer antes?

   ____

3. ¿De qué se alegra la maestra?

   ____

4. ¿Qué es necesario que haga Carmen?

   ____

5. ¿Por qué no sabe Raúl la respuesta?

   ____

6. ¿Por qué no pueden continuar la lección hoy?

   ____

 **Hablemos** With a partner, take turns asking each other the following questions.

1. ¿Les enseña Ud. geometría a sus alumnos? ¿De qué grado?
2. ¿Tiene que repasar a veces con sus estudiantes?
3. ¿Les da Ud. a sus estudiantes exámenes difíciles o fáciles?
4. ¿Es necesario que sus estudiantes levanten la mano antes de contestar?

Nombre ______________________ Sección ______________ Fecha ______________

5. ¿Faltan mucho a clase sus estudiantes?
6. ¿Qué es necesario que hagan sus estudiantes antes de contestar una pregunta?
7. ¿Qué saben sus alumnos de geometría?
8. ¿Cómo les explica Ud. a sus alumnos lo que es la circunferencia?
9. ¿Con qué concepto de geometría tienen más dificultad sus alumnos?

Quiz

Vamos a practicar

A Rewrite the following sentences, using the new beginnings. Follow the model.

MODELO Ella adelanta mucho en geometría.
Me alegro de que **ella adelante mucho en geometría.**

1. Los alumnos no saben los nombres de las figuras geométricas.
   Es una lástima que ______________________.
2. Repasamos los conceptos básicos.
   Es necesario que ______________________.
3. Mides todos los ángulos.
   No es necesario que ______________________.
4. Entiende la lección de geometría.
   Dudo que ______________________.
5. Él está entre los alumnos.
   Ojalá que ______________________.
6. ¡Yo estudio tanto!
   ¡Se alegran de que ______________________!
7. Ellos no adelantan.
   Sentimos que ______________________.
8. Tú no puedes comenzar ahora.
   Temo que ______________________.

Nombre ______________________ Sección ____________ Fecha ____________

B Complete the following sentences with the adverbial form of the adjectives in parentheses.

Modelo Ella __________ (raro) viene a clase.
Ella **raramente** viene a clase.

1. ____________________ (seguro) me va a llamar hoy.
2. Voy a estudiar ____________________ (nuevo) la lección.
3. Él escribe ____________________ (claro).
4. Ellos comen aquí ____________________ (general).
5. ____________________ (desgraciado) no podemos ir.

Conversaciones breves

Complete the following dialogue, using your imagination and the vocabulary from this lesson.

El Sr. Roca repasa con sus alumnos algunos conceptos básicos de geometría.

Maestro —¿Quién recuerda qué es un ángulo recto? ¿Ricardo?

Ricardo —____________________

Maestro —Muy bien. ¿Cómo se llama el punto donde se unen dos líneas que se encuentran? ¿Gonzalo?

Gonzalo —____________________

Maestro —Muy bien. Si sumo la longitud de los lados de un cuadrado, ¿qué encuentro?

Rafael —____________________

Maestro —Y si en un rectángulo multiplico el largo por el ancho, ¿qué encuentro?

Margarita —____________________

Maestro —¿Cómo se llama el perímetro del círculo?

Ana —____________________

Maestro —La circunferencia, ¿es una línea recta o curva?

Estela —____________________

Maestro —Bien, desgraciadamente tenemos que terminar. Para mañana estudien qué son las líneas perpendiculares y las líneas paralelas.

Nombre ________________ **Sección** ________ **Fecha** ________

En estas situaciones
With two or more classmates, act out the following situations in Spanish.

1. One of your students is giving an oral report about angles to the class. The report must include a definition of an angle and a vertex, as well as an explanation of a right angle.
2. In your geometry class, you tell your students how to find the area of a rectangle and a triangle, and you introduce them to the concept of perimeter.
3. One of your students has missed too many classes and is not doing his/her work. You encourage your student not to miss any more classes and to study, and you suggest that the two of you meet after class tomorrow so you can help him/her with classwork.

Casos
With you and a partner playing the roles, work through the following scenarios.

1. Two students quiz each other before a geometry test.
2. A teacher gives extra help to a student who is having trouble with the concepts of angles and parallel lines.
3. A teacher discusses a student's absences with a parent.

Un paso más
Review the **Vocabulario adicional** in this lesson and write the name of each figure.

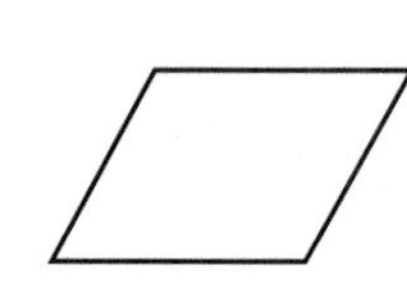

1. ________

2. ________

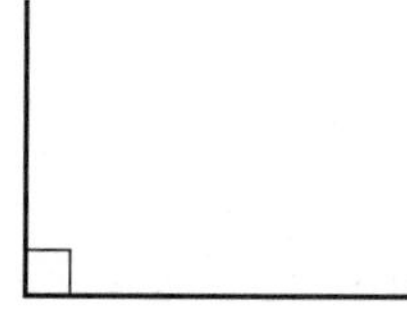

3. ________

4. ________

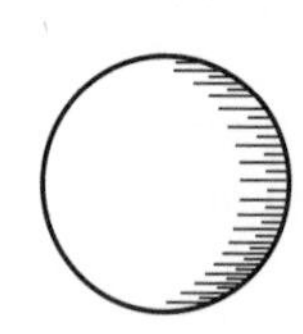

5. ________

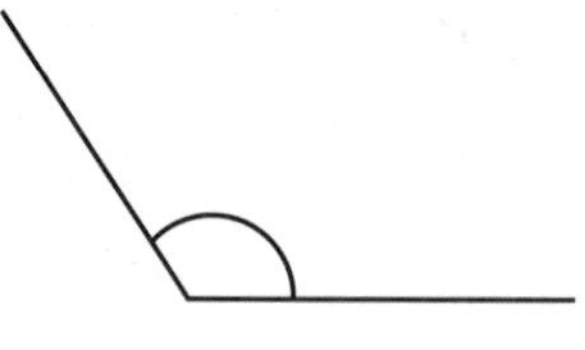

6. ________

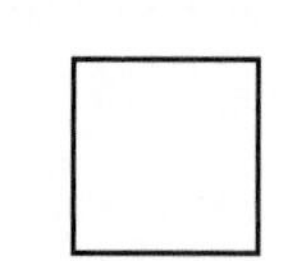

7. ________

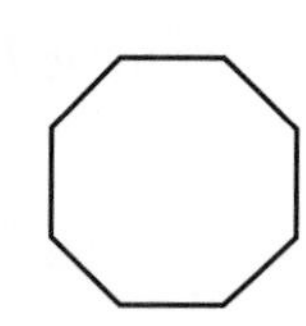

8. ________

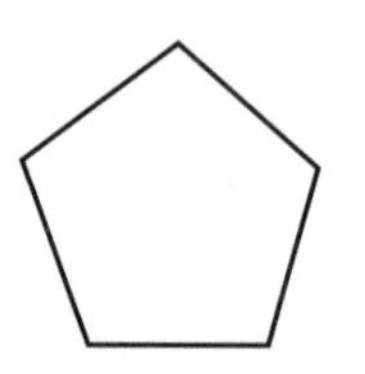

9. ________

Nombre ______________________ Sección ____________ Fecha ____________

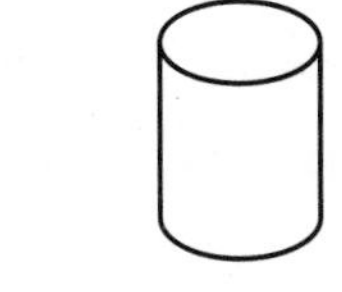

10. ____________

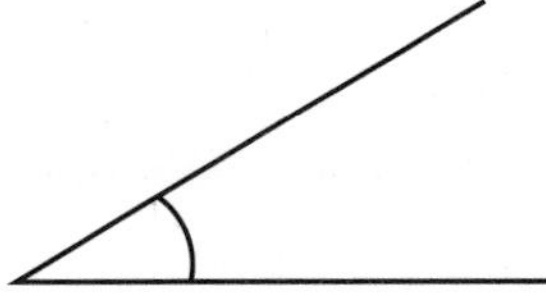

11. ____________

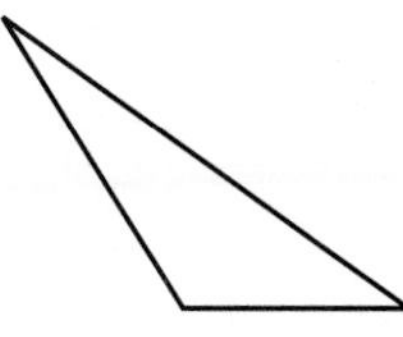

12. ____________

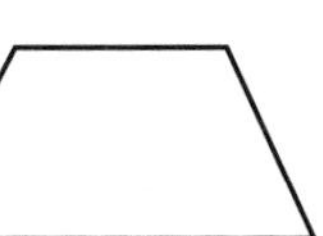

13. ____________

14. ____________

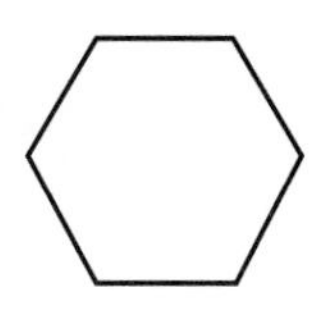

15. ____________

16. ____________

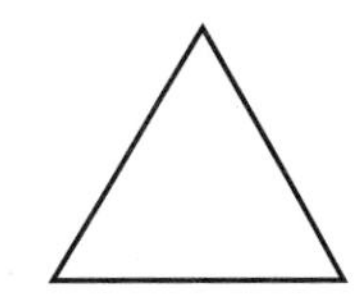

17. ____________

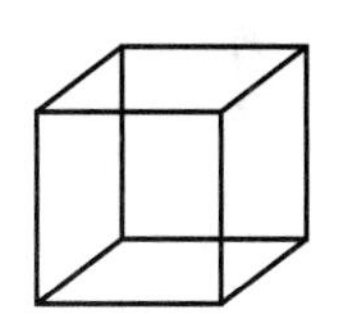

18. ____________

Actividad en grupo In groups of three or four, prepare a quiz on geometry, in which students have to provide information to complete sentences.

Lección 18

¡Es la hora del recreo!

Objectives

Structures

- The subjunctive to express doubt, disbelief, and denial
- The subjunctive to express indefiniteness and nonexistence
- Diminutive suffixes

Communication

- Recess: supervising children during recess
- Mediating among children

iLrn™

La Srta. Paz está vigilando a los niños durante el recreo. Camina por el patio de la escuela para ver si hay alguien que la necesite o algún problema que ella tenga que resolver. Ahora está cerca de los columpios.

Srta. Paz —¡Juancito![1] No te pares en el columpio. Siéntate.
Rosita —¡Ahora me toca a mí! ¡Bájate, Juancito!
Srta. Paz —Cuenta hasta veinticinco y después deja que otro niño use el columpio.
Juancito —¡No hay nadie que quiera usar este columpio! Todos están en las barras...
Rosita —¡Bájate! ¡Yo quiero usarlo! ¿Por qué no saltas a la cuerda?
Juancito —¡Déjame en paz!
Srta. Paz —¡Rosita! ¡Cuidado! ¡No te pares delante del columpio!
Adela —¡Srta. Paz! José me empujó y me caí. ¡Me lastimé!
Srta. Paz —¡Ay, no llores! Ve a la oficina ahora mismo y dile a la Sra. Torres que te ponga una curita.
Raúl —Srta. Paz, las niñas están tirando arena.
Srta. Paz —Diles que voy a mandarlas a la oficina de la directora si siguen haciéndolo.

Vienen dos niñas: una está comiendo dulces y la otra está mascando chicle.

Srta. Paz —Teresa, pon ese chicle en el basurero. ¡Carmen! ¡No traigas dulces a la escuela!
Carmen —Pero Srta. Paz, tengo hambre...

---

[1]**Juanito** is also used.

Srta. Paz	—No creo que tengas hambre cuando acabas de almorzar...
Carmen	—Es que... no almorcé. Mamá me preparó un sándwich de atún y a mí no me gusta el atún...
Srta. Paz	—Díselo a tu mamá. Ahora ve al aula. Allí en mi escritorio tengo unas galletas. Puedes comerlas.
Carmen	—¡Gracias, Srta. Paz!
Srta. Paz	—¿Adónde vas, Teresa?
Teresa	—Al baño.
Adela	—No vayas a ése. Es el baño de los maestros.
Teresa	—No es verdad que sea sólo para los maestros. Los niños pueden usarlo también.

Ya es hora de volver a la clase. Los estudiantes se ponen en fila delante de sus clases y esperan a sus maestros. Pronto el patio está vacío. "¡Qué paz!", dice la Srta. Paz.

¡Escuchemos!

While listening to the dialogue, circle **V (verdadero)** if the statement is true and **F (falso)** if it is false.

1.	Los niños están en el patio.	V	F
2.	Rosita quiere usar el columpio.	V	F
3.	La Srta. Paz quiere que Rosita se pare delante del columpio.	V	F
4.	Adela está llorando porque se cayó.	V	F
5.	La Srta. Paz está tirando arena.	V	F
6.	La maestra está mascando chicle.	V	F
7.	A Carmen no le gusta el atún.	V	F
8.	La maestra le dice a Carmen que no puede comer galletas.	V	F
9.	Los maestros tienen un baño especial para ellos.	V	F
10.	Cuando termina el recreo, los niños se ponen en fila.	V	F

Nombre ______________________ Sección ____________ Fecha ____________

VOCABULARIO

Nombres

la arena *sand*
el atún *tuna fish*
las barras *bars*
el basurero *trash can*
el columpio *swing*
el cuarto *room*
la cuerda *rope*
la curita *adhesive bandage*
el dulce, la golosina *sweet, candy*
la galleta (*Méx.*), **la galletita** *cookie*
el patio *playground*
la paz *peace*
el sándwich, el bocadillo (*España*), **el emparedado, la torta** (*Méx.*) *sandwich*

Verbos

caer(se)[1] *to fall*
dejar *to let, to allow, to leave*
empujar *to push*
lastimar(se) *to hurt (oneself), to get hurt*
llorar *to cry*
mandar *to send*
tirar *to throw*
vigilar *to watch*

Adjetivo

vacío(a) *empty*

Otras palabras y expresiones

cerca de *near*
¡Cuidado! *Look out!, Be careful!*
¡Déjame en paz! *Leave me alone!*
delante de *in front of*
es que... *the fact is . . . , it's just that . . .*
nadie *nobody, no one*
¡Qué paz! *What peace!, Such peace!*
saltar (brincar) a la cuerda *to jump rope*
tener hambre *to be hungry*

VOCABULARIO ADICIONAL

Algunas comidas y bebidas (*Some foods and beverages*)

el batido *milkshake, smoothie*
la hamburguesa *hamburger*
el helado de chocolate *chocolate ice cream*
el helado de vainilla *vanilla ice cream*
el jugo de { **manzana** *apple* / **naranja** *orange* / **tomate** *tomato* } *juice*
la limonada *lemonade*
las papas fritas *French fries*
las papitas *potato chips*
el pastel *pie*
el perro caliente *hot dog*
el refresco *soda pop*
el sándwich de ensalada de huevo *egg salad sandwich*
el sándwich de jamón y queso *ham and cheese sandwich*
el sándwich de mantequilla de maní[2] **y jalea**[3] *peanut butter and jelly sandwich*
el sándwich de pollo *chicken sandwich*
la torta, el bizcocho (*Puerto Rico*) *cake*

---

[1]Irregular first person: **(me) caigo**
[2]**el cacahuate** (*Méx.*)
[3]**la mermelada**

Nombre ______________________ Sección ____________ Fecha ____________

Notas Culturales

- In most Spanish-speaking countries breakfast generally consists of coffee with milk and bread with butter. Lunch, which is the main meal of the day, is served between 1:00 and 2:00. At 4:00, most people have a **merienda,** an afternoon snack. Dinner is generally not served before 9:00.
- Latin American countries have a great variety of dishes that are influenced by European food.

Actividades

Dígame... Answer the following questions, basing your answers on the dialogue.

1. ¿Qué está haciendo Juancito en el columpio?

   ____

2. ¿Qué quiere Rosita que haga Juancito?

   ____

3. ¿Por qué dice Juancito que puede quedarse en el columpio? ¿Tiene razón?

   ____

4. ¿Qué le sugiere Rosita a Juancito?

   ____

5. ¿Qué no quiere la Srta. Paz que haga Rosita?

   ____

6. ¿Cómo se cayó Adela?

   ____

7. La maestra va a mandar a las niñas a la oficina. ¿Por qué?

   ____

8. ¿De qué era el sándwich que preparó la mamá de Carmen?

   ____

Nombre ______________________________ Sección ______________ Fecha ______________

9. ¿Qué va a comer Carmen?

____

10. ¿Por qué dice "¡Qué paz!" la maestra?

____

Hablemos With a partner, take turns asking each other the following questions.

1. ¿Cuánto dura el recreo en su escuela?
2. ¿Qué días le toca a Ud. vigilar a los niños durante el recreo?
3. ¿Hay barras y columpios en su escuela?
4. Si un(a) niño(a) se lastima, ¿qué hace Ud.?
5. ¿Sus alumnos se ponen en fila antes de entrar en la clase?
6. ¿Permite Ud. que sus alumnos masquen chicle en la clase?
7. ¿Ud. deja que los niños coman dulces en la clase?
8. ¿Quién le prepara a Ud. el almuerzo?
9. ¿Le gusta a Ud. el atún? ¿Le gusta comer dulces?
10. ¿Salta Ud. a la cuerda para hacer ejercicio?

Quiz

Vamos a practicar

A Rewrite each of these sentences, making any changes required by the cues provided.

Modelo Estoy segura de que puede venir.
No estoy segura **de que pueda venir.**

1. Aquí hay muchos niños que saben saltar a la cuerda.
   ¿Hay alguien aquí ______________________________?
2. Hay dos niños que quieren usar los columpios.
   No hay nadie ______________________________.
3. Busco un lugar donde vendan sándwiches de atún.
   Conozco ______________________________.

4. Estoy segura de que podemos resolver los problemas.
   Dudo ______________________.

5. Creo que están tirando arena.
   No creo ______________________.

6. No dudo que ellos están lastimados.
   Dudo ______________________.

7. No creo que ella llore mucho.
   Creo ______________________.

8. Estudian en una escuela que es buena.
   Buscan una escuela ______________________.

B Complete each sentence in an original manner using the subjunctive.

MODELO No creo que tú ___________.
No creo que tú **puedas ir.**

1. Dudo que la maestra ______________________.
2. No es verdad que los niños ______________________.
3. No hay nadie aquí que ______________________.
4. No es verdad que mis estudiantes ______________________.
5. En la clase hay muchos niños que ______________________.

C Provide an affectionate form for each of the following names, using a diminutive suffix.

MODELO Rafael **Rafaelito**

1. Ana ______________
2. Pepe ______________
3. Carmen ______________
4. Jesús ______________
5. Juan ______________
6. Juliana ______________
7. Raúl ______________
8. Rosa ______________
9. Tomás ______________
10. Yolanda ______________

Nombre ______________________ Sección ____________ Fecha ____________

Conversaciones breves

Complete the following dialogue, using your imagination and the vocabulary from this lesson.

En el patio de la escuela, durante el recreo.

Maestra —¡Elenita! ¡Bájate del columpio!

Elenita —______________________________

Maestra —Porque ahora le toca a Teresa.

Elenita —______________________________

Teresa —No, yo no quiero saltar a la cuerda. Yo quiero usar el columpio.

Maestra —¡Carmen! ¿Por qué lloras?

Carmen —______________________________

Maestra —No llores. Ve a ver a la enfermera. Ella te va a poner una curita.

Rosa —Señorita, tengo hambre. ¿Puedo ir a comprar un dulce?

Maestra —______________________________

Rosa —Pero señorita... A mí me gustan los dulces...

Rafael —______________________________

Maestra —Sí, Rafael. Ya sonó el timbre. Deben ponerse en fila.

En estas situaciones

With two or more classmates, act out the following situations in Spanish.

You have playground duty at your school. Tell each child what to do or not to do.

1. Pedro is chewing gum, and Olga is eating sweets.
2. Roberto is pushing a girl.
3. Juancito is standing on the swing.
4. Paco won't get off the swing, and it is María's turn.
5. Raquel is standing in front of a swing.
6. Carlos is throwing sand.
7. Jorge cut himself and needs a Band-Aid.
8. Beto is walking toward the teachers' bathrooms.
9. Marta's hands are dirty.
10. Teresa isn't eating her lunch.

Nombre ______________________ Sección ____________ Fecha ____________

Casos

Casos With you and a partner playing the roles, work through the following scenarios.

1. Two teachers who are sharing playground duty comment on all the activities and problems they encounter during recess and lunch time.
2. Two students argue over the use of various pieces of playground equipment.
3. A student reports various playground problems to the teacher on duty.

Un paso más

Un paso más Review the **Vocabulario adicional** in the lesson and help some English-speaking friends by ordering their meals for them in Spanish.

1. John wants: ______________________
   a. a hamburger ______________________
   b. French fries ______________________
   c. tomato juice ______________________
   d. apple pie ______________________
2. Bill wants: ______________________
   a. a hot dog ______________________
   b. potato chips ______________________
   c. orange juice ______________________
   d. chocolate ice cream ______________________
3. Michelle wants: ______________________
   a. a chicken salad sandwich ______________________
   b. a soda pop ______________________
   c. apple pie ______________________
4. Wendy wants: ______________________
   a. a ham and cheese sandwich ______________________
   b. grapefruit juice ______________________
   c. vanilla milkshake ______________________

5. Jim wants: ______________________
   a. a peanut butter and jelly sandwich ______________________
   b. apple juice ______________________

6. Sandra wants: ______________________
   a. an egg salad sandwich ______________________
   b. lemonade ______________________

Actividad en grupo You and two or three other students are in charge of six Spanish-speaking children who are ready to go out to the schoolyard to play. Together, prepare a list of the things they can and cannot do. Be strict, but flexible!

____

____

____

____

____

La clase de educación para la salud

Objectives

Structures

- The subjunctive after certain conjunctions
- The present perfect subjunctive
- Uses of the present perfect subjunctive

Communication

- Health education: talking to children about nutrition and personal hygiene

iLrn™

El Sr. Chávez, maestro de cuarto grado, está en el salón de clase. En cuanto los niños vuelvan del recreo, les va a hablar de algo muy importante: la salud. ¡Ah! Aquí llegan los niños y se sientan, listos para escuchar al maestro.

Maestro —Espero que hayan leído el capítulo diez, como les dije ayer. ¿De qué trata ese capítulo?
Oscar —De la nutrición y de los buenos hábitos de limpieza.
Maestro —¡Muy bien, Oscar! Una dieta balanceada es esencial para la buena salud. ¿Por qué es eso? ¿Silvia?
Silvia —Porque necesitamos comer diferentes clases de alimentos para que nuestro cuerpo tenga las vitaminas que necesita.
Maestro —Sí, es verdad... pero, ¿qué otros elementos nutritivos necesita el cuerpo?
Ana —Proteína, minerales y... y...
Maestro —...Y carbohidratos. ¡Muy bien, Ana! ¿Para qué necesitamos proteína?
Ester —Para el crecimiento, la reparación y el mantenimiento de los tejidos.
Maestro —¡Excelente, Ester! ¿Y los carbohidratos?
Hugo —Los carbohidratos dan energía. Tan pronto como llegue a casa voy a comer un pedazo de pastel, porque estoy muy débil.
Maestro —(*Se ríe con los niños.*) Bueno, un pedazo de pastel de vez en cuando está bien. Pero... ¿qué pasa cuando se consumen demasiados carbohidratos y grasas?
Teresa —El cuerpo retiene lo que no se necesita y lo convierte en grasa.

Nombre ______________________ Sección ____________ Fecha ____________

Alberto —Y entonces la persona engorda...
Maestro —¡Exactamente! En realidad, el cuerpo no necesita mucha grasa. ¿Qué minerales son importantes para la salud?
Febe —El hierro, el calcio y el fósforo.
Maestro —Muy bien. Hay catorce minerales que son esenciales para una buena dieta.
Carlos —También es importante comer despacio y masticar bien la comida.
Maestro —Me alegro de que te hayas acordado de eso, Carlos. Es muy importante. ¿Qué otras cosas son importantes?
Raúl —Practicar deportes... hacer ejercicio...
Nora —-También necesitamos aire puro. Un cuarto debe tener buena ventilación.
Estela —La limpieza es muy importante...
Maestro —¡Muy bien! La higiene personal es importantísima. ¿Qué se debe hacer todos los días?
María —¡Bañarse! Y cepillarse los dientes tres veces al día, y lavarse las manos antes de comer.
Ana —Mamá no nos permite sentarnos a la mesa a menos que nos lavemos las manos...
Maestro —¡Muy bien! Mañana vamos a hablar de algunas enfermedades y de cómo prevenirlas. Ya saben el dicho: "Es mejor prevenir que curar."

¡Escuchemos!

While listening to the dialogue, circle **V (verdadero)** if the statement is true and **F (falso)** if it is false.

1.	El capítulo diez trata de la nutrición.	V	F
2.	Una dieta balanceada es la que tiene diferentes clases de alimentos.	V	F
3.	Las proteínas sirven para darnos energía.	V	F
4.	Cuando comemos muchas grasas y carbohidratos, engordamos.	V	F
5.	Solamente hay tres minerales que son esenciales para la salud.	V	F
6.	Para mantener la buena salud no es necesario hacer ejercicio.	V	F
7.	Es importante comer rápidamente.	V	F
8.	Debemos cepillarnos los dientes solamente una vez al día.	V	F
9.	Es importante tener buena ventilación.	V	F
10.	Las vitaminas son necesarias para tener una buena salud.	V	F

Nombre ______________ Sección ______________ Fecha ______________

VOCABULARIO

Cognados

el aire
balanceado(a)
el calcio
el carbohidrato
la dieta
esencial
el fósforo
el hábito
la higiene
el mineral
la nutrición
personal
la proteína
la ventilación
la vitamina

Nombres

el capítulo *chapter*
el crecimiento *growth*
el deporte *sport*
el dicho *saying*
el diente *tooth*
la enfermedad *sickness, disease*
la grasa *fat*
el hierro *iron*
la limpieza *cleanliness*
el mantenimiento *maintenance*
el pastel *pie*
el pedazo, el trozo *piece*
la reparación *repair*
la salud *health*
el tejido *tissue*
la vez *time (in a series)*

Verbos

acordarse (o:ue) *to remember*
bañarse *to bathe*
cepillar(se) *to brush*
consumir *to consume*
convertir (e:ie) en *to turn into*
curar *to cure*
engordar *to get fat*
lavar(se) *to wash*
permitir *to allow, to let, to permit*
prevenir[1] *to prevent*
reír(se)[2] *to laugh*
retener[3] *to retain*
tratar (de) *to deal (with), to be about*

Adjetivos

débil *weak*
nutritivo(a) *nourishing*
puro(a) *pure, fresh*

Otras palabras y expresiones

a menos que *unless*
al día *a day, per day*
de vez en cuando *from time to time*
despacio *slowly*
en cuanto, tan pronto como *as soon as*
en realidad *in fact, in reality*
exactamente *exactly*
hacer ejercicios *to exercise*
para que *so that*
practicar deportes *to take part in sports*

---

[1]Conjugated like **venir**
[2]Present indicative: **(me) río, (te) ríes, (se) ríe, (nos) reímos, (se) ríen**
[3]Conjugated like **tener**

Nombre ______________________ Sección ____________ Fecha ____________

VOCABULARIO ADICIONAL

Algunos deportes que practicamos (*Some sports we play*)

el básquetbol, el baloncesto *basketball*
el béisbol *baseball*
el fútbol *soccer*
el fútbol americano *football*
la gimnasia *gymnastics*
la natación *swimming*
el vóleibol *volleyball*

Algunas enfermedades (*Some diseases*)

la difteria *diphtheria*
las paperas *mumps*
la polio *polio*
la rubéola *German measles, rubella*
el sarampión *measles*
el tétano *tetanus*
la tos ferina *whooping cough*
la varicela *chicken pox*
la viruela *small pox*

Otras palabras útiles

alérgico(a) *allergic*
contagioso(a) *contagious*
enfermo(a) *sick, ill*
estar vacunado(a) contra *to be vaccinated against*
la medicina *medicine*
los piojos *head lice*
la vacunación *vaccination*

Notas Culturales

In Spanish-speaking countries, the separation of roles played by parents and educators in a child's life has traditionally been more rigidly defined than in the United States. The parents' job is to teach respect for authority and social skills such as cooperation and discipline; the teacher's job is to impart knowledge. The notion that parents are their child's first teachers may be an unfamiliar one to many less acculturated Hispanic American parents, depending upon their level of education. Some Latino children in the United States start school without having learned such academic basics as the alphabet or counting numbers and with little exposure to books. Less than 25% of Hispanic American children have any preschool or day care experience before entering kindergarten. Once their children are in school, some Latino parents who look upon their children's teachers as experts not to be challenged may assume that they have no role to play in school unless their children are having problems.

Nombre ______________________ Sección ____________ Fecha ____________

Actividades

Dígame... Answer the following questions, basing your answers on the dialogue.

1. ¿Qué grado enseña el Sr. Chávez?

   ____

2. ¿De qué les va a hablar el Sr. Chávez a los niños en cuanto vuelvan del recreo?

   ____

3. ¿De qué trata el capítulo diez?

   ____

4. ¿Qué va a hacer Hugo en cuanto llegue a su casa?

   ____

5. ¿Qué dice Raúl que es importante?

   ____

6. ¿Qué dice Nora que necesitamos?

   ____

7. ¿Qué dice María que se debe hacer todos los días?

   ____

8. ¿De qué van a hablar mañana en la clase del Sr. Chávez?

   ____

9. ¿Qué dicho menciona el maestro?

   ____

 **Hablemos** With a partner, take turns asking each other the following questions.

1. ¿Qué cree Ud. que es esencial para la buena salud?
2. ¿Qué hábitos de higiene personal cree Ud. que son importantes?
3. ¿Sabe Ud. qué necesitamos para el mantenimiento, la reparación y el crecimiento de los tejidos?
4. ¿Tiene Ud. una dieta balanceada?
5. ¿Qué comidas cree Ud. que engordan mucho?
6. ¿Qué actividades (*activities*) tienen sus alumnos? ¿Son buenas para la salud?
7. ¿Come Ud. un pedazo de pastel de vez en cuando?

8. ¿Qué hace Ud. cuando se siente débil?
9. ¿Practica Ud. deportes? ¿Cuáles?
10. ¿Tiene buena ventilación el aula de Uds.?
11. ¿Les habla Ud. a sus alumnos de los buenos hábitos de limpieza?
12. ¿Se ríe Ud. con sus alumnos a veces? ¿De qué?
13. ¿Qué va a hacer Ud. en cuanto llegue a su casa?
14. ¿Les dice Ud. a sus alumnos que se laven las manos antes de comer?
15. ¿Qué hace Ud. si uno de sus alumnos no se baña?
16. ¿Toma Ud. vitaminas? ¿Cuáles y para qué son?

Quiz

Vamos a practicar

A Complete the following sentences using the indicative or the subjunctive of the verbs given.

Modelo Voy a hacer un pastel en caso de que __________ (venir) los chicos.
Voy a hacer un pastel en caso de que **vengan** los chicos.

1. Vamos a tener la clase de educación para la salud tan pronto como él __________ (regresar).
2. Necesitas seguir una dieta balanceada para que tu cuerpo __________ (tener) las vitaminas necesarias.
3. Ellos siempre se cepillan los dientes cuando __________ (terminar) de comer.
4. No puede comer a menos que __________ (lavarse) las manos.
5. No va a ir hasta que __________ (terminar) la limpieza.
6. Voy a tratar de salir sin que los niños __________ (verme).
7. Ella siempre me espera hasta que yo __________ (terminar).
8. Voy a hacer ejercicio con tal que tú también __________ (hacerlo).

B Rewrite each of the sentences, making any changes required by the cues provided.

Modelo Ella ha engordado.
No es verdad que **ella haya engordado.**

1. Él no ha tenido una dieta balanceada.

   Temo (*I fear*) que ____.

2. Los niños han vuelto del recreo.

   Dudo que ______________________________.

3. Tú no te has lavado las manos.

   No es verdad que ______________________________.

4. Yo he leído la lección.

   Ellos dudan que ______________________________.

5. Nosotros hemos limpiado el cuarto.

   No creen que ______________________________.

6. Él no ha venido hoy.

   Sentimos que ______________________________.

Conversaciones breves

Complete the following dialogue, using your imagination and the vocabulary from this lesson.

Los niños han terminado de estudiar el capítulo que trata de la salud, y la maestra les hace algunas preguntas para ver si lo han comprendido.

Maestra —______________________________

Inés —Debemos cepillarnos los dientes tres veces al día.

Maestra —______________________________

Rita —No, nuestro cuerpo no necesita mucha grasa.

Maestra —______________________________

Flora —Los carbohidratos nos dan energía.

Maestra —______________________________

Tomás —Necesitamos las proteínas para el crecimiento y el mantenimiento de los tejidos.

Maestra —______________________________

Fernando —Son minerales muy importantes.

Maestra —______________________________

Paco —Debemos bañarnos y cepillarnos los dientes todos los días.

Nombre ______________________________ Sección ____________ Fecha ____________

En estas situaciones

With two or more classmates, act out the following situations in Spanish.

1. You explain to your students the relationship between a balanced diet and good health and why their bodies need vitamins, protein, minerals, and carbohydrates.
2. One of your students asks you what the saying "An ounce of prevention is worth a pound of cure" means, and you explain by mentioning the need to get fresh air, to exercise, to take part in sports, and to practice good habits of personal hygiene.

Casos

With you and a partner playing the roles, work through the following scenarios.

1. A teacher and a student discuss nutrition.
2. A teacher shares his/her views on personal hygiene with a group of parents.
3. Two students analyze their lunches to see how nutritious they are.

Un paso más

Review the **Vocabulario adicional** in this lesson and complete the following sentences, using the Spanish equivalent of the words in parentheses.

1. No jugamos al __________ (*soccer*); jugamos al __________ (*football*). También nos gusta mucho la __________ (*gymnastics*).
2. La __________ (*whooping cough*) y la __________ (*chicken pox*) son enfermedades muy __________ (*contagious*).
3. Mis hijos __________ (*are vaccinated against*) el __________ (*tetanus*), la __________ (*polio*) y la __________ (*diphtheria*).
4. No podemos jugar al __________ (*basketball*) ni al __________ (*volleyball*) porque no tenemos las pelotas.
5. ¿Es Ud. __________ (*allergic*) a alguna __________ (*medicine*)?
6. Mis __________ (*sports*) favoritos son la __________ (*swimming*) y el __________ (*baseball*).
7. Cuando yo era niña, tuve __________ (*mumps*) y __________ (*German measles*).
8. Mañana tengo que traer a la escuela mi récord de __________ (*vaccination*).
9. Mi hijo menor está muy __________ (*sick*). Tiene __________ (*measles*).
10. Algunos niños tienen __________ (*head lice*).

Nombre ______________________ Sección ____________ Fecha ____________

Actividad en grupo In groups of three or four, write the ten most important rules to maintain a healthy body and live a healthy life. Use the **tú** command form when preparing the list.

Nombre ______ Sección ______ Fecha ______

Lección 20 ¡Trabajemos juntos!

Objectives

Structures

- The imperfect subjunctive
- Uses of the imperfect subjunctive
- *If* clauses

Communication

- Cooperation between school and parents: talking to parents about school rules
- Soliciting parent support to enforce school rules

iLrn™

La Srta. García, vicedirectora de la escuela, está hablando con un grupo de padres sobre algunas de las reglas de la escuela, y está pidiéndoles su cooperación para que, juntos, padres y maestros, puedan hacer que los niños se beneficien y aprovechen bien el año escolar.

Srta. García —Un problema que tenemos es que algunos niños llegan a la escuela demasiado temprano. Si están aquí una hora antes de que empiecen las clases, no tienen supervisión.

Sra. Vargas —Yo tengo que ir a trabajar, y no quiero dejar a mi hija sola en casa.

Srta. García —Comprendo, pero sería mejor si su hija pudiera quedarse en la casa de alguna amiga o vecina hasta la hora de venir a la escuela.

Sr. Torres —Srta. García, mi hijo trajo su bicicleta el mes pasado y se la robaron...

Srta. García —Si los niños vienen en bicicleta, tienen que tener un candado y ponerlas en el lugar donde se guardan las bicicletas.

Sra. Gómez —Mi hijo viene en el autobús escolar, y el otro día lo perdió y tuvo que quedarse en casa.

Srta. García —¡Qué lástima! Eso no pasaría si el niño estuviera en la parada de autobuses unos diez minutos antes de la llegada del autobús.

Sr. Soto —El otro día mi hija llegó tarde porque tuvo que ir al dentista y la maestra la dejó sin recreo.

Srta. García —Si un niño tiene cita con el médico o con el dentista, hagan el favor de darle una notita para el maestro.

Sra. Vargas —¿Y si mis hijos estuvieran enfermos pero no fueran al médico?

Nombre ______________________ Sección ______________ Fecha ______________

Srta. García —Nosotros les dijimos a los niños que siempre trajeran una nota de los padres al volver a la escuela, explicando la razón de la ausencia.

Sr. Torres —Bueno, cambiando de tema... yo creo que el almuerzo de la cafetería es muy caro. Yo tengo tres hijos en la escuela, y es mucho dinero para mí.

Srta. García —Ud. puede solicitar un almuerzo más barato o gratis, según el sueldo que reciba... Yo puedo darle una planilla para llenar.

Sra. Gómez —Mi hijo muchas veces pierde el dinero que le doy para el almuerzo.

Srta. García —Sería mejor si pusiera el dinero en un sobre cerrado antes de dárselo al niño.

Sr. Soto —Tenemos una sobrina que está de visita en casa. ¿Puede venir a la escuela con mi hija?

Srta. García —Lo siento, Sr. Soto, pero si permitiéramos visitas de niños que no están matriculados en la escuela, los maestros tendrían mucho más trabajo. Además, tendríamos problemas con el seguro.

Al final de la reunión, la Srta. García les agradece a los padres que hayan venido y les pide que, si es posible, trabajen como voluntarios para ayudar a los niños de la escuela.

¡Escuchemos! While listening to the dialogue, circle **V (verdadero)** if the statement is true and **F (falso)** if it is false.

1. La vicedirectora quiere que los padres y los maestros trabajen juntos. V F
2. Los niños deben llegar a la escuela una hora antes de que empiecen las clases. V F
3. Los niños deben estar en la parada de autobuses media hora antes de que llegue el autobús. V F
4. Cuando los niños faltan a la escuela deben traer una nota de los padres cuando vuelven a clase. V F
5. Muchos padres piensan que la comida en la cafetería es barata. V F
6. Los niños deben darle al maestro el dinero que llevan para el almuerzo. V F
7. Los niños que no están matriculados en la escuela no pueden asistir a las clases. V F
8. A algunos niños les roban cosas en la escuela. V F
9. En la escuela no hay un lugar especial para poner las bicicletas de los niños. V F
10. La vicedirectora les pide a los padres que trabajen como voluntarios en la escuela. V F

Nombre ______________________ Sección ____________ Fecha ____________

VOCABULARIO

Cognados

la bicicleta
la cooperación
el (la) dentista
posible
la supervisión
el (la) voluntario(a)

Nombres

el almuerzo *lunch*
el (la) amigo(a) *friend*
la ausencia, la falta (*Méx.*) *absence*
el candado *padlock*
la cita *appointment*
el día *day*
el dinero *money*
la llegada *arrival*
el (la) médico(a) *doctor, M.D.*
el mes *month*
los padres *parents*
la parada *stop*
la planilla, la forma, el formulario (*Puerto Rico*) *form*
la razón *reason*
la reunión, la junta *meeting, get-together*
el seguro, la aseguranza (*Méx.*) *insurance*
el sobre *envelope*
la sobrina *niece*
el sobrino *nephew*
el sueldo *salary*
el tema *subject, topic*
el (la) vecino(a) *neighbor*
el (la) vicedirector(a) *vice-principal*

Verbos

agradecer[1] *to thank*
aprovechar *to make good use of, to take advantage of*
beneficiarse *to benefit*
comprender *to understand*
llenar *to fill, to fill out*
matricularse *to enroll, to register*
perder (e:ie) *to miss (i.e., the bus), to lose*
recibir *to receive*
robar *to steal*
solicitar *to apply (for)*

Adjetivos

caro(a) *expensive*
cerrado(a) *sealed, closed*
enfermo(a) *sick, ill*
escolar *school, scholastic, school-related*
juntos(as) *together*
matriculado(a) *enrolled, registered*

Otras palabras y expresiones

de visita *visiting*
haga(n) (haz) el favor (de + ***inf.*****)** *please (do . . .)*
llegar temprano[2] *to be early*
Lo siento. *I'm sorry.*
¡Qué lástima! *That's too bad!, What a pity!*

---

[1]Irregular first person: **yo agradezco**
[2]**llegar tarde:** *to be late*

Nombre ______________________ Sección ____________ Fecha ____________

VOCABULARIO ADICIONAL

Cosas que diría al hablar con un padre (*Things you would say when speaking to a parent*)

Su hijo(a) tiene que...

aprender a respetar la propiedad de otros *learn to respect other people's property*

asistir a clase regularmente *attend class regularly*

devolver los libros de la biblioteca *return library books*

repetir el ________ grado, año (*Méx.*) *repeat the ________ grade*

ser más considerado(a) con sus compañeros *be more considerate with his/her classmates*

terminar el trabajo en el tiempo asignado *finish the work in the allotted time*

volver a tomar el examen *take the exam again*

Su hijo(a)...

es muy amistoso(a) *is very friendly*

es muy inteligente *is very intelligent*

es muy popular *is very popular*

es muy trabajador(a) *is very hardworking*

está en el grupo más adelantado *is in the most advanced group*

ha mejorado mucho *has improved a great deal*

pasa al ________ grado *is promoted to the ________ grade*

tiene muchas ideas interesantes *has many interesting ideas*

Es (Ha sido) un placer tener a ________ en mi clase. *It is (It has been) a pleasure having ________ in my class.*

Notas Culturales

Personal space—the distance at which people feel comfortable talking or otherwise interacting with one another—is generally smaller in Spanish-speaking countries than in the United States. Physical contact is more common in the course of daily life, and both parents and teachers tend to be quite physically expressive with young children. Young Latino children who are used to this may interpret a less physical personal style as an expression of coldness or rejection, particularly if their education began in a Latin American school, where teachers are more likely to reward good behavior or a correct answer with a gentle touch or a hug.

Nombre ______________________ Sección ____________ Fecha ____________

Actividades

Dígame... Answer the following questions, basing your answers on the dialogue.

1. ¿Para qué necesita la vicedirectora la cooperación de los padres?

   ____

2. ¿Dónde sería mejor que se quedara la hija de la Sra. Vargas?

   ____

3. ¿A quién le robaron la bicicleta el mes pasado?

   ____

4. ¿Qué deben hacer los niños que vienen a la escuela en bicicleta?

   ____

5. El otro día, el hijo de la Sra. Gómez tuvo que quedarse en casa. ¿Por qué?

   ____

6. ¿Qué les sugiere la Srta. García a los niños que vienen en autobús?

   ____

7. ¿Por qué llegó tarde a clase la hija del Sr. Soto?

   ____

8. ¿Cuándo deben traer los niños una nota de sus padres?

   ____

9. ¿Qué dice el Sr. Torres sobre el almuerzo en la cafetería? ¿Qué puede solicitar él?

   ____

10. ¿Qué sería mejor que hiciera la Sra. Gómez antes de darle el dinero a su hijo?

    ____

Hablemos With a partner, take turns asking each other the following questions.

1. ¿Cómo se llama el director (la directora) de su escuela? ¿Y el (la) vicedirector(a)?
2. ¿Cree Ud. que sus alumnos aprovechan bien el año escolar?
3. Generalmente, ¿sus estudiantes llegan a la escuela demasiado tarde o demasiado temprano?
4. Si un alumno llegara tarde, ¿lo dejaría Ud. sin recreo?

Nombre ______________________ Sección ______________ Fecha ______________

5. ¿Cuántos alumnos están matriculados en su clase?
6. ¿Permitiría su director(a) que un niño que no estuviera matriculado en la escuela asistiera a su clase?
7. ¿Les pide Ud. a los padres de sus alumnos que trabajen como voluntarios en su clase?
8. ¿Les agradece Ud. a los padres su cooperación?
9. Si Ud. tuviera que mandarles una nota a los padres de un alumno, ¿podría escribirla en español?
10. ¿Va Ud. a la escuela en bicicleta, en autobús o en coche?
11. ¿Cree Ud. que los maestros reciben un buen sueldo?
12. ¿Cree Ud. que ha aprendido bastante (*enough*) español en esta clase?

Quiz

Vamos a practicar

A Rewrite the following sentences, using the new beginnings provided and making all necessary changes.

Modelo Dudo que ella pueda ir.
Dudaba **que ella pudiera ir.**

1. Quiere que yo traiga un candado.
   Quería ______________________.
2. No creo que tú sepas llenar la planilla.
   No creía ______________________.
3. No es verdad que estén de visita en casa.
   No era verdad ______________________.
4. Esperamos que se matriculen esta semana.
   Esperábamos ______________________.
5. Quieren que esperemos la llegada de los estudiantes.
   Querían ______________________.
6. Te sugiero que llames al vicedirector.
   Te sugerí ______________________.

7. No hay nadie que me comprenda.

   No había nadie ______________________________.

8. Busco un voluntario que nos ayude.

   Buscaba ______________________________.

B Answer the following questions, using **si** and the appropriate form of the verbs provided in parentheses.

MODELO ¿Por qué no compras la bicicleta? (tener dinero)
La compraría si tuviera dinero.

1. ¿Por qué no llamas al médico? (estar enfermo)

   ____

2. ¿Por qué no llenas la planilla? (saber llenarla)

   ____

3. ¿Por qué no le pones un candado a la bicicleta? (tenerlo)

   ____

4. ¿Por qué no vas a clase? (poder)

   ____

5. ¿Por qué no llamas a la vicedirectora? (estar en la escuela)

   ____

Conversaciones breves

Complete the following dialogue, using your imagination and the vocabulary from this lesson.

El maestro de quinto grado tiene hoy una reunión con los padres de sus alumnos.

Sra. Paz —______________________________

Maestro —No, es mejor que no llegue demasiado temprano porque entonces no tiene supervisión.

Sra. Paz —______________________________

Maestro —Si Ud. empieza a trabajar muy temprano, podría dejarla en casa de una vecina o de una amiga.

Sr. López —______________________________

Maestro —Los niños deben estar en la parada de autobuses diez minutos antes de la llegada del autobús.

Nombre ______________________ **Sección** __________ **Fecha** __________

Sra. Roca —______________________________

Maestro —Si un niño no viene a clase, debe traer una nota al día siguiente, explicando su ausencia.

Sr. Díaz —______________________________

Maestro —¡Qué lástima! Siento mucho que le robaran la bicicleta.

Sr. Pérez —______________________________

Maestro —¡Buena idea! Todos los niños deberían tener un candado para la bicicleta.

Sra. Gómez —______________________________

Maestro —Si Ud. no puede pagar el almuerzo, debe llenar una forma para pedirlo gratis.

Sr. Rojas —Cambiando de tema... ¿Ud. permite que un niño que no esté matriculado en esta escuela asista a su clase?

Maestro —______________________________

Sra. Díaz —Ud. tiene razón. Eso sería un problema.

Maestro —Muchas gracias por estar aquí con nosotros.

En estas situaciones

With two or more classmates, act out the following situations in Spanish.

At the request of your principal, you are addressing a group of parents at a PTA meeting. You start your speech by asking the parents for their cooperation so that the children will benefit and will make good use of the school year. Before you close your speech by thanking the parents for coming, you explain some of the school's regulations and you give them some suggestions.

1. Children should not get to school too early because they don't have any supervision.
2. It is suggested that children who bring their bicycles to school have a padlock.
3. Many children miss the bus, and that would not happen if they were at the bus stop early.
4. If a child has a doctor's appointment, he/she should bring a note from his/her parents explaining the reason for being late or for being absent.
5. A parent may apply for a cheaper or free lunch for his/her children, according to his/her salary.
6. Some children lose their lunch money, so it is suggested that parents put lunch money in a sealed envelope before giving it to the child.

Casos

With you and a partner playing the roles, work through the following scenarios.

1. A principal and a parent discuss various problems. The principal explains school regulations and offers solutions.
2. A parent approaches his/her child's teacher about the price of school lunches.
3. Two parents make arrangements for getting their children to school on time.

Nombre ______________________ Sección ____________ Fecha ____________

Un paso más Review the **Vocabulario adicional** in this lesson and write Spanish statements that you might use in parent-teacher conferences if your students were exhibiting these behaviors.

1. Oscar misses too many classes, and takes library books home, but never brings them back.

2. Elena always works diligently and is very friendly.

3. Luis is very intelligent and is now in the highest reading group, but he needs to be more considerate of others.

4. Alicia never finishes her work on time. She also often borrows others' supplies without returning them.

5. Teresa is now doing much better. She's promoted to the fifth grade.

6. Ramón didn't do well on the proficiency test, and he might have to be retained in the fourth grade.

7. Antonio always contributes interesting ideas during class discussions. All the other children like him.

8. Ana is a child that you enjoy having in your class.

Nombre ______________________ Sección ____________ Fecha ____________

Actividad en grupo In groups of three or four, discuss in Spanish the problems that teachers encounter with students in the classroom and problems that may arise with parents. In each case, explain how you might handle the problem.

¿Cómo pueden los padres participar en las actividades escolares?

Read the following information from a handout about parental involvement at school. Try to guess the meaning of all cognates.

Entrevistas con los maestros

Usted puede pedir una entrevista privada con el maestro de su hijo para hablar sobre cómo le va al niño en la escuela. Los maestros también pueden ponerse en contacto[1] con un padre o un tutor para hablar de cualquier[2] problema relacionado con el niño.

De regreso a la escuela

Todas las escuelas ofrecen anualmente lo que en inglés se llama "Open House". Esta reunión tiene lugar[3] por la noche y allí los padres o tutores tienen la oportunidad de conocer a los maestros de sus hijos, de visitar el aula y de obtener información sobre el programa de estudios.

El Consejo[4] Escolar

El Consejo Escolar está formado por padres, directores, maestros y otros miembros del personal escolar. Está encargado de[5] decidir cuáles serán las metas[6] y los objetivos de la escuela, el presupuesto[7] y los programas para mejorar[8] la educación de los alumnos, así como también[9] supervisar el éxito[10] de los estudiantes. Si usted desea ser miembro del Consejo Escolar, llame a la oficina del director para obtener más información.

[1]**ponerse en contacto** *to contact*
[2]**cualquier** *any*
[3]**tiene lugar** *takes place*
[4]**Consejo** *Council*
[5]**encargado de** *in charge of*
[6]**metas** *goals*
[7]**presupuesto** *budget*
[8]**mejorar** *to improve*
[9]**así como también** *as well as*
[10]**éxito** *success*

Nombre ______________________ Sección ____________ Fecha ____________

Actividades

Dígame... Answer the following questions based on the handout.

1. ¿Para qué puede un padre pedir una entrevista con el maestro de su hijo(a)?
____
2. ¿Para qué puede un(a) maestro(a) ponerse en contacto con un padre o tutor?
____
3. ¿Qué ofrecen todas las escuelas anualmente?
____
4. ¿Estas reuniones son durante el día?
____
5. ¿Cuál es el propósito de estas reuniones?
____
6. ¿Quiénes forman el Consejo Escolar?
____
7. ¿De qué está encargado el Consejo Escolar? Dé una lista.
   a. ____
   b. ____
   c. ____
   d. ____
8. ¿Qué debe hacer un padre si quiere ser miembro del Consejo Escolar?
____

Nombre ______________________ Sección ____________ Fecha ____________

Repaso

Práctica de vocabulario

A Circle the word or phrase that does not belong in each group.

1. basurero barras columpio
2. paz guerra arena
3. empujar observar vigilar
4. estudio diámetro radio
5. muy bien excelente mal
6. reunión candado junta
7. cuento contar cantar
8. base dicho altura
9. concepto idea bloque
10. línea segmento ancho
11. desgraciadamente qué lástima en realidad
12. ventilación aire puro curita
13. personal solo juntos
14. ¡Cuidado! ¡No te lastimes! ¡Ven aquí!
15. asiste a clases viene mañana está matriculado
16. naranja junta manzana
17. esperar saltar brincar
18. ojalá consumo espero

Nombre ______________________ **Sección** __________ **Fecha** __________

B Circle the word or phrase that best completes each sentence.

1. En una dieta balanceada necesitamos (carbohidratos / ventilación / hábitos) y proteínas.
2. Para jugar tienen (muñecas / citas / cuentos) y pelotas.
3. Debe (cepillarse / consumirse / convertirse) los dientes tres veces al día.
4. Es necesario tener buenos hábitos de higiene y nutrición para el mantenimiento de la (grasa / limpieza / salud).
5. Encontramos el área de un triángulo multiplicando la mitad de la base por (la altura / el lado / la abertura).
6. Si comes demasiados dulces vas a (engordar / reírte / mandar).
7. Es mejor (permitir / retener / prevenir) que curar.
8. El calcio y el fósforo son minerales (débiles / graciosos / esenciales) para la salud.
9. Esa línea no es horizontal ni vertical; es (nutritiva / inclinada / vacía).
10. El lugar donde se unen los lados de un ángulo se llama (área / vértice / plano).
11. Te voy a (vender / vendar / adivinar) los ojos.
12. Voy a (correr / armar / apagar) la luz.
13. No me puedo (abrochar / parar / enojar) la chaqueta. Haz el favor de ayudarme.
14. Me (lastimé / quedé / olvidé) de traer los libros.
15. Siéntate aquí, en la alfombra, (según / hacia / al lado) mío.
16. Los niños se portan mal cuando no tienen (punto / tema / supervisión).
17. ¿Quieres tomar una clase en la universidad? Ve a (beneficiarte / sentarte / matricularte) hoy mismo.
18. Los niños deben ponerse en fila delante (de la razón / de la clase / del sobre).
19. Quiero (solicitar / aprovechar / robar) la oportunidad para hablar con los padres.
20. Si faltó a clase, tiene que traer (una nota / títeres / imaginación) de los padres.
21. ¿Quieres beber una (limpieza / salud / limonada)?
22. Los días de repaso, los niños generalmente le (hacen / vuelven / ponen) muchas preguntas a la maestra.

C Match the questions in column **A** with the answers in column **B**.

	A		B
______	**1.** ¿Dónde pusiste el rompecabezas?	**a.**	Sí, tengo hambre.
______	**2.** ¿Qué vas a preparar para el almuerzo?	**b.**	El tercero.
______	**3.** ¿Por qué hay tanto ruido en tu cuarto?	**c.**	No, con sus padres.
______	**4.** ¿Tiene un buen sueldo?	**d.**	Sí, estoy de acuerdo.
______	**5.** ¿Qué te vas a poner?	**e.**	No, perpendiculares.
______	**6.** ¿Cómo se llama tu compañero de clase?	**f.**	No, gana sólo $30 al día.
______	**7.** ¿Qué deporte practicas?	**g.**	Sí, hasta mil.
______	**8.** ¿Dónde tiraste los papeles?	**h.**	No, era muy difícil.
______	**9.** ¿A quién le toca?	**i.**	Carlos Rivas Soto.
______	**10.** ¿Qué capítulo estás leyendo?	**j.**	En la caja.
______	**11.** ¿Pudiste resolver el problema?	**k.**	Esta planilla.
______	**12.** ¿Son paralelas?	**l.**	En el basurero.
______	**13.** ¿Crees que tengo razón?	**m.**	Porque estoy jugando con los niños.
______	**14.** ¿Sabes contar en español?	**n.**	El tenis.
______	**15.** ¿Vas a trabajar de voluntario?	**o.**	Sándwiches y un pastel.
______	**16.** ¿Qué debo llenar?	**p.**	Veinte entre cinco.
______	**17.** ¿Por qué llegaste tarde?	**q.**	Perdí el autobús.
______	**18.** ¿Qué tengo que dividir?	**r.**	Sí, porque necesitan mi cooperación.
______	**19.** ¿Vienen solos?	**s.**	A mí.
______	**20.** ¿Vas a comer ahora?	**t.**	El abrigo.

Nombre ______________ Sección ______________ Fecha ______________

D Crucigrama

Horizontales

1. Hoy tengo una ___________ con el dentista.
3. Vamos a ___________ una canción.
5. verbo: llegar; nombre: ___________
7. lo que hace el médico
8. Las líneas ___________ nunca se encuentran.
11. Voy a saltar a la ___________.
12. visitar: estar de ___________
16. trozo
17. después
18. opuesto de **recto**
19. mineral muy importante
20. largo
21. El calcio y el fósforo son ___________ muy importantes.
22. Voy a ___________ a la niña a la oficina.
27. adjetivo: ausente; nombre: ___________
30. opuesto de **vertical**
31. opuesto de **rápido**
33. dar gracias
34. forma
35. Él nunca habla; siempre está ___________.
36. La usamos para tomar café.
37. El triángulo y el rectángulo son figuras ___________.
38. ¡Vete! ¡Déjame en ___________!

Verticales

1. perímetro del círculo
2. No cuesta (*costs*) nada; es ___________.
4. progresar
6. adjetivo: enfermo; nombre: ___________
9. Tiene cinco años; va al ___________ de infantes.
10. Para hacer ejercicios, podemos practicar ___________.
13. La leche tiene ___________ D.
14. opuesto de **barato**
15. entender
18. *swing,* en español
21. Necesitamos proteína para el crecimiento, la reparación y el ___________ de los tejidos.
23. *sweet,* en español
24. relativo a la escuela
25. piso
26. permitir
28. verbo: limpiar; nombre: ___________
29. opuesto de **reír**
32. Está en la ___________ de autobuses.

Nombre ______________________ Sección ____________ Fecha ____________

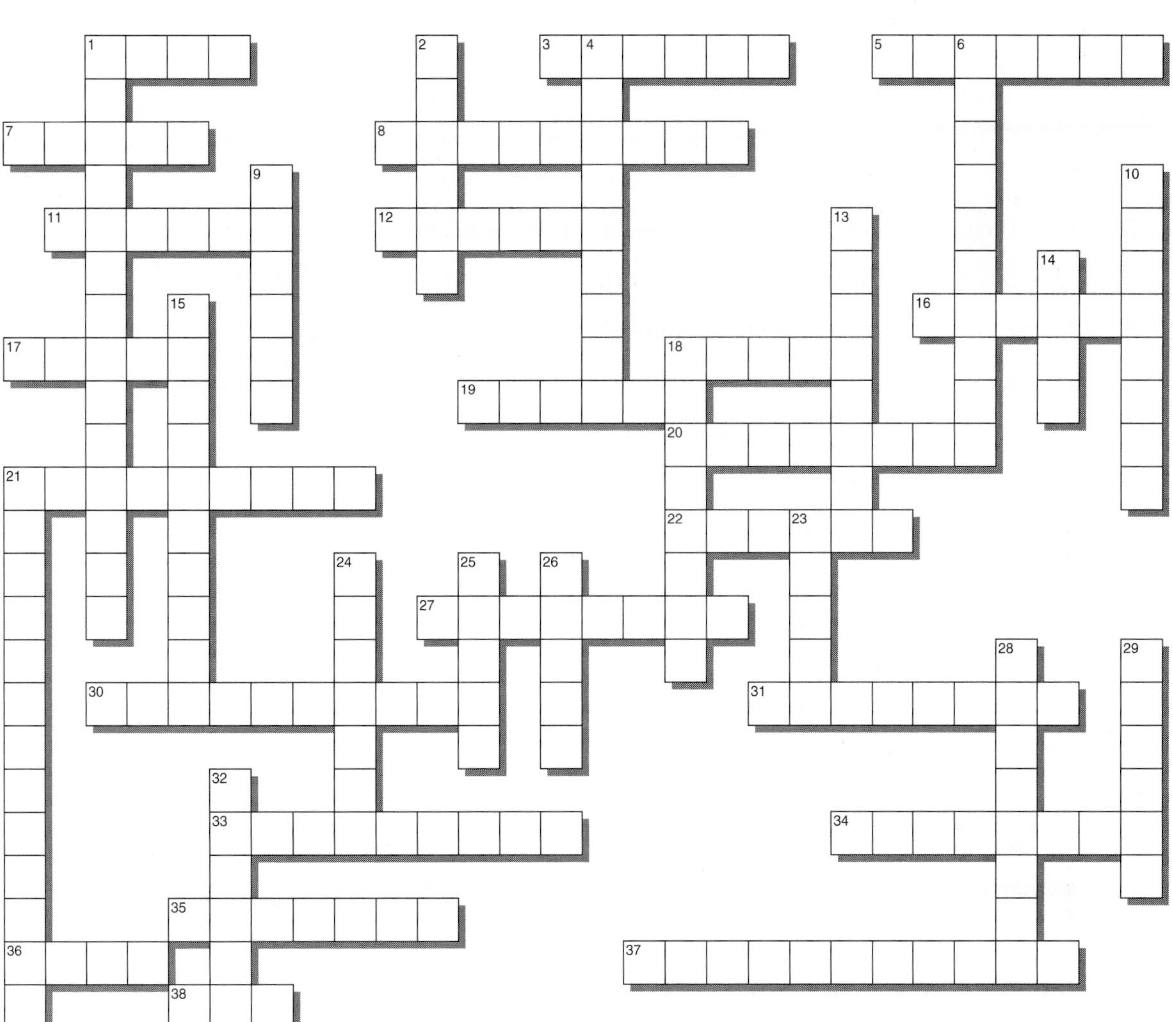

Nombre ______________________ Sección ____________ Fecha ____________

Práctica oral Listen to the following exercise in the audio program. The speaker will ask you some questions. Answer the questions, using the cues provided. The speaker will confirm the correct answer. Repeat the correct answer.

1. ¿De qué les va a hablar Ud. a sus alumnos el lunes? (de la salud)
2. ¿De qué trata el capítulo que Ud. va a enseñar? (de los elementos nutritivos)
3. ¿Qué tipo de dieta debemos tener para tener buena salud? (una dieta balanceada)
4. ¿Qué hace Ud. cuando uno de sus alumnos se corta un dedo? (le pongo una curita)
5. ¿Adónde manda Ud. a sus alumnos cuando se portan mal? (a la oficina de la directora)
6. ¿Le gusta a Ud. armar rompecabezas a veces? (sí)
7. ¿Usa Ud. títeres cuando les cuenta un cuento a sus alumnos? (sí)
8. ¿Quiénes vigilan a los niños durante el recreo? (los maestros)
9. ¿A sus alumnos les gusta más usar los columpios o las barras? (los columpios)
10. ¿Puede asistir un niño a su escuela si no está matriculado? (no)
11. ¿Qué va a hacer Ud. tan pronto como llegue a su casa? (estudiar geometría)
12. ¿Come Ud. dulces y pasteles? (sí, de vez en cuando)
13. ¿Qué le gusta comer cuando tiene hambre? (sándwiches)
14. ¿Es muy caro el almuerzo en la cafetería de la escuela? (no)
15. ¿Cuántas veces por semana hace Ud. ejercicio? (tres veces por semana)
16. ¿Juega Ud. al tenis, al básquetbol o al vóleibol? (al tenis)
17. ¿Ud. se baña por la mañana, por la tarde o por la noche? (por la mañana)
18. ¿Cuántas veces al día se cepilla Ud. los dientes? (tres veces)
19. ¿Cuándo fue la última vez que Ud. tuvo una cita con el médico? (el mes pasado)
20. ¿Cuándo va a tener Ud. una reunión con la madre de un estudiante? (la semana que viene)

Appendix A

Introduction to Spanish Sounds and the Alphabet

Sections marked with an audio icon are available on the iLrn that accompanies this text. Repeat each Spanish word after the speaker, imitating as closely as possible the correct pronunciation.

The Alphabet

Letter	Name	Letter	Name	Letter	Name	Letter	Name
a	a	h	hache	ñ	eñe	t	te
b	be (larga)	i	i	o	o	u	u
c	ce	j	jota	p	pe	v	ve, uve
d	de	k	ka	q	cu	w	doble ve, doble uve
e	e	l	ele	r	ere, erre	x	equis
f	efe	m	eme			y	i griega, ye
g	ge	n	ene	s	ese	z	zeta

The Vowels

1. The Spanish **a** has a sound similar to the English *a* in the word *father.* Repeat:

   Ana casa banana mala dama mata

2. The Spanish **e** is pronounced like the English *e* in the word *eight.* Repeat:

   este René teme deme entre bebe

3. The Spanish **i** is pronounced like the English *ee* in the word *see.* Repeat:

   sí difícil Mimí ir dividir Fifí

4. The Spanish **o** is similar to the English *o* in the word *no,* but without the glide. Repeat:

   solo poco como toco con monólogo

5. The Spanish **u** is similar to the English *ue* sound in the word *Sue.* Repeat:

   Lulú un su universo murciélago

The Consonants

1. The Spanish **p** is pronounced like the English *p* in the word *spot.* Repeat:

pan papá Pepe pila poco pude

2. The Spanish **c** in front of **a, o, u, l,** or **r** sounds similar to the English *k.* Repeat:

casa como cuna clima crimen cromo

3. The Spanish **q** is only used in the combinations **que** and **qui,** in which the **u** is silent, and also has a sound similar to the English *k.* Repeat:

que queso Quique quinto quema quiso

4. The Spanish **t** is pronounced like the English *t* in the word *stop.* Repeat:

toma mata tela tipo atún Tito

5. The Spanish **d** at the beginning of an utterance or after **n** or **l** sounds somewhat similar to the English *d* in the word *David.* Repeat:

día dedo duelo anda Aldo

In all other positions, the **d** has a sound similar to the English *th* in the word *they.* Repeat:

medida todo nada Ana dice Eva duda

6. The Spanish **g** also has two sounds. At the beginning of an utterance and in all other positions, except before **e** or **i,** the Spanish **g** sounds similar to the English *g* in the word *sugar.* Repeat:

goma gato tengo lago algo aguja

In the combinations **gue** and **gui,** the **u** is silent. Repeat:

guerra guineo guiso ligue la guía

7. The Spanish **j,** and **g** before **e** or **i,** sounds similar to the English *h* in the word *home.* Repeat:

jamás juego jota Julio gente Genaro gime

8. The Spanish **b** and **v** have no difference in sound. Both are pronounced alike. At the beginning of the utterance or after **m** or **n,** they sound similar to the English *b* in the word *obey.* Repeat:

Beto vaga bote vela también un vaso

Between vowels, they are pronounced with the lips barely closed. Repeat:

sábado yo voy sabe Ávalos Eso vale

9. In most Spanish-speaking countries, the **y** and the **ll** are similar to the English *y* in the word *yet.* Repeat:

yo llama yema lleno ya lluvia llega

10. The Spanish **r** is pronounced like the English *tt* in the word *gutter.* Repeat:

cara	pero	arena	carie	Laredo	Aruba

The Spanish **r** in an initial position and after **l, n,** or **s,** and **rr** in the middle of a word are pronounced with a strong trill. Repeat:

Rita	Rosa	torre	ruina	Enrique	Israel
perro	parra	rubio	alrededor	derrama	

11. The Spanish **s** sound is represented in most of the Spanish-speaking world by the letters **s, z,** and **c** before **e** or **i.** The sound is very similar to the English sibilant *s* in the word *sink.* Repeat:

sale	sitio	solo	seda	suelo
zapato	cerveza	ciudad	cena	

In most of Spain, the **z,** and **c** before **e** or **i,** is pronounced like the English *th* in the word *think.* Repeat:

zarzuela	cielo	docena

12. The letter **h** is silent in Spanish except when it's preceded by **c** to form the phoneme **ch**. Repeat:

hilo	Hugo	ahora	Hilda	almohada	hermano

13. The Spanish **ch** is pronounced like the English *ch* in the word *chief.* Repeat:

muchacho	chico	coche	chueco	chaparro

14. The Spanish **f** is identical in sound to the English *f.* Repeat:

famoso	feo	difícil	fuego	foto

15. The Spanish **l** is pronounced like the English *l* in the word *lean* except in the combination **ll** (see item 9). Repeat:

dolor	ángel	fácil	sueldo	salgo	chaval

16. The Spanish **m** is pronounced like the English *m* in the word *mother.* Repeat:

mamá	moda	multa	médico	mima

17. In most cases, the Spanish **n** has a sound similar to the English *n.* Repeat:

nada	norte	nunca	entra	nene

The sound of the Spanish **n** is often affected by the sounds that occur around it. When it appears before **b, v,** or **p,** it is pronounced like the English *m.* Repeat:

invierno	tan bueno	un vaso	un bebé	un perro

18. The Spanish **ñ (eñe)** has a sound similar to the English *ny* in the word *canyon.* Repeat:

muñeca	leña	año	señorita	piña	señor

19. The Spanish **x** has two pronunciations, depending on its position. Between vowels, the sound is similar to the English *ks*. Repeat:

examen   boxeo   exigente   éxito

Before a consonant, the Spanish **x** sounds like the English *s*. Repeat:

expreso   excusa   exquisito   extraño

Linking

In spoken Spanish, the various words in a phrase or sentence are not pronounced as isolated elements, but they are combined. This is called *linking*.

1. The final consonant of a word is pronounced together with the initial vowel of the following word. Repeat:

   Carlos‿anda   un‿ángel   el‿otoño   unos‿estudiantes

2. The final vowel of a word is pronounced together with the initial vowel of the following word. Repeat:
   su‿esposo   la‿hermana   ardua‿empresa   la‿invita

3. When the final vowel of a word and the initial vowel of the following word are identical, they are pronounced slightly longer than one vowel. Repeat:
   Ana‿alcanza   me‿espera   mi‿hijo   lo‿olvida

   The same rule applies when two identical vowels appear within a word. Repeat:
   cooperación   crees   leemos   coordinación

4. When the final consonant of a word and the initial consonant of the following word are the same, they are pronounced as one consonant with slightly longer-than-normal duration. Repeat:

   el‿lado   un‿novio   Carlos‿salta   tienes‿sed   al‿leer

Rhythm

Rhythm is the variation of sound intensity that we usually associate with music. Spanish and English each regulate these variations in speech differently, because they have different patterns of syllable length. In Spanish the length of the stressed and unstressed syllables remains almost the same, while in English stressed syllables are considerably longer than unstressed ones. Pronounce the following Spanish words, enunciating each syllable clearly.

es-tu-dian-te   bue-no   Úr-su-la
com-po-si-ción   di-fí-cil   ki-ló-me-tro
po-li-cí-a   Pa-ra-guay

Because the length of the Spanish syllables remains constant, the greater the number of syllables in a given word or phrase, the longer the phrase will be.

Intonation

Intonation is the rise and fall of pitch in the delivery of a phrase or a sentence. In general, Spanish pitch tends to change less than English, giving the impression that the language is less emphatic.

As a rule, the intonation for normal statements in Spanish starts in a low tone, raises to a higher one on the first stressed syllable, maintains that tone until the last stressed syllable, and then goes back to the initial low tone, with still another drop at the very end.

Tu amigo viene mañana. José come pan.
Ada está en casa. Carlos toma café.

Syllable Formation in Spanish

General rules for dividing words into syllables are as follows.

Vowels

1. A vowel or a vowel combination can constitute a syllable.

   a-lum-no a-bue-la Eu-ro-pa

2. Diphthongs and triphthongs are considered single vowels and cannot be divided.

   bai-le puen-te Dia-na es-tu-diáis an-ti-guo

3. Two strong vowels **(a, e, o)** do not form a diphthong and are separated into two syllables.

   em-ple-ar vol-te-ar lo-a

4. A written accent on a weak vowel **(i** or **u)** breaks the diphthong, thus the vowels are separated into two syllables.

   trí-o dú-o Ma-rí-a

Consonants

1. A single consonant forms a syllable with the vowel that follows it.

   po-der ma-no mi-nu-to

   NOTE: **rr** is considered a single consonant: **pe-rro.**

2. When two consonants appear between two vowels, they are separated into two syllables.
   al-fa-be-to cam-pe-ón me-ter-se mo-les-tia

   EXCEPTION: When a consonant cluster composed of **b, c, d, f, g, p,** or **t** with **l** or **r** appears between two vowels, the cluster joins the following vowel: **so-bre, o-tros, ca-ble, te-lé-gra-fo.**

3. When three consonants appear between two vowels, only the last one goes with the following vowel.

ins-pec-tor trans-por-te trans-for-mar

EXCEPTION: When there is a cluster of three consonants in the combinations described in rule 2, the first consonant joins the preceding vowel, and the cluster joins the following vowel: **es-cri-bir, ex-tran-je-ro, im-plo-rar, es-tre-cho.**

Accentuation

In Spanish, all words are stressed according to specific rules. Words that do not follow the rules must have a written accent to indicate the change of stress. The basic rules for accentuation are as follows.

1. Words ending in a vowel, **n,** or **s** are stressed on the next-to-the-last syllable.

hi-jo **ca**-lle **me**-sa fa-**mo**-sos

flo-**re**-cen **pla**-ya **ve**-ces

2. Words ending in a consonant, except **n** or **s,** are stressed on the last syllable.

ma-**yor** a-**mor** tro-pi-**cal** na-**riz** re-**loj** co-rre-**dor**

3. All words that do not follow these rules must have the written accent.

ca-**fé**	**lá**-piz	**mú**-si-ca	sa-**lón**
án-gel	**lí**-qui-do	fran-**cés**	**Víc**-tor
sim-**pá**-ti-co	rin-**cón**	a-**zú**-car	**dár**-se-lo
sa-**lió**	**dé**-bil	e-**xá**-me-nes	**dí**-me-lo

4. Pronouns and adverbs of interrogation and exclamation have a written accent to distinguish them from relative pronouns.

—¿**Qué** comes? —La pera que él no comió.	*"What are you eating?"* *"The pear that he did not eat."*
—¿**Quién** está ahí? —El hombre a quien tú llamaste.	*"Who is there?"* *"The man whom you called."*
—¿**Dónde** está? —En el lugar donde trabaja.	*"Where is he?"* *"At the place where he works."*

5. Words that have the same spelling but different meanings take a written accent to differentiate one from the other.

el	*the*	**él**	*he, him*	**te**	*you*	**té**	*tea*
mi	*my*	**mí**	*me*	**si**	*if*	**sí**	*yes*
tu	*your*	**tú**	*you*	**mas**	*but*	**más**	*more*

VERBS

REGULAR VERBS

Model -ar, -er, -ir *verbs*

	INFINITIVE	
amar *(to love)*	**comer** *(to eat)*	**vivir** *(to live)*
	GERUND	
amando *(loving)*	**comiendo** *(eating)*	**viviendo** *(living)*
	PAST PARTICIPLE	
amado *(loved)*	**comido** *(eaten)*	**vivido** *(lived)*

SIMPLE TENSES		
	Indicative Mood	
	PRESENT	
(I love)	*(I eat)*	*(I live)*
am**o**	com**o**	viv**o**
am**as**	com**es**	viv**es**
am**a**	com**e**	viv**e**
am**amos**	com**emos**	viv**imos**
am**áis**[1]	com**éis**	viv**ís**
am**an**	com**en**	viv**en**
	IMPERFECT	
(I used to love)	*(I used to eat)*	*(I used to live)*
am**aba**	com**ía**	viv**ía**
am**abas**	com**ías**	viv**ías**
am**aba**	com**ía**	viv**ía**
am**ábamos**	com**íamos**	viv**íamos**
am**abais**	com**íais**	viv**íais**
am**aban**	com**ían**	viv**ían**

[1]**Vosotros amáis:** The **vosotros** form of the verb is used primarily in Spain. This form has not been used in this text.

	PRETERIT	
(I loved)	*(I ate)*	*(I lived)*
am**é**	com**í**	viv**í**
am**aste**	com**iste**	viv**iste**
am**ó**	com**ió**	viv**ió**
am**amos**	com**imos**	viv**imos**
am**asteis**	com**isteis**	viv**isteis**
am**aron**	com**ieron**	viv**ieron**

	FUTURE	
(I will love)	*(I will eat)*	*(I will live)*
amar**é**	comer**é**	vivir**é**
amar**ás**	comer**ás**	vivir**ás**
amar**á**	comer**á**	vivir**á**
amar**emos**	comer**emos**	vivir**emos**
amar**éis**	comer**éis**	vivir**éis**
amar**án**	comer**án**	vivir**án**

	CONDITIONAL	
(I would love)	*(I would eat)*	*(I would live)*
amar**ía**	comer**ía**	vivir**ía**
amar**ías**	comer**ías**	vivir**ías**
amar**ía**	comer**ía**	vivir**ía**
amar**íamos**	comer**íamos**	vivir**íamos**
amar**íais**	comer**íais**	vivir**íais**
amar**ían**	comer**ían**	vivir**ían**

Subjunctive Mood

	PRESENT	
([that] I [may] love)	*([that] I [may] eat)*	*([that] I [may] live)*
am**e**	com**a**	viv**a**
am**es**	com**as**	viv**as**
am**e**	com**a**	viv**a**
am**emos**	com**amos**	viv**amos**
am**éis**	com**áis**	viv**áis**
am**en**	com**an**	viv**an**

	IMPERFECT (two forms: **-ra**, **-se**)	
([that] I [might] love)	*([that] I [might] eat)*	*([that] I [might] live)*
am**ara(-ase)**	com**iera(-iese)**	viv**iera(-iese)**
am**aras(-ases)**	com**ieras(-ieses)**	viv**ieras(-ieses)**
am**ara(-ase)**	com**iera(-iese)**	viv**iera(-iese)**
am**áramos (-ásemos)**	com**iéramos (-iésemos)**	viv**iéramos (-iésemos)**
am**arais(-aseis)**	com**ierais(-ieseis)**	viv**ierais(-ieseis)**
am**aran(-asen)**	com**ieran(-iesen)**	viv**ieran(-iesen)**

Imperative Mood (Command Forms)

(love)	*(eat)*	*(live)*
am**a** (tú)	com**e** (tú)	viv**e** (tú)
am**e** (Ud.)	com**a** (Ud.)	viv**a** (Ud.)
am**emos** (nosotros)	com**amos** (nosotros)	viv**amos** (nosotros)
am**ad** (vosotros)	com**ed** (vosotros)	viv**id** (vosotros)
am**en** (Uds.)	com**an** (Uds.)	viv**an** (Uds.)

COMPOUND TENSES

	PERFECT INFINITIVE	
haber amado	**haber comido**	**haber vivido**

	PERFECT PARTICIPLE	
habiendo amado	**habiendo comido**	**habiendo vivido**

Indicative Mood

	PRESENT PERFECT	
(I have loved)	*(I have eaten)*	*(I have lived)*
he amado	he comido	he vivido
has amado	has comido	has vivido
ha amado	ha comido	ha vivido
hemos amado	hemos comido	hemos vivido
habéis amado	habéis comido	habéis vivido
han amado	han comido	han vivido

	PLUPERFECT	
(*I had loved*)	(*I had eaten*)	(*I had lived*)
había amado	había comido	había vivido
habías amado	habías comido	habías vivido
había amado	había comido	había vivido
habíamos amado	habíamos comido	habíamos vivido
habíais amado	habíais comido	habíais vivido
habían amado	habían comido	habían vivido
	FUTURE PERFECT	
(*I will have loved*)	(*I will have eaten*)	(*I will have lived*)
habré amado	habré comido	habré vivido
habrás amado	habrás comido	habrás vivido
habrá amado	habrá comido	habrá vivido
habremos amado	habremos comido	habremos vivido
habréis amado	habréis comido	habréis vivido
habrán amado	habrán comido	habrán vivido
	CONDITIONAL PERFECT	
(*I would have loved*)	(*I would have eaten*)	(*I would have lived*)
habría amado	habría comido	habría vivido
habrías amado	habrías comido	habrías vivido
habría amado	habría comido	habría vivido
habríamos amado	habríamos comido	habríamos vivido
habríais amado	habríais comido	habríais vivido
habrían amado	habrían comido	habrían vivido

Subjunctive Mood

	PRESENT PERFECT	
([*that*] *I* [*may*] *have loved*)	([*that*] *I* [*may*] *have eaten*)	([*that*] *I* [*may*] *have lived*)
haya amado	haya comido	haya vivido
hayas amado	hayas comido	hayas vivido
haya amado	haya comido	haya vivido
hayamos amado	hayamos comido	hayamos vivido
hayáis amado	hayáis comido	hayáis vivido
hayan amado	hayan comido	hayan vivido

PLUPERFECT (two forms: -ra, -se)		
([that] I [might] have loved)	*([that] I [might] have eaten)*	*([that] I [might] have lived)*
hubiera(-iese) amado	hubiera(-iese) comido	hubiera(-iese) vivido
hubieras(-ieses) amado	hubieras(-ieses) comido	hubieras(-ieses) vivido
hubiera(-iese) amado	hubiera(-iese) comido	hubiera(-iese) vivido
hubiéramos(-iésemos) amado	hubiéramos(-iésemos) comido	hubiéramos(-iésemos) vivido
hubierais(-ieseis) amado	hubierais(-ieseis) comido	hubierais(-ieseis) vivido
hubieran(-iesen) amado	hubieran(-iesen) comido	hubieran(-iesen) vivido

Stem-Changing Verbs

The -ar *and* -er *stem-changing verbs*

Stem-changing verbs are those that have a change in the root of the verb. Verbs that end in **-ar** and **-er** change the stressed vowel **e** to **ie** and the stressed **o** to **ue.** These changes occur in all persons, except the first and second persons plural of the present indicative, present subjunctive, and command.

INFINITIVE	PRESENT INDICATIVE	IMPERATIVE	PRESENT SUBJUNCTIVE
cerrar	cierro	—	cierre
(*to close*)	cierras	cierra	cierres
	cierra	(Ud.) cierre	cierre
	cerramos	cerremos	cerremos
	cerráis	cerrad	cerréis
	cierran	(Uds.) cierren	cierren

INFINITIVE	PRESENT INDICATIVE	IMPERATIVE	PRESENT SUBJUNCTIVE
perder (*to lose*)	**pier**do **pier**des **pier**de perdemos perdéis **pier**den	— **pier**de (Ud.) **pier**da perdamos perded (Uds.) **pier**dan	**pier**da **pier**das **pier**da perdamos perdáis **pier**dan
contar (*to count, to tell*)	**cuen**to **cuen**tas **cuen**ta contamos contáis **cuen**tan	— **cuen**ta (Ud.) **cuen**te contemos contad (Uds.) **cuen**ten	**cuen**te **cuen**tes **cuen**te contemos contéis **cuen**ten
volver (*to return*)	**vuel**vo **vuel**ves **vuel**ve volvemos volvéis **vuel**ven	— **vuel**ve (Ud.) **vuel**va volvamos volved (Uds.) **vuel**van	**vuel**va **vuel**vas **vuel**va volvamos volváis **vuel**van

Verbs that follow the same pattern include the following.

acertar	*to guess right*	**entender**	*to understand*
acordarse	*to remember*	**llover**	*to rain*
acostar(se)	*to go to bed*	**mostrar**	*to show*
almorzar	*to have lunch*	**mover**	*to move*
atravesar	*to go through*	**negar**	*to deny*
cegar	*to blind*	**nevar**	*to snow*
cocer	*to cook*	**pensar**	*to think, to plan*
colgar	*to hang*	**probar**	*to prove, to taste*
comenzar	*to begin*	**recordar**	*to remember*
confesar	*to confess*	**resolver**	*to decide on*
costar	*to cost*	**rogar**	*to beg*
demostrar	*to demonstrate, to show*	**sentar(se)**	*to sit down*
despertar(se)	*to wake up*	**soler**	*to be in the habit of*
empezar	*to begin*	**soñar**	*to dream*
encender	*to light, to turn on*	**tender**	*to stretch, to unfold*
encontrar	*to find*	**torcer**	*to twist*

The -ir *stem-changing verbs*

There are two types of stem-changing verbs that end in **-ir:** one type changes stressed **e** to **ie** in some tenses and to **i** in others and stressed **o** to **ue** or **u;** the second type always changes stressed **e** to **i** in the irregular forms of the verb.

Type I				
		e:ie	or	**i**
	-ir:			
		o:ue	or	**u**

These changes occur as follows.

Present Indicative: all persons except the first and second plural change **e** to **ie** and **o** to **ue.** *Preterit:* third person, singular and plural, changes **e** to **i** and **o** to **u.** *Present Subjunctive:* all persons change **e** to **ie** and **o** to **ue,** except the first and second persons plural, which change **e** to **i** and **o** to **u.** *Imperfect Subjunctive:* all persons change **e** to **i** and **o** to **u.** *Imperative:* all persons except the second person plural change **e** to **ie** and **o** to **ue;** first person plural changes **e** to **i** and **o** to **u.** *Present Participle:* changes **e** to **i** and **o** to **u.**

	Indicative		*Imperative*	*Subjunctive*	
INFINITIVE	PRESENT	PRETERIT		PRESENT	IMPERFECT
sentir	siento	sentí	—	sienta	sintiera(-iese)
(*to feel*)	sientes	sentiste	siente	sientas	sintieras
	siente	sintió	(Ud.) sienta	sienta	sintiera
PRESENT	sentimos	sentimos	sintamos	sintamos	sintiéramos
PARTICIPLE	sentís	sentisteis	sentid	sintáis	sintierais
sintiendo	sienten	sintieron	(Uds.) sientan	sientan	sintieran
dormir	duermo	dormí	—	duerma	durmiera(-iese)
(*to sleep*)	duermes	dormiste	duerme	duermas	durmieras
	duerme	durmió	(Ud.) duerma	duerma	durmiera
PRESENT	dormimos	dormimos	durmamos	durmamos	durmiéramos
PARTICIPLE	dormís	dormisteis	dormid	durmáis	durmierais
durmiendo	duermen	durmieron	(Uds.) duerman	duerman	durmieran

Other verbs that follow the same pattern include the following.

advertir	*to warn*	**herir**	*to wound, to hurt*
arrepentir(se)	*to repent*	**mentir**	*to lie*
consentir	*to consent, to pamper*	**morir**	*to die*
convertir(se)	*to turn into*	**preferir**	*to prefer*
discernir	*to discern*	**referir**	*to refer*
divertir(se)	*to amuse oneself*	**sugerir**	*to suggest*

Type II **-ir: e:i**

The verbs in this second category are irregular in the same tenses as those of the first type. The only difference is that they only have one change: **e:i** in all irregular persons.

	Indicative		***Imperative***	***Subjunctive***	
INFINITIVE	**PRESENT**	**PRETERIT**		**PRESENT**	**IMPERFECT**
pedir	p**i**do	pedí	—	p**i**da	p**i**diera(-iese)
(*to ask for,*	p**i**des	pediste	p**i**de	p**i**das	p**i**dieras
to request)	p**i**de	p**i**dió	(Ud.) p**i**da	p**i**da	p**i**diera
PRESENT	pedimos	pedimos	p**i**damos	p**i**damos	p**i**diéramos
PARTICIPLE	pedís	pedisteis	pedid	p**i**dáis	p**i**dierais
p**i**diendo	p**i**den	p**i**dieron	(Uds.) p**i**dan	p**i**dan	p**i**dieran

Verbs that follow this pattern include the following.

competir	*to compete*	**reír(se)**	*to laugh*
concebir	*to conceive*	**reñir**	*to fight*
despedir(se)	*to say good-bye*	**repetir**	*to repeat*
elegir	*to choose*	**seguir**	*to follow*
impedir	*to prevent*	**servir**	*to serve*
perseguir	*to pursue*	**vestir(se)**	*to dress*

Orthographic-Changing Verbs

Some verbs undergo a change in the spelling of the stem in certain tenses in order to maintain the original sound of the final consonant. The most common verbs of this type are those with the consonants **g** and **c.** Remember that **g** and **c** have a soft sound in front of **e** or **i** and a hard sound in front of **a, o,** or **u.** In order to maintain the soft sound in front of **a, o,** and **u, g** and **c** change to **j** and **z,** respectively. And in order to maintain the hard sound of **g** and **c** in front of **e** and **i, u** is added to the **g** (**gu**) and **c** changes to **qu.**

The following important verbs undergo spelling changes in the tenses listed below.

1. Verbs ending in **-gar** change **g** to **gu** before **e** in the first person of the preterit and in all persons of the present subjunctive.

   pagar (*to pay*)
   Preterit: pa**gu**é, pagaste, pagó, etc.
   Pres. Subj.: pa**gu**e, pa**gu**es, pa**gu**e, pa**gu**emos, pa**gu**éis, pa**gu**en

   Verbs that follow the same pattern: **colgar, jugar, llegar, navegar, negar, regar, rogar.**

2. Verbs ending in **-ger** and **-gir** change **g** to **j** before **o** and **a** in the first person of the present indicative and in all persons of the present subjunctive.

   proteger (*to protect*)
   Pres. Ind.: prote**j**o, proteges, protege, etc.
   Pres. Subj.: prote**j**a, prote**j**as, prote**j**a, prote**j**amos, prote**j**áis, prote**j**an

   Verbs that follow the same pattern: **coger, corregir, dirigir, elegir, escoger, exigir, recoger.**

3. Verbs ending in **-guar** change **gu** to **gü** before **e** in the first person of the preterit and in all persons of the present subjunctive.

   averiguar (*to find out*)
   Preterit: averi**gü**é, averiguaste, averiguó, etc.
   Pres. Subj.: averi**gü**e, averi**gü**es, averi**güe,** averi**güemos,** averi**gü**éis, averi**gü**en

   The verb **apaciguar** follows the same pattern.

4. Verbs ending in **-guir** change **gu** to **g** before **o** and **a** in the first person of the present indicative and in all persons of the present subjunctive.

   conseguir (*to get*)
   Pres. Ind.: consi**g**o, consigues, consigue, etc.
   Pres. Subj.: consi**g**a, consi**g**as, consi**g**a, consi**g**amos, consi**g**áis, consi**g**an

   Verbs that follow the same pattern: **distinguir, perseguir, proseguir, seguir.**

5. Verbs ending in **-car** change **c** to **qu** before **e** in the first person of the preterit and in all persons of the present subjunctive.

tocar (*to touch, to play [a musical instrument]*)
Preterit: to**qu**é, tocaste, tocó, etc.
Pres. Subj.: to**qu**e, to**qu**es, to**qu**e, to**qu**emos, to**qu**éis, to**qu**en

Verbs that follow the same pattern: **atacar, buscar, comunicar, explicar, indicar, pescar, sacar.**

6. Verbs ending in **-cer** and **-cir** preceded by a consonant change **c** to **z** before **o** and **a** in the first person of the present indicative and in all persons of the present subjunctive.

torcer (*to twist*)
Pres. Ind.: tuer**zo**, tuerces, tuerce, etc.
Pres. Subj.: tuer**za**, tuer**zas**, tuer**za**, tor**za**mos, tor**zá**is, tuer**za**n

Verbs that follow the same pattern: **convencer, esparcir, vencer.**

7. Verbs ending in **-cer** and **-cir** preceded by a vowel change **c** to **zc** before **o** and **a** in the first person of the present indicative and in all persons of the present subjunctive.

conocer (*to know, to be acquainted with*)
Pres. Ind.: cono**zc**o, conoces, conoce, etc.
Pres. Subj.: cono**zc**a, cono**zc**as, cono**zc**a, cono**zc**amos, cono**zc**áis, cono**zc**an

Verbs that follow the same pattern: **agradecer, aparecer, carecer, entristecer, establecer, lucir, nacer, obedecer, ofrecer, padecer, parecer, pertenecer, reconocer, relucir.**

8. Verbs ending in **-zar** change **z** to **c** before **e** in the first person of the preterit and in all persons of the present subjunctive.

rezar (*to pray*)
Preterit: re**c**é, rezaste, rezó, etc.
Pres. Subj.: re**c**e, re**c**es, re**c**e, re**c**emos, re**c**éis, re**c**en

Verbs that follow the same pattern: **abrazar, alcanzar, almorzar, comenzar, cruzar, empezar, forzar, gozar.**

9. Verbs ending in **-eer** change the unstressed **i** to **y** between vowels in the third person singular and plural of the preterit, in all persons of the imperfect subjunctive, and in the present participle.

creer (*to believe*)
Preterit: creí, creíste, cre**y**ó, creímos, creísteis, cre**y**eron
Imp. Subj.: cre**y**era(ese), cre**y**eras, cre**y**era, cre**y**éramos, cre**y**erais, cre**y**eran
Pres. Part.: cre**y**endo

Leer and **poseer** follow the same pattern.

10. Verbs ending in **-uir** change the unstressed **i** to **y** between vowels (except **-quir,** which has the silent **u**) in the following tenses and persons.

huir (*to escape, to flee*)
Pres. Part.: huyendo
Past Part.: huido
Pres. Ind.: huyo, huyes, huye, huimos, huís, huyen
Preterit: huí, huiste, huyó, huimos, huisteis, huyeron
Imperative: huye, huya, huyamos, huid, huyan
Pres. Subj.: huya, huyas, huya, huyamos, huyáis, huyan
Imp. Subj.: huyera(ese), huyeras, huyera, huyéramos, huyerais, huyeran

Verbs that follow the same pattern: **atribuir, concluir, constituir, construir, contribuir, destituir, destruir, disminuir, distribuir, excluir, incluir, influir, instruir, restituir, sustituir.**

11. Verbs ending in **-eír** lose one **e** in the third person singular and plural of the preterit, in all persons of the imperfect subjunctive, and in the present participle.

reír(se) (*to laugh*)
Preterit: reí, reíste, rió, reímos, reísteis, rieron
Imp. Subj.: riera(ese), rieras, riera, riéramos, rierais, rieran
Pres. Part.: riendo

Freír and **sonreír** follow the same pattern.

12. Verbs ending in **-iar** add a written accent to the **i,** except in the first and second persons plural of the present indicative and subjunctive.

fiar(se) (*to trust*)
Pres. Ind.: fío, fías, fía, fiamos, fiáis, fían
Pres. Subj.: fíe, fíes, fíe, fiemos, fiéis, fíen

Verbs that follow the same pattern: **ampliar, criar, desviar, enfriar, enviar, esquiar, guiar, telegrafiar, vaciar, variar.**

13. Verbs ending in **-uar** (except **-guar**) add a written accent to the **u,** except in the first and second persons plural of the present indicative and subjunctive.

actuar (*to act*)
Pres. Ind.: actúo, actúas, actúa, actuamos, actuáis, actúan
Pres. Subj.: actúe, actúes, actúe, actuemos, actuéis, actúen

Verbs that follow the same pattern: **acentuar, continuar, efectuar, exceptuar, graduar, habituar, insinuar, situar.**

14. Verbs ending in **-ñir** remove the **i** of the diphthongs **ie** and **ió** in the third person singular and plural of the preterit and in all persons of the imperfect subjunctive. They also change the **e** of the stem to **i** in the same persons.

teñir (*to dye*)
Preterit: teñí, teñiste, **tiñó,** teñimos, teñisteis, **tiñeron**
Imp. Subj.: t**iñe**ra(ese), t**iñe**ras, t**iñe**ra, t**iñé**ramos, t**iñe**rais, t**iñe**ran

Verbs that follow the same pattern: **ceñir, constreñir, desteñir, estreñir, reñir.**

Some Common Irregular Verbs

Only those tenses with irregular forms are given below.

adquirir (*to acquire*)
Pres. Ind.: adquiero, adquieres, adquiere, adquirimos, adquirís, adquieren
Pres. Subj.: adquiera, adquieras, adquiera, adquiramos, adquiráis, adquieran
Imperative: adquiere, adquiera, adquiramos, adquirid, adquieran

andar (*to walk*)
Preterit: anduve, anduviste, anduvo, anduvimos, anduvisteis, anduvieron
Imp. Subj.: anduviera (anduviese), anduvieras, anduviera, anduviéramos, anduvierais, anduvieran

avergonzarse (*to be ashamed, to be embarrassed*)
Pres. Ind.: me avergüenzo, te avergüenzas, se avergüenza, nos avergonzamos, os avergonzáis, se avergüenzan
Pres. Subj.: me avergüence, te avergüences, se avergüence, nos avergoncemos, os avergoncéis, se avergüencen
Imperative: avergüénzate, avergüéncese, avergoncémonos, avergonzaos, avergüéncense

caber (*to fit, to have enough room*)
Pres. Ind.: quepo, cabes, cabe, cabemos, cabéis, caben
Preterit: cupe, cupiste, cupo, cupimos, cupisteis, cupieron
Future: cabré, cabrás, cabrá, cabremos, cabréis, cabrán
Conditional: cabría, cabrías, cabría, cabríamos, cabríais, cabrían
Imperative: cabe, quepa, quepamos, cabed, quepan
Pres. Subj.: quepa, quepas, quepa, quepamos, quepáis, quepan
Imp. Subj.: cupiera (cupiese), cupieras, cupiera, cupiéramos, cupierais, cupieran

caer (*to fall*)
Pres. Ind.: caigo, caes, cae, caemos, caéis, caen
Preterit: caí, caíste, cayó, caímos, caísteis, cayeron
Imperative: cae, caiga, caigamos, caed, caigan
Pres. Subj.: caiga, caigas, caiga, caigamos, caigáis, caigan
Imp. Subj.: cayera (cayese), cayeras, cayera, cayéramos, cayerais, cayeran
Past Part.: caído

conducir (*to guide, to drive*)

Pres. Ind.: conduzco, conduces, conduce, conducimos, conducís, conducen
Preterit: conduje, condujiste, condujo, condujimos, condujisteis, condujeron
Imperative: conduce, conduzca, conduzcamos, conducid, conduzcan
Pres. Subj.: conduzca, conduzcas, conduzca, conduzcamos, conduzcáis, conduzcan
Imp. Subj.: condujera (condujese), condujeras, condujera, condujéramos, condujerais, condujeran

(All verbs ending in **-ducir** follow this pattern.)

convenir (*to agree*) See **venir.**

dar (*to give*)

Pres. Ind.: doy, das, da, damos, dais, dan
Preterit: di, diste, dio, dimos, disteis, dieron
Imperative: da, dé, demos, dad, den
Pres. Subj.: dé, des, dé, demos, deis, den
Imp. Subj.: diera (diese), dieras, diera, diéramos, dierais, dieran

decir (*to say, to tell*)

Pres. Ind.: digo, dices, dice, decimos, decís, dicen
Preterit: dije, dijiste, dijo, dijimos, dijisteis, dijeron
Future: diré, dirás, dirá, diremos, diréis, dirán
Conditional: diría, dirías, diría, diríamos, diríais, dirían
Imperative: di, diga, digamos, decid, digan
Pres. Subj.: diga, digas, diga, digamos, digáis, digan
Imp. Subj.: dijera (dijese), dijeras, dijera, dijéramos, dijerais, dijeran
Pres. Part.: diciendo
Past Part.: dicho

detener (*to stop, to hold, to arrest*) See **tener.**

entretener (*to entertain, to amuse*) See **tener.**

errar (*to err, to miss*)

Pres. Ind.: yerro, yerras, yerra, erramos, erráis, yerran
Imperative: yerra, yerre, erremos, errad, yerren
Pres. Subj.: yerre, yerres, yerre, erremos, erréis, yerren

estar (*to be*)

Pres. Ind.: estoy, estás, está, estamos, estáis, están
Preterit: estuve, estuviste, estuvo, estuvimos, estuvisteis, estuvieron
Imperative: está, esté, estemos, estad, estén
Pres. Subj.: esté, estés, esté, estemos, estéis, estén
Imp. Subj.: estuviera (estuviese), estuvieras, estuviera, estuviéramos, estuvierais, estuvieran

haber (*to have*)

Pres. Ind.: he, has, ha, hemos, habéis, han
Preterit: hube, hubiste, hubo, hubimos, hubisteis, hubieron
Future: habré, habrás, habrá, habremos, habréis, habrán
Conditional: habría, habrías, habría, habríamos, habríais, habrían

Imperative:	he, haya, hayamos, habed, hayan
Pres. Subj.:	haya, hayas, haya, hayamos, hayáis, hayan
Imp. Subj.:	hubiera (hubiese), hubieras, hubiera, hubiéramos, hubierais, hubieran

hacer (*to do, to make*)

Pres. Ind.:	hago, haces, hace, hacemos, hacéis, hacen
Preterit:	hice, hiciste, hizo, hicimos, hicisteis, hicieron
Future:	haré, harás, hará, haremos, haréis, harán
Conditional:	haría, harías, haría, haríamos, haríais, harían
Imperative:	haz, haga, hagamos, haced, hagan
Pres. Subj.:	haga, hagas, haga, hagamos, hagáis, hagan
Imp. Subj.:	hiciera (hiciese), hicieras, hiciera, hiciéramos, hicierais, hicieran
Past Part.:	hecho

imponer (*to impose, to deposit*) See **poner.**

introducir (*to introduce, to insert, to gain access*) See **conducir.**

ir (*to go*)

Pres. Ind.:	voy, vas, va, vamos, vais, van
Imp. Ind.:	iba, ibas, iba, íbamos, ibais, iban
Preterit:	fui, fuiste, fue, fuimos, fuisteis, fueron
Imperative:	ve, vaya, vayamos, id, vayan
Pres. Subj.:	vaya, vayas, vaya, vayamos, vayáis, vayan
Imp. Subj.:	fuera (fuese), fueras, fuera, fuéramos, fuerais, fueran

jugar (*to play*)

Pres. Ind.:	juego, juegas, juega, jugamos, jugáis, juegan
Imperative:	juega, juegue, juguemos, jugad, jueguen
Pres. Subj.:	juegue, juegues, juegue, juguemos, juguéis, jueguen

obtener (*to obtain*) See **tener.**

oír (*to hear*)

Pres. Ind.:	oigo, oyes, oye, oímos, oís, oyen
Preterit:	oí, oíste, oyó, oímos, oísteis, oyeron
Imperative:	oye, oiga, oigamos, oíd, oigan
Pres. Subj.:	oiga, oigas, oiga, oigamos, oigáis, oigan
Imp. Subj.:	oyera (oyese), oyeras, oyera, oyéramos, oyerais, oyeran
Pres. Part.:	oyendo
Past Part.:	oído

oler (*to smell*)

Pres. Ind.:	huelo, hueles, huele, olemos, oléis, huelen
Imperative:	huele, huela, olamos, oled, huelan
Pres. Subj.:	huela, huelas, huela, olamos, oláis, huelan

poder (*to be able*)

Pres. Ind.:	puedo, puedes, puede, podemos, podéis, pueden

Preterit:	pude, pudiste, pudo, pudimos, pudisteis, pudieron
Future:	podré, podrás, podrá, podremos, podréis, podrán
Conditional:	podría, podrías, podría, podríamos, podríais, podrían
Imperative:	puede, pueda, podamos, poded, puedan
Pres. Subj.:	pueda, puedas, pueda, podamos, podáis, puedan
Imp. Subj.:	pudiera (pudiese), pudieras, pudiera, pudiéramos, pudierais, pudieran
Pres. Part.:	pudiendo

poner (*to place, to put*)

Pres. Ind.:	pongo, pones, pone, ponemos, ponéis, ponen
Preterit:	puse, pusiste, puso, pusimos, pusisteis, pusieron
Future:	pondré, pondrás, pondrá, pondremos, pondréis, pondrán
Conditional:	pondría, pondrías, pondría, pondríamos, pondríais, pondrían
Imperative:	pon, ponga, pongamos, poned, pongan
Pres. Subj.:	ponga, pongas, ponga, pongamos, pongáis, pongan
Imp. Subj.:	pusiera (pusiese), pusieras, pusiera, pusiéramos, pusierais, pusieran
Past Part.:	puesto

querer (*to want, to wish, to like*)

Pres. Ind.:	quiero, quieres, quiere, queremos, queréis, quieren
Preterit:	quise, quisiste, quiso, quisimos, quisisteis, quisieron
Future:	querré, querrás, querrá, querremos, querréis, querrán
Conditional:	querría, querrías, querría, querríamos, querríais, querrían
Imperative:	quiere, quiera, queramos, quered, quieran
Pres. Subj.:	quiera, quieras, quiera, queramos, queráis, quieran
Imp. Subj.:	quisiera (quisiese), quisieras, quisiera, quisiéramos, quisierais, quisieran

resolver (*to decide on*)

Past Part.:	resuelto

saber (*to know*)

Pres. Ind.:	sé, sabes, sabe, sabemos, sabéis, saben
Preterit:	supe, supiste, supo, supimos, supisteis, supieron
Future:	sabré, sabrás, sabrá, sabremos, sabréis, sabrán
Conditional:	sabría, sabrías, sabría, sabríamos, sabríais, sabrían
Imperative:	sabe, sepa, sepamos, sabed, sepan
Pres. Subj.:	sepa, sepas, sepa, sepamos, sepáis, sepan
Imp. Subj.:	supiera (supiese), supieras, supiera, supiéramos, supierais, supieran

salir (*to leave, to go out*)

Pres. Ind.:	salgo, sales, sale, salimos, salís, salen
Future:	saldré, saldrás, saldrá, saldremos, saldréis, saldrán
Conditional:	saldría, saldrías, saldría, saldríamos, saldríais, saldrían
Imperative:	sal, salga, salgamos, salid, salgan
Pres. Subj.:	salga, salgas, salga, salgamos, salgáis, salgan

ser (*to be*)

Pres. Ind.:	soy, eres, es, somos, sois, son
Imp. Ind.:	era, eras, era, éramos, erais, eran
Preterit:	fui, fuiste, fue, fuimos, fuisteis, fueron
Imperative:	sé, sea, seamos, sed, sean
Pres. Subj.:	sea, seas, sea, seamos, seáis, sean
Imp. Subj.:	fuera (fuese), fueras, fuera, fuéramos, fuerais, fueran

suponer (*to assume*) See **poner.**

tener (*to have*)

Pres. Ind.:	tengo, tienes, tiene, tenemos, tenéis, tienen
Preterit:	tuve, tuviste, tuvo, tuvimos, tuvisteis, tuvieron
Future:	tendré, tendrás, tendrá, tendremos, tendréis, tendrán
Conditional:	tendría, tendrías, tendría, tendríamos, tendríais, tendrían
Imperative:	ten, tenga, tengamos, tened, tengan
Pres. Subj.:	tenga, tengas, tenga, tengamos, tengáis, tengan
Imp. Subj.:	tuviera (tuviese), tuvieras, tuviera, tuviéramos, tuvierais, tuvieran

traducir (*to translate*) See **conducir.**

traer (*to bring*)

Pres. Ind.:	traigo, traes, trae, traemos, traéis, traen
Preterit:	traje, trajiste, trajo, trajimos, trajisteis, trajeron
Imperative:	trae, traiga, traigamos, traed, traigan
Pres. Subj.:	traiga, traigas, traiga, traigamos, traigáis, traigan
Imp. Subj.:	trajera (trajese), trajeras, trajera, trajéramos, trajerais, trajeran
Pres. Part.:	trayendo
Past Part.:	traído

valer (*to be worth*)

Pres. Ind.:	valgo, vales, vale, valemos, valéis, valen
Future:	valdré, valdrás, valdrá, valdremos, valdréis, valdrán
Conditional:	valdría, valdrías, valdría, valdríamos, valdríais, valdrían
Imperative:	vale, valga, valgamos, valed, valgan
Pres. Subj.:	valga, valgas, valga, valgamos, valgáis, valgan

venir (*to come*)

Pres. Ind.:	vengo, vienes, viene, venimos, venís, vienen
Preterit:	vine, viniste, vino, vinimos, vinisteis, vinieron
Future:	vendré, vendrás, vendrá, vendremos, vendréis, vendrán
Conditional:	vendría, vendrías, vendría, vendríamos, vendríais, vendrían
Imperative:	ven, venga, vengamos, venid, vengan
Pres. Subj.:	venga, vengas, venga, vengamos, vengáis, vengan
Imp. Subj.:	viniera (viniese), vinieras, viniera, viniéramos, vinierais, vinieran
Pres. Part.:	viniendo

ver (*to see*)

Pres. Ind.:	veo, ves, ve, vemos, veis, ven
Imp. Ind.:	veía, veías, veía, veíamos, veíais, veían
Preterit:	vi, viste, vio, vimos, visteis, vieron
Imperative:	ve, vea, veamos, ved, vean
Pres. Subj.:	vea, veas, vea, veamos, veáis, vean
Imp. Subj.:	viera (viese), vieras, viera, viéramos, vierais, vieran
Past. Part.:	visto

volver (*to return*)

Past Part.:	vuelto

Appendix C

Useful Classroom Expressions

You will hear your teacher use the following directions and general terms in class. Take time to familiarize yourself with them.

- When the teacher is speaking to the whole class:

Abran sus libros, por favor.	*Open your books, please.*
Cierren sus libros, por favor.	*Close your books, please.*
Escriban, por favor.	*Write, please.*
Escuchen, por favor.	*Listen, please.*
Estudien la lección...	*Study Lesson . . .*
Hagan el ejercicio número...	*Do exercise number . . .*
Levanten la mano.	*Raise your hands.*
Repasen el vocabulario.	*Review the vocabulary.*
Repitan, por favor.	*Repeat, please.*
Siéntense, por favor.	*Sit down, please.*
Vayan a la página...	*Go to page . . .*

- When the teacher is speaking to one student:

Continúe, por favor.	*Go on, please.*
Lea, por favor.	*Read, please.*
Vaya a la pizarra, por favor.	*Go to the chalkboard, please.*

- Some other words used in the classroom.

diccionario	*dictionary*	**palabra**	*word*
dictado	*dictation*	**presente**	*present, here*
examen	*exam*	**prueba**	*quiz*
horario de clases	*class schedule*	**tarea**	*homework*

Appendix D Weights and Measures

Length

la pulgada = *inch*
el pie = *foot*
la yarda = *yard*
la milla = *mile*

1 centímetro (cm) = .3937 pulgadas (*less than 1/2 inch*)
1 metro (m) = 39.37 pulgadas (*1 yard, 3 inches*)
1 kilómetro (km) (1.000 metros) = .6214 millas (*5/8 mile*)

Weight

la onza = *ounce*
la libra = *pound*
la tonelada = *ton*

1 gramo (g) = .03527 onzas
100 gramos = 3.527 onzas (*less than 1/4 pound*)
1 kilogramo (kg) (1.000 gramos) = 2.2 libras

Liquid Measure

la pinta = *pint*
el cuarto (de galón) = *quart*
el galón = *gallon*

1 litro (l) = 1.0567 cuartos (de galón) (*slightly more than a quart*)

Surface

el acre = *acre*
1 hectárea = 2.471 acres

Temperature

°C = Celsius (*Celsius*) or centigrade (*centígrado*); °F = Fahrenheit (*Fahrenheit*)
0 °C = 32 °F (*freezing point of water*)
37 °C = 98.6 °F (*normal body temperature*)
100 °C = 212 °F (*boiling point of water*)

Conversión de grados Fahrenheit a grados centígrados °C = 5/9 (°F −32)
Conversión de grados centígrados a grados Fahrenheit °F = 9/5 (°C) + 32

Spanish-English Vocabulary

The Spanish-English and English-Spanish vocabularies contain all active and passive vocabulary that appears in the manual. Active vocabulary includes words and expressions appearing in the **Vocabulario** lists. These items are followed by a number indicating the lesson in which each word is introduced in the dialogues. Passive vocabulary consists of words and expressions included in the **Vocabulario adicional** lists and those that are given an English gloss in readings, exercises, activities, and authentic documents.

The following abbreviations are used in the vocabularies:

adj.	adjective	*L.A.*	Latin America
adv.	adverb	*m.*	masculine noun
col.	colloquial	*Méx.*	Mexico
f.	feminine noun	*pl.*	plural noun
form.	formal	*sing.*	singular noun
inf.	infinitive		

A

a at, 1; to
— **casa** home, 1
— **fines de** at the end of, 12
— **la escuela** to school, 2
— **la vez** at the same time, 11; simultaneously, 11
— **principios de** at the beginning of, 12
— **veces** sometimes, 1
— **ver** let's see, 11
abajo down; downstairs
abecedario (*m.*) alphabet
abeja (*f.*) bee
abertura (*f.*) opening, 17
abolir to abolish, 12
abreviatura (*f.*) abbreviation
abrigo (*m.*) coat, 16
abrir to open, 2
abrochar to fasten, 16; to button, 16
acabar to finish, 1
— **de (+*inf.*)** to have just (done something), 13
Acción de Gracias (Día de) (*m.*) Thanksgiving (Day)
acento (*m.*) accent, 11; stress, 11
acerca de about, 10
acontecimiento (*m.*) event, 12
acordarse (o:ue) to remember, 19
acre (*m.*) acre
actividad (*f.*) activity
— **de grupo** group activity, 1
acuarela (*f.*) watercolor
adelantado(a) ahead of the class, advanced
adelantar to progress, 17
además de besides, 9; in addition to, 16
adentro inside
adicional additional
adiós good-bye, P
adivinar to guess, 16
adjetivo (*m.*) adjective, 3
adónde where (to), 3
adverbio (*m.*) adverb, 11
África Africa
afuera outside
agallas (*f. pl.*) gills, 8; branchiae, 8
agradecer to thank, 20
agregar to add
agricultura (*f.*) agriculture, 4
agua (*f.* but **el agua**) water, 5
aguacate (*m.*) avocado
agudo(a) acute
aguja (*f.*) needle
ahora now, 3
— **mismo** right now, 3
aire (*m.*) air, 19
ají (*m.*) bell pepper
ajo (*m.*) garlic
alcalde (*m.*) mayor
alcaldesa (*f.*) mayor
alegrarse (de) to be glad, 17; to rejoice (at), 17
alérgico(a) allergic
alfabeto (*m.*) alphabet
alfombra (*f.*) carpet, 16; rug, 16
algo something, 5
algodón (*m.*) cotton, 5
alguien someone, 6; somebody, 6
algún any, 1
alguna vez ever
algunos(as) some, 2
aliados(as) (*m. pl., f. pl.*) allies
alimentar(se) to feed, 10; to nourish, 10; to take nourishment, 10
alimento (*m.*) nourishment, 10; food, 10; nutrient, 10
almorzar (o:ue) to have lunch, 7
almuerzo (*m.*) lunch, 20
alrededor (de) around, 5
alto(a) high, 4; tall, 4
altura (*f.*) height, 17
alumno(a) (*m., f.*) student, P
allí there, 4
amarillo(a) yellow, 2
América America, 12
— **Central** Central America
— **del Norte** North America
— **del Sur** South America
americano(a) (*m., f.*) American, 4
amigo(a) (*m., f.*) friend, 20
amistoso(a) friendly
anaranjado(a) orange, 2
anatomía (*f.*) anatomy, 6
ancho (*m.*) width, 17
anexo(a) annexed
anfibio (*m.*) amphibian, 8
ángulo (*m.*) angle, 17
— **agudo** acute angle
— **obtuso** obtuse angle
— **recto** right angle, 17
animal (*m.*) animal, 8
— **de la finca** farm animal
— **doméstico** pet
Antártida Antarctica
anteojos (*m. pl.*) eyeglasses, 9
antes de before, 6
antónimo (*m.*) antonym
añadir to add
año (*m.*) year, 10
— **luz** (*m.*) light-year
apagar to turn off, 16
aparato (*m.*) system
— **circulatorio** circulatory system, 7
— **digestivo** digestive system
— **respiratorio** respiratory system, 7
aparecer to appear, 12
apellido (*m.*) surname
apio (*m.*) celery
apóstrofe (*m.*) apostrophe
aprender to learn, 3

aprendizaje (*m.*) learning
problema de — (*m.*) learning disability, 9
aprovechar to make good use of, 20; to take advantage of, 20
apurarse to hurry up, 10
aquí here, 1
— tiene... here is . . . , 2
arábigo(a) arabic, 13
araña (*f.*) spider
árbol (*m.*) tree, 5
archipiélago (*m.*) archipelago
área (*f.* but **el área**) area, 4
arena (*f.*) sand, 18
aritmética (*f.*) arithmetic
armar to put together, 16
armario (*m.*) cabinet, 5
armazón (*f.*) frame, 6
arriba (de) up, upstairs
de — top, 5; upper, 5
arte (*m.* but **las artes**) art, 5
arteria (*f.*) artery, 7
articulación (*f.*) joint, 6
artículo (*m.*) article
— definido (*m.*) definite article
— indefinido (*m.*) indefinite article
aseguranza (*f.*) insurance (*Méx.*), 20
así like this, 3
— que so, 9
Asia (*m.*) Asia
asiento (*m.*) seat
tome — have a seat, P
asignado(a) allotted
asistir (a) to attend
astronomía (*f.*) astronomy, 15
atención (*f.*) attention
Atlántico (*m.*) Atlantic, 4
átomo (*m.*) atom, 15
atrasado(a) behind, 9
atún (*m.*) tuna fish, 18
aula (*m.*) classroom, P
ausencia (*f.*) absence, 20
ausente absent, 2
Australia Australia
autobús (*m.*) bus, 10
ave (*f.* but **el ave**) bird, 8; fowl, 8
averiguar to find out
avispa (*f.*) wasp
ayer yesterday, 11
ayuda (*f.*) help, 1
ayudar to help, 2
azúcar (*m.*) sugar, 4
azul blue, 2
— celeste sky blue
— marino navy blue

B

bajar(se) to get off, 10
bajo under, 12
bajo(a) low, 9
balanceado(a) balanced, 19
baloncesto (*m.*) basketball
banana (*f.*) banana
bandera (*f.*) flag
bañar(se) to bathe (oneself), 19
baño (*m.*) bathroom, 2
barato(a) inexpensive, 12; cheap, 12
barras (*f. pl.*) bars, 18; slashes
base (*f.*) base, 17
básico(a) basic, 15
básquetbol (*m.*) basketball
bastante enough
bastar (con) to be enough, 11
basurero (*m.*) trash can, 18
batalla (*f.*) battle
batería (*f.*) battery
batido (*m.*) milkshake, smoothie
beber to drink
bebida (*f.*) drink, beverage
beige beige
béisbol (*m.*) baseball
beneficiarse (de) to benefit by, 20
biblioteca (*f.*) library, 6
bibliotecario(a) (*m., f.*) librarian
bicicleta (*f.*) bicycle, 20
bien well, P; fine, P
muy — very well
bizcocho (*m.*) cake (*Puerto Rico*)
blanco(a) white, 7
bloque (*m.*) block, 16
blusa (*f.*) blouse
boca (*f.*) mouth, 8
bocadillo (*m.*) sandwich (*Spain*), 18
boleta de calificaciones (*f.*) report card (*Méx.*), 1
bombardear to bomb, 12
bonito(a) pretty, 3; beautiful, 3
borrador (*m.*) eraser, P
borrar to erase, 2
botánico(a) botanical
branquias (*f.*) gills, 8; branchiae, 8
brazo (*m.*) arm
breve brief, P
bronquio (*m.*) bronchial tube, 7
bueno(a) good
buenas noches good evening, P; good night (*when leaving*), P
buenas tardes good afternoon, P
bueno... well . . . , 1
buenos días good morning, P
bufanda (*f.*) scarf
buscar to look for, 3; to look up; to pick up

C

caballo (*m.*) horse
cabello (*m.*) hair
cabeza (*f.*) head, 6
cabo (*m.*) cape
cabra (*f.*) goat
cacto (*m.*) cactus, 10
cada each, 3
caer(se) to fall, 18
café brown (Méx.), 2
cafetería (*f.*) cafeteria, 2
caja (*f.*) box, 16
cajón (*m.*) drawer, 5
calcar to trace
calcetines (*m. pl.*) socks
calcio (*m.*) calcium, 19
calentura (*f.*) fever
cálido(a) warm, hot
caliente hot, 8
calor (*m.*) heat, 15
calladito(a) quiet; silent
callado(a) quiet, 16; silent, 16
camarón (*m.*) shrimp
cambiar to change, 9
cambio (*m.*) change, 15
camelia (*f.*) camellia
camello (*m.*) camel
caminar to walk, 10
camión (*m.*) bus (*Méx.*), 10
camisa (*f.*) shirt
camiseta (*f.*) T-shirt
campana (*f.*) bell, 6
canción (*f.*) song, 16
candado (*m.*) padlock, 20
cangrejo (*m.*) crab
cantar to sing, 16
cantidad (*f.*) quantity, 6
capa de agua (*f.*) raincoat (*Puerto Rico, Cuba*)
capital (*f.*) capital (city), 4
capitalismo capitalism
capítulo (*m.*) chapter, 19
cara (*f.*) face
caracol (*m.*) snail
característica (*f.*) characteristic, 8
carbohidrato (*m.*) carbohydrate, 19
carmelita brown (*Cuba*), 2
caro(a) expensive, 20
cartel (*m.*) poster, 4; chart, 4
cartón (*m.*) cardboard
cartulina (*f.*) construction paper
casa (*f.*) house, 13; home, 13
castigar to punish, 9
cebolla (*f.*) onion
cebra (*f.*) zebra
centena (*f.*) hundred
centésima (*f.*) hundredth, 14
centímetro (*m.*) centimeter
centro (*m.*) center, 17
Centroamérica Central America
cepillar(se) to brush, 19
cerdo(a) (*m., f.*) pig
cerebelo (*m.*) cerebellum
cerebro (*m.*) brain, 6
cereza (*f.*) cherry
cerrado(a) sealed, 20; closed, 20
cerrar (e:ie) to close, 5
chamarra (*f.*) jacket (*Méx.*), 16
chango (*m.*) monkey (*Méx.*)
chaqueta (*f.*) jacket, 16
chau bye, P
chicle (*m.*) chewing gum, 5
chile (*m.*) pepper
— verde bell pepper (*Méx.*)
china (*f.*) orange (*Puerto Rico*)
chivo (*m.*) goat
chocolate (*m.*) chocolate
ciclón (*m.*) cyclone
cien milésimo(a) hundred thousandth
ciencia (*f.*) science, 8

científico(a) scientific, 15
cifra (*f.*) number
cilindro (*m.*) cylinder
cinto (*m.*) belt
cinturón (*m.*) belt
círculo (*m.*) circle, 16
circunferencia (*f.*) circumference, 17
cita (*f.*) appointment, 20
ciudad (*f.*) city
civil civil, 12
claro(a) clear, 3; light (*in color*)
clase (*f.*) class, 1; kind, 8; type, 8
clavel (*m.*) carnation
clima (*m.*) weather
cloro (*m.*) chlorine, 15
cloruro de sodio (*m.*) sodium chloride, 15
coagular to coagulate, 7
cochino(a) (*m., f.*) pig
cociente (*m.*) quotient
cocina (*f.*) kitchen, 15
cocodrilo (*m.*) crocodile, 8
codo (*m.*) elbow, 6
cognado (*m.*) cognate
colgar (o:ue) to hang up, 16
colindar (con) to border (*Méx.*), 4
Colón (Cristóbal) (Christopher) Columbus, 12
colonia (*f.*) colony, 12
colonizar to colonize, 12
color (*m.*) color, 5
colorear to color, 2
columna vertebral (*f.*) spine, 8
columpio (*m.*) swing, 18
coma (*f.*) comma
comedor (*m.*) cafeteria (*Méx.*), 2
comenzar (e:ie) to begin, 5; to start, 5
comer to eat, 2
cómico(a) funny, 16
comida (*f.*) food, 6
comillas (*f. pl.*) quotation marks
  — latinas Spanish quotation marks
como as, 7; since, 9; like, 11
cómo how
  ¿— está Ud.? How are you?, P
  ¿— se dice...? How do you say . . . ?, 3
  ¿— se escribe...? How do you spell . . . ?, 3
  ¿— se llama...? What is . . . called?, 6
compañero(a) de clase (*m., f.*) classmate, 9
compás (*m.*) compass
complemento (*m.*) object
componer to compose, 15; to be found in, 15
comportamiento (*m.*) behavior
composición (*f.*) composition, 3
comprender to understand, 20
comprensión (*f.*) comprehension
comprobar (o:ue) to verify, 15
compuesto(a) compound, 15
común common
comunismo (*m.*) communism
con with, 1
  — la vista silently (reading), 2
  — más cuidado more carefully, 3; with more care, 3
  — permiso excuse me, P
concepto (*m.*) concept, 17
concurso (*m.*) contest, 11
  — de ortografía spelling bee, 11
condensación (*f.*) condensation
conducta (*f.*) conduct; citizenship
conejo(a) (*m., f.*) rabbit
conferencia (*f.*) conference, 9
congreso (*m.*) congress, 12
conjunción (*f.*) conjunction
conmigo with me, 6
cono (*m.*) cone
conocer to know, 7; to be acquainted with, 7
conocimiento (*m.*) knowledge, 15
conquistar to conquer
consejo (*m.*) council
conserje (*m., f.*) janitor
considerado(a) considerate
consistente consistent
consonante (*f.*) consonant, 11
constitución (*f.*) constitution, 12
consumir to consume, 19
contagioso(a) contagious
contar (o:ue) to count, 13; to tell, 16
contestar to answer, 6
continente (*m.*) continent, 4
continuar to continue, 5
contra against, 12; versus, 12
contracción (*f.*) contraction
conversación (*f.*) conversation, P
  — breve brief conversation, P
conversar to converse
convertir (en) (e:ie) to turn into, 19
cooperación (*f.*) cooperation, 20
copiar to copy, 2
corazón (*m.*) heart, 7
corchetes (*m. pl.*) brackets
cordillera (*f.*) chain of mountains
correcto(a) correct, 3
corregir (e:i) to correct, 11
correr to run, 16
cortar to cut, 5
cosa (*f.*) thing
coser to sew
costa (*f.*) coast, 12
coyuntura (*f.*) joint, 6
cráneo (*m.*) skull, 6
crecimiento (*m.*) growth, 19
creer to think, 9; to believe, 9
  — que sí to think so, 11
cuaderno (*m.*) notebook, P
  — de ejercicios workbook, 2
cuadrado (*m.*) square
cuadrado(a) square
cuál(es) which, 3; what, 3
cuándo when, 6
cuánto(a) how much
cuántos(as) how many, 4
cuarto (*m.*) room, 18; quart
cuarto(a) fourth, 14
cúbico(a) cubic
cubierto(a) (de) covered (with), 8
cubo (*m.*) cube
cubrir to cover, 6
cuello (*m.*) neck
cuento (*m.*) story, 16; short story, 16
cuerda (*f.*) rope, 18
cuerpo (*m.*) body, 6
cuidado (*m.*) care
  con más — more carefully, 3
  ¡cuidado! look out!, 18; be careful!, 18
cultural cultural
curar to cure, 19
curita (*f.*) adhesive bandage, 18
curvo(a) curved, 17

D

dar to give, 3
darse prisa to hurry up, 10
de from, P
  — arriba top, 5; upper, 5
  — dónde? (from) where?, P
  — dos en dos two by two, 10
  — vez en cuando once in a while, 9
debajo (de) under
deber must, 2; should, 2
  se debe(n) a... is (are) due to . . . , 9
débil weak, 19
década (*f.*) decade, 12
decena (*f.*) ten (quantity of ten objects), 13
décima (*f.*) tenth, 14
decimal decimal, 13
decímetro (*m.*) decimeter
décimo (*m.*) one-tenth
decir (e:i) to say, 7; to tell, 7
declarar to declare, 12
dedo (*m.*) finger
  — del pie toe
definición (*f.*) definition
dejar to leave (behind), 9; to let, 18; to allow, 18
  — en paz to leave alone, 18
delante (de) in front of, 18
deletrear to spell, 11
demás other, rest
  los (las) — the others, 1
demasiado(a) too, 16; too much, 16
democracia (*f.*) democracy
denominador (*m.*) denominator, 14
dentista (*m., f.*) dentist, 20
dentro in, 4; inside, 4
depender to depend, 6
deporte (*m.*) sport, 19
depresión (*f.*) depression, 12
derecho(a) right
  a la derecha to the right, 5
derrotar to defeat
desayuno (*m.*) breakfast, 9
descubrir to discover, 12
desdoblar unfold
desgraciadamente unfortunately, 17
desierto (*m.*) desert, 10
despacio slowly, 19
despedida (*f.*) farewell, P
despedirse (e:i) (de) to say good-bye to, 11
después (de) after, 2; afterwards, 4

detrás (de) behind
devolver (o:ue) to return
día (*m.*) day, 20
al — a day, 19; per day, 19
— de Acción de Gracias Thanksgiving Day
— de la Independencia Independence Day
— de la Madre Mother's Day
— de los Enamorados Valentine's Day
— de los Trabajadores Labor Day
— de los Veteranos Veteran's Day
— del Padre Father's Day
— festivo holiday
diámetro (*m.*) diameter, 17
dibujar to draw, 5
dibujo (*m.*) drawing, 5
diccionario (*m.*) dictionary, 3
dictado (*m.*) dictation
dicho (*m.*) saying, 19
diente (*m.*) tooth, 19
dieta (*f.*) diet, 19
diez milésimo(a) ten thousandth
diferencia (*f.*) difference
diferente different, 5
difícil difficult, 3
dificultad (*f.*) difficulty, 9
difteria (*f.*) diphtheria
digerir (e:ie) to digest, 6
digestión (*f.*) digestion, 6
digestivo(a) digestive
dígito (*m.*) digit, 13
dimensión (*f.*) dimension
dinero (*m.*) money, 20
dirección (*f.*) principal's office, 2
director(a) (*m., f.*) principal, 3
disculpar(se) to excuse (oneself), 3
dislexia (*f.*) dyslexia, 9
disolver (o:ue) to dissolve
distinto(a) different, 6
dividendo (*m.*) dividend
dividido(a) divided, 8
divisible divisible, 13
división (*f.*) division
divisor divisor
doblado(a) folded, 5
doblar to fold, 5
doctor(a) (Dr.)(Dra.) (*m., f.*) doctor, P
doler (o:ue) to hurt, 8; to ache, 8
dónde where, 1
dorado(a) golden
dormir (o:ue) to sleep, 6
dos two
de — en — two by two, 10; in pairs, 10
— puntos (*m.*) colon
dulce (*m.*) sweet, candy, 18
durante during, 12
durar to last, 12

E

edad (*f.*) age, 13
educación física (*f.*) physical education
ejemplo (*m.*) example, 15
ejercicio (*m.*) exercise, 3
elección (*f.*) election, 12
electricidad (*f.*) electricity, 15
electrón (*m.*) electron, 15
elefante (*m.*) elephant
elegir (e:i) to elect, 12; to choose, 12
elemento (*m.*) element, 7
emergencia (*f.*) emergency, 3
emparedado (*m.*) sandwich, 18
empezar (e:ie) to begin, 5; to start, 5
empujar to push, 18
en in, 1; on; at, 2
— cuanto as soon as, 19
— forma de in the shape of, 8
— mi casa at home, 3
— orden alfabético in alphabetical order, 3
— realidad in fact, 19
— silencio silently, 2
— voz alta aloud, 2
encender (e:ie) to turn on
encima de on top of
encontrar (o:ue) to find, 10
encontrarse (o:ue) to meet (each other), 17
energía (*f.*) energy, 15
enfermedad (*f.*) sickness, 19; disease, 19
enfermero(a) (*m., f.*) nurse, 8
enfermo(a) sick, 20; ill, 20
engordar to get fat, 19
enojarse to get angry, 16
ensalada (*f.*) salad
enseguida right away, 6
enseñar to show, 8; to teach, 10
entender (e:ie) to understand, 5
entero (*m.*) whole, 14
entonces then, 11; in that case, 11
entrar (en) to enter, 2
entre by, 14; between, 17; among, 17
entregar to turn in
enviar to send, 7
época (*f.*) time
en esa— at that time, 12
equilátero(a) equilateral
equivalencia (*f.*) equivalence, 14
es que... the fact is . . . , 18; it's just that . . . , 18
escaleno scalene (*triangle*)
escama (*f.*) scale, 8
esclavitud (*f.*) slavery, 12
esclavo(a) (*m., f.*) slave
escolar (*adj.*) school, 20; scholastic, 20; school-related, 20
escribir to write, 2
escrito(a) written, 13
escritorio (*m.*) desk, P
escuchar to listen, 1
escuela (*f.*) school, 2
— primaria (elemental) grade school, 10
ese(a) that, 8
esencial essential, 19
esfera (*f.*) sphere
esforzarse (o:ue) to try, 9; to make an effort, 9
esfuerzo (*m.*) effort
eso that, 8
esófago (*m.*) esophagus
espacio (*m.*) space, 15
espalda (*f.*) back
España Spain, 12
especial special
espejuelos (*m. pl.*) eyeglasses (*Cuba, Puerto Rico*), 9
esperar to wait, 2; to hope, 17
esposo(a) (*m., f.*) spouse; 9, husband; 9, wife, 9
esqueleto (*m.*) skeleton, 6
establecido(a) established, 12
estaciones del año (*f. pl.*) seasons of the year
estado (*m.*) state, 4
Estados Unidos United States, 4
estallar (guerra) to start (war), 12
estambre (*m.*) yarn, 5
estante (*m.*) shelf, 5
estar to be, 3
— adelantado(a) to be ahead of the class, 9
— escrito(a) to be written, 13
— formado(a) to be made up, 6; to be formed, 6
— progresando to be progressing, 9
este (*m.*) east, 4
este(a) this, 7
estómago (*m.*) stomach, 6
estos(as) these
estrella (*f.*) star, 15
estudiante (*m., f.*) student, P
estudiar to study, 1
estudio (*m.*) study, 17
estudios sociales (*m. pl.*) social studies
Europa (*f.*) Europe
evaluación (*f.*) evaluation, 9
evaporación (*f.*) evaporation, 15
exactamente exactly, 19
examen (*m.*) exam; 3
excelente excellent, 11
excepción (*f.*) exception, 11
excursión (*f.*) field trip, 10
ir de — to go on a tour (excursion), 10
existir to exist, 8
éxito (*m.*) success
experimento (*m.*) experiment, 15
explicar to explain, 8
expresión (*f.*) expression, P
— de cortesía polite expression, P

F

fácil easy, 3
factor (*m.*) factor
falda (*f.*) skirt
falta (*m.*) absence (*Méx.*), 20
faltar to be missing, 17
fecha (*f.*) date, 2
¿qué — es hoy? what's the date today?, P
fenómeno (*m.*) phenomenon
fiebre (*f.*) fever
fieltro (*m.*) felt, 5

figura (*f.*) figure, 17
fila (*f.*) line, 10
filtrar to filter
finca (*f.*) farm
firmar to sign, 1
física (*f.*) physics, 15
flor (*f.*) flower, 10
forma (*f.*) shape, 8; form, 20
formado(a) made up, 6; formed, 6
formar to form, 11
 — parte de to be (a) part of, 7
fórmula (*f.*) formula, 15
formulario (*m.*) form (*Puerto Rico*), 20
fósforo (*m.*) phosphorus, 19
fotografía (*f.*) photograph, 8
fracción (*f.*) fraction, 13
Francia (*f.*) France, 12
frente front
 al — de to the front (of), 7
fresa (*f.*) strawberry
frío(a) cold, 8
fruto (*m.*) fruit (*on tree*), 10
fuego (*m.*) fire, 4
fuente (*f.*) source, 4
 — de riqueza source of income, 4
fundar to found, 12
fútbol (*m.*) soccer
 — americano football
futuro (*m.*) future

G

gabinete (*m.*) cabinet (*Méx.*), 5
gafas (*f. pl.*) eyeglasses (*Spain*), 9
galaxia (*f.*) galaxy, 15
galón (*m.*) gallon
galleta (*f.*) cookie (*Méx.*), 18
galletita (*f.*) cookie, 18
gallina (*f.*) hen
gallo (*m.*) rooster
ganadería (*f.*) livestock, 4
ganso(a) (*m., f.*) gander, 8; goose, 8
gas (*m.*) gas, 15
gaseoso(a) gaseous, 15
gato(a) (*m., f.*) cat
gaveta (*f.*) drawer (*Cuba, Puerto Rico*), 5
generalmente generally, 17
gente (*f.*) people, 12
geografía (*f.*) geography, 4
geometría (*f.*) geometry, 17
geométrico(a) geometric, 17
gimnasia (*f.*) gymnastics
glándula (*f.*) gland
 — salival salivary gland
globo terráqueo (*m.*) globe, 4
glóbulo blanco (rojo) (*m.*) white (red) blood cell, 7
gobernador(a) governor
gobierno (*m.*) government
golfo (*m.*) gulf, 4
golosina (*f.*) sweet, candy, 18
goma (*f.*) gum
 — de mascar chewing gum, 5
 — de pegar glue, 5
grabadora (*f.*) tape recorder
gracias thank you, P
 — por venir thank you for coming, 1
gracioso(a) funny, 16
grado (*m.*) grade, 5; degree, 17
gramática (*f.*) grammar
gramo (*m.*) gram, 14
grande big, 4; large, 4
grasa (*f.*) fat, 19
gratis free (of charge), 9
gris gray
gritar to shout
grupo (*m.*) group, 2
guagua (*f.*) bus (*Cuba, Puerto Rico*), 10
guajolote (*m.*) turkey (*Méx.*)
guanajo (*m.*) turkey (*Cuba*)
guante (*m.*) glove
guardar to put away, 3; to keep, 3
guerra (*f.*) war, 12
guineo (*m.*) banana
guión (*m.*) hyphen
gustar to be pleasing to, 8; to like, 8; to please, 13
gusto (*m.*) taste; sense of taste; pleasure
 el — es mío the pleasure is mine, P
 mucho — it's a pleasure to meet you, P

H

había there was 12; there were 12
habilidad (*f.*) ability, 9
habitante (*m., f.*) inhabitant, 4
hábito (*m.*) habit, 19
hablar to speak, 1
hacer to do, 5; to make, 5
 — ejercicio to exercise, 19
 — un viaje to take a trip, 15
 — una cita to make an appointment, 9
hacia toward, 16
hamburguesa (*f.*) hamburger
hasta until, 4
 — la vista see you around, P
 — luego I'll see you later, P
hay there is, 2; there are, 2
 ¿qué — de nuevo? what's new?, P
helado (*m.*) ice cream
hexágono (*m.*) hexagon
hidrógeno (*m.*) hydrogen, 15
hierro (*m.*) iron, 19
hígado (*m.*) liver
higiene (*f.*) hygiene, 19
hijo(a) (*m., f.*) child, 9; son, 9; daughter, 9
hilo (*m.*) thread
hipopótamo (*m.*) hippopotamus
historia (*f.*) history, 12
hoja (*f.*) leaf, 10
hola hello, P; hi, P
Holanda Holland, 12
hombre (*m.*) man, 7
hora (*f.*) time; hour
 — de lectura reading time, 2
 — de recreo recess time, 3
 — de salida time to go, 5
 ¿qué — es? what time is it?
horizontal horizontal, 17
hormiga (*f.*) ant
hoy today, P
hubo there was, 12; there were, 12
hueso (*m.*) bone, 6
huevo (*m.*) egg, 8
huracán (*m.*) hurricane

I

idea (*f.*) idea
igual equal, 17; the same
ilustración (*f.*) picture, 4; illustration, 4
imaginación (*f.*) imagination, 16
impar odd (*number*), 13
impermeable (*m.*) raincoat
importante important, 7
impropio(a) improper, 14
incendio (*m.*) fire, 4
inclinado(a) inclined, 17
independencia (*f.*) independence, 12
independientemente independently, 1
indios (*m.*) Indians
industria (*f.*) industry, 4
información (*f.*) information, 12
Inglaterra England, 12
inglés (*m.*) English (language), 3
inorgánico(a) inorganic
insecto (*m.*) insect, 8
instrucción (*f.*) instruction, 1
inteligente intelligent, 1
interjección (*f.*) interjection
interrumpir to disturb; to interrupt, 12
 — la clase to disturb the class
intestino (*m.*) intestine, 6
 — delgado small intestine
 — grueso large intestine
inundación (*f.*) flood
invertebrado (*m.*) invertebrate, 8
invierno (*m.*) winter
ir to go, 3
 — al baño to go to the bathroom, 2
irregular irregular, 11
irse to leave, 9; to go away, 9
isla (*f.*) island, 4
isósceles isoceles (*triangle*)
izquierdo(a) left
 a la izquierda to the left, 5

J

jalea (*f.*) jelly
jamón (*m.*) ham
Japón (*m.*) Japan, 12
japonés(esa) Japanese, 12
jardín (*m.*) garden, 10;
 — botánico botanical garden
 — de infantes kindergarten, 16
 — de niños kindergarten (*Méx.*), 16
jirafa (*f.*) giraffe
jugo (*m.*) juice
 — de manzana apple juice
 — de naranja orange juice
 — de tomate tomato juice

junta (*f.*) meeting, 20; get-together, 20
juntos(as) together, 20

K

kilogramo (*m.*) kilo, 14; kilogram, 14
kilómetro (*m.*) kilometer
kindergarten (*m.*) kindergarten, 16

L

lado (*m.*) side, 17
  al — de beside, 16; next to, 16
lagartija (*f.*) lizard, 8
lago (*m.*) lake
lámina (*f.*) picture, 4; illustration, 4
lana de tejer (*f.*) yarn, 5
langosta (*f.*) lobster
lápiz (*m.*) pencil, P
  — de color colored pencil, 2
largo (*m.*) length, 17
largo(a) long, 4
lastimar(se) to hurt (oneself), 18; to get hurt, 18
lavar(se) to wash, 19
lección (*f.*) lesson, 3
  — para hoy today's lesson, 3
lectura (*f.*) reading, 1
  — oral oral reading, reading aloud
leche (*f.*) milk
  — malteada milkshake (*Méx.*)
lechuga (*f.*) lettuce
leer to read, 1
  — más to read more, 1
lengua (*f.*) tongue
lenguaje (*m.*) language
lentes (*m. pl.*) eyeglasses, 9
león (*m.*) lion
letra (*f.*) handwriting, 3; letter, 3
levantar to raise
  — la mano to raise one's hand, 6
ley (*f.*) law
liberar to liberate
libra (*f.*) pound, 14
librarse (de) to be (become) free (from), 12
libre free
libreta de calificaciones (*f.*) report card, 1
libro (*m.*) book, P
  — de lectura reading book, 2
limitar (con) to border, 4
límite (*m.*) boundary, 4
limón (*m.*) lemon
limonada (*f.*) lemonade
limpiar to clean, 5
limpieza (*f.*) cleanliness, 19
línea (*f.*) line, 5
  — de puntos dotted line
lineal linear, 13
líquido(a) liquid, 15
lista (*f.*) list, 2
listo(a) ready, 5
literatura (*f.*) literature
litro (*m.*) liter

llamar to call, 3
  — por teléfono to call on the telephone, 3
llamarse to be called, 6
llegada (*f.*) arrival, 20
llegar to arrive, 12
  — tarde to be late, 9
  — temprano to be early, 20
llenar to fill, 20; to fill out, 20
llevar to take (someone or something somewhere), 1; to carry, 1
  — (tiempo) + *gerund* to have been doing for (*time*), 11
llevarse to take away, 10; to carry out, 10
  — bien to get along, 9
llorar to cry, 18
llover (o:ue) to rain, 10
lluvia torrencial (*f.*) cloudburst
lo it
  — siento I'm sorry, 20
longitud (*f.*) length, 14
los (las) que the ones who, 12
luchar to fight
luego then, 13; later, 13
lugar (*m.*) place, 13,
luna (*f.*) moon, 15
luz (*f.*) light, P
  — del sol sunlight, 10

M

madera (*f.*) wood, 10
madre (*f.*) mother
maestro(a) (*m., f.*) teacher, P
maíz (*m.*) corn
mal badly, 3; wrong, 3
mamá (*f.*) mom, 8; mother, 8
mamífero (*m.*) mammal, 8
mandar to send, 18
manera (*f.*) manner, 11; way, 11
mano (*f.*) hand
mantener(se) to keep (oneself), 12; to maintain (oneself), 12
mantenimiento (*m.*) maintenance, 19
mantequilla (*f.*) butter
  — de cacahuete peanut butter (*Méx.*)
  — de maní peanut butter
manzana (*f.*) apple
mañana tomorrow, 4
mapa (*m.*) map, P
máquina (*f.*) machine, 15
mar (*m.*) sea
margarita (*f.*) daisy
mariposa (*f.*) butterfly
marrón brown, 2
más more, 1; plus (+); further
  — o menos more or less, 4
  — tarde later, 2
mascar to chew, 5
masticar to chew, 5
matemáticas (*f. pl.*) math, 12
materia (*f.*) subject, 1; matter, 15
material (*m.*) material, 3
matriculado(a) enrolled, 20; registered, 20

matricularse to enroll, 20; to register, 20
mayor bigger, 13; larger, 13; greater, 13
mayúscula uppercase (capital) letter, 3
medias (*f. pl.*) stockings
  — de hombre socks (*Puerto Rico*)
medicina (*f.*) medicine
médico(a) (*m., f.*) doctor, 20; M.D., 20
medida (*f.*) measure, 9; measurement, 13
  — cuadrada square measurement
  — cúbica cubic measurement
  — de capacidad liquid measure
  — de longitud lineal measure
  — de peso weight measure
  — de superficie square measurement
  — de volumen cubic measurement
  — lineal lineal measure
medio (*m.*) one-half, 14
medir (e:i) to measure, 17
médula espinal (*f.*) spinal cord
mejor better, 1
mejorar to improve, 1; to get better, 1
mejorar(se) to improve (oneself), 9; to get better, 9
memoria (*f.*) memory
menor smaller, 13; less, 13
menos minus (−)
  a — que unless, 19
meridiano (*m.*) meridian
merienda (*f.*) snack
mermelada (*f.*) jelly
mes (*m.*) month, 20
mesa (*f.*) table, 5
métrico(a) metric
metro (*m.*) meter
mezcla (*f.*) mixture
microbio (*m.*) germ, 6
mientras while
milésima (*f.*) thousandth
milímetro (*m.*) millimeter
milla (*f.*) mile, 4
millar (*m.*) thousand
millón (*m.*) million, 4
mineral (*m.*) mineral, 19
minería (*f.*) mining, 4
minuendo (*m.*) minuend
minúscula lowercase (small) letter, 3
minuto (*m.*) minute, 2
mirar to look (at), 9
mismo(a) same, 11; self, 17
mitad (*f.*) half, 5
  por la — in half, 5
mixto(a) mixed, 14
modelo (*m.*) pattern, 5; model, 5
molécula (*f.*) molecule, 15
momento (*m.*) moment, 2
monarquía (*f.*) monarchy
mono(a) (*m., f.*) monkey
montaña (*f.*) mountain, 4
monte (*m.*) mount, 4
morado(a) purple
morir (o:ue) to die, 13
mosca (*f.*) fly
mosquito (*m.*) mosquito
mostrar (o:ue) to show, 8

mover (o:ue) to move, 6
muchas veces many times, 9
mucho(a) much, P; a lot, 1; a great deal
mucho gusto it's a pleasure (to meet you), P
muchos (as) many, 1
mudo(a) silent
muebles (*m. pl.*) furniture, 10
multiplicación (*f.*) multiplication
multiplicador (*m.*) multiplier
multiplicando (*m.*) multiplicand
multiplicar to multiply, 1
múltiplo (*m.*) multiple, 13
mundial (*adj.*) world, 12; world-wide, 12
mundo (*m.*) world, 4
muñeca (*f.*) doll, 16
músculo (*m.*) muscle, 6
música (*f.*) music
muy very, P
  — bien, ¿y usted? very well, and you?, P
  — poco very little, 1

N

nacer to be born, 8
nacimiento (*m.*) birth
nacionalidad (*f.*) nationality, 12
nada nothing, 6
nadie nobody, 18; no one, 18
naranja (*f.*) orange
naranjo (*m.*) orange tree, 10
nariz (*f.*) nose, 7
natación (*f.*) swimming
natural natural
naturaleza (*f.*) nature, 15
Navidad (*f.*) Christmas, 5
necesario(a) necessary, 16
necesitar to need, 1
negro(a) black
nervio (*m.*) nerve
neutral neutral, 12
neutrón (*m.*) neutron, 15
ninguno(a) not any, 17; none, 17
niño(a) (*m., f.*) child, 1; boy; girl
niños(as) (*m., f.*) children, 2
nivel (*m.*) level, 9
  — del grado grade level, 9
no no, P; not, P
  — devolver (o:ue) los libros not to return the books
  — sentirse (e:ie) bien not to be feeling well
Nochebuena (*f.*) Christmas Eve
nombrar to name, 7
nombre (*m.*) noun, 3
  — común common noun
  — propio proper noun, 3
norte (*m.*) north, 4
Norteamérica North America, 4
norteamericano(a) (*m., f.*) North American, 12
nota (*f.*) note
noveno (*m.*) one-ninth
nuevo(a) new, 2
numerador (*m.*) numerator, 14
número (*m.*) number, 4
nunca never, 1
nutrición (*f.*) nutrition, 19
nutritivo(a) nourishing, 19

O

observar to observe, 9
obtuso(a) obtuse (*triangle*)
océano (*m.*) ocean, 4
octógono (*m.*) octagon
octavo (*m.*) one-eighth
oculista (*m., f.*) eye doctor, 9
ocurrir to happen, 11
oeste (*m.*) west, 4
oficina (*f.*) office, 3
oído (*m.*) inner ear; sense of hearing
ojalá... I hope . . . , 17; If only . . . , 17
ojo (*m.*) eye, 16
olfato (*m.*) sense of smell
olvidar(se) (de) to forget (to), 16
ómnibus (*m.*) bus, 10
onceavo (*m.*) one-eleventh
onda (*f.*) wave
  — corta short wave
  — larga long wave
onza (*f.*) ounce, 14
operación (*f.*) operation, 13
operar to operate, 7
oración (*f.*) sentence, 3
oral oral
orden alfabético (*m.*) alphabetical order
oreja (*f.*) ear
orgánico(a) organic
órgano (*m.*) organ, 7
orgulloso(a) proud, 15
original original
orquídea (*f.*) orchid
ortografía (*f.*) spelling, 3
  concurso de — (*m.*) spelling bee, 11
oscuro(a) dark, 6
otoño (*m.*) fall, autumn, 10
otro(a) other, 1; another, 1
  otra cosa something else, 8
  otra vez again
oveja (*f.*) sheep
oxígeno (*m.*) oxygen, 6

P

Pacífico (*m.*) Pacific, 4
padecer (de) to suffer (from, with), 7
  — del corazón to have heart trouble, 7
padre (*m.*) father
padres (*m. pl.*) parents, 20
pagar to pay
página (*f.*) page, 2
país (*m.*) country, 4; nation, 4
pájaro (*m.*) bird
palabra (*f.*) word, 2
palanca (*f.*) lever, 15
páncreas (*m.*) pancreas
pantalones (*m. pl.*) pants
papa (*f.*) potato
papas fritas French fries
papel (*m.*) paper, 2
papita (*f.*) potato chip
par even (*number*), 13
para for, 3; in order to, 6
  — que so that, 19
  ¿— qué? what for?, 5; why?, 5
  ¿— qué sirven...? what are . . . good for?, 7
parada (*f.*) stop, 20
paralelo(a) parallel, 17
paralelogramo (*m.*) parallelogram
pararse to stand, 16
paréntesis (*m. pl.*) parentheses
parte (*f.*) part, 3
participación (*f.*) participation
participar to participate, 1
pasado (*m.*) past, 11
pasar to come in, P; to happen, 7; to spend time, 10; to pass; to go; to be promoted
  — lista to take roll (attendance), 2
Pascua Florida (*f.*) Easter
paso (*m.*) step
pastel (*m.*) pie, 19
patata (*f.*) potato (*Spain*)
patio (*m.*) school yard, 3; backyard, 10; playground, 18
pato (*m.*) duck
patrón (*m.*) pattern, 5; model, 5
pavo (*m.*) turkey
paz (*f.*) peace, 18
pecho (*m.*) chest
pedazo (*m.*) piece, 19
pedir (e:i) to ask (for), 8; to request, 8; to order
  — prestado(a) to borrow, 13
  — turno to make an appointment, 9
pegar to glue, 5; to hit, 9
pelear(se) to fight, 9
película (*f.*) movie; film
pelo (*m.*) hair, 8
pelota (*f.*) ball, 16
península (*f.*) peninsula
pensamiento (*m.*) pansy
pensar (e:ie) to think, 6
pentágono (*m.*) pentagon
penúltimo(a) next to last, 11; penultimate, 11
pequeño(a) small, 5; little, 5
pera (*f.*) pear
perder (e:ie) to miss, 20; to lose, 20
perdonar la molestia to excuse the interruption, 2
peregrino(a) (*m., f.*) pilgrim, 12
perfecto(a) perfect, 13
perímetro (*m.*) perimeter, 17
permitir to allow, 19; to let, 19; to permit, 19
pero but, 1
perpendicular perpendicular, 17
perro (*m.*) dog
  — caliente hot dog
persecución (*f.*) persecution, 12
persona (*f.*) person, 6

personal personal, 19
pertenecer to belong, 8
pesca (*f.*) fishing, 4
pescado (*m.*) fish
peso (*m.*) weight, 14
pez (*m.*) fish (live), 8
pico (*m.*) beak, 8
pie (*m.*) foot, 14
piel (*f.*) skin, 6
pierna (*f.*) leg
pigmento (*m.*) pigment, 6
pila (*f.*) battery
pincel (*m.*) brush
pinta (*f.*) pint
pintar to paint
pintura (*f.*) paint; painting
piojos (*m. pl.*) head lice
pionero(a) (*m., f.*) pioneer
pirámide (*f.*) pyramid
piso (*m.*) floor, 16
pizarra (*f.*) (black)board, P
pizarrón (*m.*) (black)board, P
placer (*m.*) pleasure
planeta (*m.*) planet, 15
planilla (*f.*) form, 20
plano (*m.*) plane, 17
  — inclinado inclined plane, 15
planta (*f.*) plant, 10
plaqueta (*f.*) blood platelet, 7
plátano (*m.*) banana
plateado(a) silver, silvery
pluma (*f.*) pen, P; feather, 8
población (*f.*) population, 4
poco(a) little (*quantity*), 6
  muy poco very little (*adv.*)
  un poco a little, 9
poder (o:ue) to be able to, 6; can, 6; may, 6
polea (*f.*) pulley, 15
polio (*f.*) polio
pollo (*m.*) chicken
polo (*m.*) pole
poner to put, 5
ponerse to put on, 16
  — en fila to get (stand) in line, 10
popular popular
por by, 14; for
  — aquí this way
  — ciento percent, 14
  — ejemplo for example, 11
  — favor please, P
  ¿— qué? why?
  — todo throughout, 6
porque because, 1
portarse to behave, 9
  — mal to misbehave, 9
posible possible, 20
posición (*f.*) position, 17
potencia (*f.*) power, 12
práctica (*f.*) drill, 4
practicar to practice, 11; to play
  — deportes to take part in sports, 19
predicado (*m.*) predicate
preferir (e:ie) to prefer, 5
prefijo (*m.*) prefix
pregunta (*f.*) question, 11
preguntar to ask (a question), 8
prender to turn on
preocuparse to worry
preparado(a) prepared, 11
preparar(se) to prepare (oneself), 11; to get ready, 11
preposición (*f.*) preposition
presente present, 2
presidente (*m.*) president, 4
prestar to lend, 13
  — atención to pay attention; 1
presupuesto (*m.*) budget
prevenir to prevent, 19
primavera (*f.*) spring
primero(a) first, 2
primo(a) prime, 13 (*m., f.*); cousin, 13
principal main, 4
principalmente mainly, 12
prisa: darse — to hurry up, 10
problema (*m.*) problem, 1
  — de aprendizaje learning disability, 9
producto (*m.*) product, 4
profesor(a) (*m., f.*) professor, P; teacher, P; instructor, P
progresando progressing
pronto soon, 13
  tan — como as soon as, 19
pronunciar to pronounce, 11
propiedad (*f.*) property
propio(a) proper
prosperidad (*f.*) prosperity, 12
proteger to protect, 6
protegido(a) protected, 6
proteína (*f.*) protein, 19
protón (*m.*) proton, 15
próximo(a) next, 4
psicólogo(a) (*m., f.*) psychologist, 9
puerta (*f.*) door, P
pulgada (*f.*) inch, 14
pulmón (*m.*) lung, 7
punto (*m.*) point, 14; period; dot
  dos puntos colon
  — y coma semicolon
pupitre (*m.*) desk, P
purificar purify, 7
puritano(a) (*m., f.*) Puritan
puro(a) pure, 19

Q

que that, 4; than, 4; who, 9
qué what, 1; how
  ¡— bien: how nice(ly)!, 4
  ¡— bonito(a)! how pretty!, 5
  ¡— contento! how happy!, 4
  ¡— fácil! how easy!, 17
  ¿— fecha es hoy? what's the day today?, P
  ¿— hay de nuevo? what's new?, P
  ¿— hora es? what time is it?, 1
  ¡— lástima! that's too bad!, 20; what a pity!, 20
  ¿— más? what else?
  ¡— paz! what peace!, 18; such peace!, 18
  ¿— significa...? what does . . . mean?
  ¿— tal? how's it going?, P
quebrado (*m.*) fraction, 13
querer (e:ie) to want, 5 to wish, 5
queso (*m.*) cheese
quién(es) who, whom
química (*f.*) chemistry, 15
quinto (*m.*) one-fifth, 14
quitar(se) to take away, 10; to remove, 10
quizá(s) maybe, 9; perhaps, 9

R

radio (*m.*) radius, 17
raíz (*f.*) root, 10
rana (*f.*) frog, 8
raya (*f.*) dash
razón (*f.*) reason, 20
recibir to receive, 20
recíproco (*m.*) reciprocal, 14
recoger to pick up, 5
recordar (o:ue) to remember, 6
recortar to cut out, 5; to trim, 5
rectángulo (*m.*) rectangle
recto(a) straight, 17; right
reducir to reduce, 14
refresco (*m.*) soda
regla (*f.*) ruler, P; rule, 11
regresar to return, 3; to go (come) back, 3
regular regular, 11
reino (*m.*) kingdom, 8
reír(se) to laugh, 19
relacionado(a) related
religioso(a) religious, 12
reloj (*m.*) clock, P
renacuajo (*m.*) tadpole, 8
reparación (*f.*) repair, 19
repasar to review, 1
repaso (*m.*) review, 3
repetir (e:i) to repeat, 11
representante (*m., f.*) congressional delegate
reptil (*m.*) reptile, 8
residuo (*m.*) remainder
resolver (o:ue) to solve, 13; to resolve, 13
respetar to respect
respirar to breathe, 7
resta (*f.*) subtraction, 13
restar to subtract, 1
resto (*m.*) difference
retener to retain, 19
reunión (*f.*) meeting, 20; get-together, 20
revisar to check, 11
rimar to rhyme
río (*m.*) river, 4
robar to steal, 20
rodilla (*f.*) knee, 6
rojo(a) red, 2
romano(a) Roman, 13
rombo (*m.*) rhombus

rompecabezas (*m. sing.* or *pl.*) puzzle, 16
ropa (*f.*) clothes, 6; clothing
rosa (*f.*) pink, 2; rose
rosado(a) pink, 2
roto(a) broken, 3
rubéola (*f.*) rubella
ruido (*m.*) noise, 16

S

saber to know, 2
sacapuntas (*m.*) pencil sharpener, P
sacar to take out, 16
sal (*f.*) salt, 15
salida (*f.*) dismissal, 6
salir to go out, 7; to get out, 7
salón de clase (*m.*) classroom, P
saltar to jump, 16
— **a la cuerda** to jump rope, 18
salud (*f.*) health, 19
saludar to salute
saludo (*m.*) greeting, P
saludos a... say hello to . . . , P
salvaje wild
sándwich (*m.*) sandwich, 18
sangre (*f.*) blood, 6
sarampión (*m.*) measles
satélite (*m.*) satellite, 15
satisfactorio(a) satisfactory, 1
secretario(a) (*m., f.*) secretary, 2
segmento (*m.*) segment, 17
seguir (e:i) to continue, 7
según according to, 17
segundo(a) second, 6
seguro (*m.*) insurance, 20
seguro(a) sure, 4
semana (*f.*) week, 4
semilla (*f.*) seed, 10
senador(a) (*m., f.*) senator
sentarse (e:ie) to sit down, 9
sentido (*m.*) sense
sentirse (e:ie) to feel, 15
señor (Sr.) (*m.*) Mr., P; Sir, P; gentleman, P
señora (Sra.) (*f.*) Mrs., P; madam, P; lady, P
señorita (Srta.) (*f.*) Miss, P; young lady (unmarried), P
separar(se) to separate, 10; get separated, 10
séptimo (*m.*) one-seventh
ser to be, 2
— **las (+*time*)** it's (+ *time*), 1
serio(a) serious, 1
serpiente (*f.*) snake, 8; serpent, 8
servir (e:i) to serve, 7; to be good for, 7
¿para qué sirve...? what is . . . good for?
sexto (*m.*) one-sixth
si if, 2
sí yes, 1
siempre always, 1
siglo (*m.*) century, 12
significado (*m.*) meaning, 3
significar to mean, 1; to stand for, 1; to signify, 1
signo (*m.*) sign
— **de admiración** exclamation mark
— **de interrogación** question mark
siguiendo following, 5
siguiente following, 11
sílaba (*f.*) syllable, 11
silencio (*m.*) silence, 2
en — silently, 2
silla (*f.*) chair, P
símbolo (*m.*) symbol
simple simple, 15
simplificar to simplify, 14
simulacro (*m.*) drill (*Méx., Puerto Rico*), 4
sin without, 7
singular singular
sinónimo (*m.*) synonym
sistema (*m.*) system
— **métrico** metric system, 14
— **nervioso** nervous system, 7
situación (*f.*) situation
situado(a) located, 4; situated, 4
sobre about, 4; on, 5; on top of, 5; (*m.*) envelope, 20
sobresaliente outstanding, 1
sobrino(a) (*m., f.*) nephew, 20; niece, 20
social social
sodio (*m.*) sodium, 15
sol (*m.*) sun, 10
solamente only, 11
solar solar, 15
solicitar to apply (for), 20
solidificación (*f.*) solidification
sólido(a) solid, 15
solo(a) alone, 16
sólo only, solely
solución (*f.*) solution, 9
sonar (o:ue) to ring, 6
— **como** to sound (like), 11
sonido (*m.*) sound, 11
sin — silent
sostener to support, 6; to hold, 6
soy I am, P
subdirector(a) (*m., f.*) vice-principal
subir(se) to get on, 10; to rise, 10
subrayar to underline, 3
substraendo (*m.*) subtrahend
Sudamérica South America
sueldo (*m.*) salary, 20
suelo (*m.*) floor, 16
suficiente sufficient, 9
sufijo (*m.*) suffix
sugerir (e:ie) to suggest, 16
sujeto (*m.*) subject
suma (*f.*) addition, 13; total
sumando (*m.*) addend
sumar to add, 1; to add up, 1
superficie (*f.*) area, 4
supervisión (*f.*) supervision, 20
suponer to suppose, 15
sur (*m.*) south, 4
sustantivo (*m.*) noun, 3
sustraendo (*m.*) subtrahend

T

tabla (*f.*) table
— **de multiplicar** multiplication table, 1
tacto (*m.*) sense of touch
tallo (*m.*) stem, 10
también also, 1
tampoco neither, 9
tan pronto como as soon as, 19
tanto so much, 17
— **por ciento** (*m.*) percentage, 14
tarde late
tarea (*f.*) homework, 1
tarjeta de notas (*f.*) report card (*Puerto Rico*), 1
taza (*f.*) cup, 16
té (*m.*) tea, 16
tejer to knit
tejido (*m.*) tissue, 19
teléfono (*m.*) telephone
televisor (*m.*) T.V. set
tema (*m.*) subject, 20; topic, 20
temblor (*m.*) earthquake
temer to fear
templado(a) temperate
tener to have, 4
— **fiebre** to have a fever
— **hambre** to be hungry, 4
— **que** (+*inf.*) to have to (do something), 4
— **razón** to be right, 4
— **sed** to be thirsty, 5
— **sueño** to be sleepy, 6
tenis (*m.*) tennis, 16
tercero (*m.*) one third
terminado(a) finished, 3
terminar to finish, 1
término (*m.*) term, 14
terremoto (*m.*) earthquake
territorio (*m.*) territory
tétano (*m.*) tetanus
tía (*f.*) aunt, 4
tiempo (*m.*) time, 12; tense
tierra (*f.*) soil, 8; earth, 8; land, 8
— **cultivable** land suitable for farming, 12
Tierra (*f.*) Earth, 15
tigre (*m.*) tiger
tijeras (*f. pl.*) scissors, 5
timbre (*m.*) bell, 6
tío (*m.*) uncle, 4
tirar to throw, 18
títere (*m.*) puppet, 16
título (*m.*) title, P
tiza (*f.*) chalk, P
tobilleras (*f. pl.*) socks (*Méx.*)
tobillo (*m.*) ankle
tocarle a uno to be one's turn, 16
todavía still, 11
— **no** not yet, 9
todo(a) all, 6
todos(as) all, 2; everybody, 2
tomar to drink, 5; to take, 7
— **asiento** to have a seat, P
tomarse de la mano to hold hands, 10

tomate (*m.*) tomato
tonelada (*f.*) ton, 14
tormenta de nieve (*f.*) (snow) blizzard
tornado (*m.*) tornado
torno (*m.*) lathe
toro (*m.*) bull
toronja (*f.*) grapefruit
torta (*f.*) sandwich, 18; cake
tortuga (*f.*) turtle, 8
tos ferina (*f.*) whooping cough
total (*m.*) total
trabajador(a) hard-working
trabajar to work, 1
trabajo (*m.*) work, 1
  — manual arts and crafts
traer to bring, 2
tragar to swallow, 6
transformar to turn into, 10; to transform, 10
trapecio (*m.*) trapezoid
tráquea (*f.*) windpipe, 7; trachea, 7
tratar (de) to try (to), 9; to deal (with), 19; to be about, 19
trazar to draw (*i.e., a line*), 5; to trace, 5
triángulo (*m.*) triangle
tronco (*m.*) (tree) trunk, 10
trozo (*m.*) piece, 19
turno (*m.*) appointment
tutor (*m.*) legal guardian

U

último(a) last, 11
único(a) only, 11
unidad (*f.*) unit, 13
unión (*f.*) joining together, 6; union, 6
unir to unite, 17; to join, 17; to connect
  — los puntos to connect the dots
urgente urgent
usar to use, 3
útil useful, P
uva (*f.*) grape
¡uy! wow!, 4

V

vaca (*f.*) cow
vacaciones (*f. pl.*) vacation, 13
vacío(a) empty, 18
vacunación (*f.*) vaccination
vacunado(a) vaccinated
vainilla (*f.*) vanilla
valer to be worth, 13
vamos a almorzar let's have lunch, 7
varicela (*f.*) chicken pox
varios(as) several, 5; various, 5
vaso capilar (*m.*) capillary vessel, 7
vecino(a) (*m., f.*) neighbor, 20
velocidad (*f.*) speed; velocity
vena (*f.*) vein, 7
vencer to defeat
vendar to blindfold, 16
venir to come, 4
ventana (*f.*) window, P
ventilación (*f.*) ventilation, 19
ver to see, 7
verano (*m.*) summer
verbo (*m.*) verb, 3
¿verdad? right?, 1; true?, 1
verde green
vertebrado (*m.*) vertebrate, 8
vertical vertical, 17
vértice (*m.*) vertex, 17
vestido (*m.*) dress
vez (*f.*) time (*in a series*), 19
  de — en cuando once in a while, 9; from time to time, 19
Vía Láctea (*f.*) Milky Way, 15
viajar to travel, 15
viaje (*m.*) trip, 15
vicedirector(a) (*m., f.*) vice-principal, 20
vida (*f.*) life, 8
video (*m.*) video
videograbadora (*f.*) VCR
vigilar to watch, 18
violeta violet; purple
viruela (*f.*) smallpox
visita: de — visiting, 20
vista (*f.*) sight, 9; eyesight, 9
vitamina (*f.*) vitamin, 19
vivir to live, 4
vivo(a) alive, 8
vocabulario (*m.*) vocabulary, 2
vocal (*f.*) vowel, 11
volar (o:ue) to fly, 8
volcán (*m.*) volcano, 4
vóleibol (*m.*) volleyball
voluntario(a) (*m., f.*) volunteer, 20
volver (o:ue) to return, 6; to go (come) back, 6
  — a (+ *inf.*) to . . . again
vomitar to throw up
votar to vote
¿voy ahora? shall I go now?, 3
Vuelvo enseguida. I'll be right back., 6

Y

y and, P
ya already, 1
yarda (*f.*) yard, 14
yegua (*f.*) mare

Z

zanahoria (*f.*) carrot
zancudo (*m.*) mosquito (*Méx.*)

English-Spanish Vocabulary

A

a (per) day al día, 19
 — lot mucho(a), 1
abbreviation abreviatura (*f.*)
ability habilidad (*f.*), 9
able
 to be — to poder (o:ue), 7
abolish abolir, 12
about sobre, 4; más o menos, 4; acerca de, 10
absence ausencia (*f.*), 20
absent ausente, 2
accent acento (*m.*) 11
according to según, 17
ache doler (o:ue), 8
acre acre (*m.*)
activity actividad (*f.*)
 group — actividad de grupo, 1
acute agudo(a)
add sumar, 1; agregar; añadir
 — up sumar, 1
addend sumando (*m.*)
addition suma (*f.*), 13
 in — to además de, 16
additional adicional
adhesive bandage curita (*f.*), 18
adjective adjetivo (*m.*), 3
adverb adverbio (*m.*), 11
Africa África
after después (de), 2
afternoon tarde (*f.*), P
afterwards después, 4
against contra, 12
age edad (*f.*), 13
agriculture agricultura (*f.*), 4
ahead (of the class) adelantado(a)
air aire (*m.*), 19
alive vivo(a), 8
all todos(as), 2; todo(a), 6
allergic alérgico(a)
allies aliados(as) (*m. pl., f. pl.*)
allotted asignado(a)
allow dejar, 18; permitir, 19
alone solo(a), 16
aloud en voz alta, 2
alphabet alfabeto (*m.*)
alphabetical alfabético(a)
 in — order en orden alfabético, 3
already ya, 1
also también, 1
America América, 12
American americano (a) (*m., f.*), 4
among entre
amphibian anfibio (*m.*), 8
anatomy anatomía (*f.*), 6
and y, P
angle ángulo (*m.*), 17
animal animal (*m.*), 8
ankle tobillo (*m.*)
another otro(a), 9
answer contestar, 6
ant hormiga (*f.*)
Antarctica Antártida
antonym antónimo (*m.*)
any algún, alguno(a), 1
 not — ninguno(a)
apostrophe apóstrofe (*m.*)
appear aparecer, 12
apple manzana (*f.*)
 — juice jugo de manzana (*m.*)
apply solicitar, 20
appointment cita (*f.*), 20; turno (*m.*)
 make an — pedir (e:i) cita, 9; pedir (e:i) turno, 9
Arabic arábigo(a), 13
archipelago archipiélago (*m.*)
area área (*f.*), 4; superficie (*f.*), 4
arithmetic aritmética (*f.*)
arm brazo (*m.*)
around alrededor (de), 5
arrival llegada (*f.*), 20
arrive llegar, 12
art arte (*m.*), 5
artery arteria (*f.*), 7
arts and crafts trabajo manual (*m.*)
as como, 7
 — soon — en cuanto, 19; tan pronto como, 19
Asia Asia
ask (for) pedir (e:i), 8; (*a question*) preguntar, 8
assemble armar, 16
astronomy astronomía (*f.*), 15
at en, 2; a, 1
 — home en casa, 3
Atlantic Atlántico, 4
atom átomo (*m.*), 15
attend asistir (a)
attendance: to take — pasar lista, 2
attention atención (*f.*)
aunt tía (*f.*), 4
Australia Australia
autumn otoño (*m.*), 10
avocado aguacate (*m.*)

B

back espalda (*f.*)
 — garden patio (*m.*), 10
backyard patio (*m.*), 10;
badly mal, 3
balanced balanceado(a), 19
ball pelota (*f.*), 16
banana banana (*f.*); plátano (*m.*); guineo (*m.*) (*Puerto Rico*)
bars barras (*f. pl.*), 18
base base (*f.*), 17
baseball béisbol (*m.*)
basic básico(a), 15
basketball básquetbol (*m.*); baloncesto (*m.*)
bathe bañar(se), 19
bathroom baño (*m.*), 2
battery pila (*f.*); batería (*f.*)
battle batalla (*f.*)
be ser, 2; estar, 3
 — about tratar (de), 19
 — acquainted with conocer, 7
 — ahead of the class estar adelantado(a), 9
 — (become) free from librarse (de), 12
 — born nacer, 8
 — careful! ¡Cuidado!, 18
 — early llegar temprano, 20
 — enough bastar, 11
 — formed estar formado(a), 6
 — found in componer, 15
 — glad alegrarse (de), 17
 — good for servir (e:i) para, 7
 — hungry tener hambre, 4
 — late llegar tarde, 9
 — made up estar formado(a), 6
 — missing faltar, 17
 — pleasing gustar, 8
 — progressing estar progresando, 9
 — promoted pasar
 — right tener razón, 4
 — worth valer, 13
 — written estar escrito(a), 13
beak pico (*m.*), 8
beautiful bonito(a), 3
because porque, 1
bee abeja (*f.*)
before antes de, 6
begin empezar (e:ie), 5; comenzar (e:ie), 5
beginning: at the — of a principios de
behave portarse, 9
behavior comportamiento (*m.*)
behind atrasado(a), 9; detrás (de)
beige beige
believe creer, 9
bell timbre (*m.*), 6; campana (*f.*), 6
belong pertenecer, 8
belt cinto (*m.*); cinturón (*m.*)
benefit (by) beneficiar(se) (de), 20
beside al lado (de), 16
besides además de, 9
better mejor, 1
between entre, 17
bicycle bicicleta (*f.*), 20
big grande, 4
bigger mayor, 13
bird ave (*f.*), 8; pájaro (*m.*)
birth nacimiento (*m.*)
black negro(a)
blackboard pizarra (*f.*); pizarrón (*m.*)
blindfold vendar, 16
block bloque (*m.*), 16
blood sangre (*f.*), 6
 — cell glóbulo (*m.*), 7

blue azul, 2
navy — azul marino
sky — azul celeste
board pizarra (*f.*); pizarrón (*m.*)
body cuerpo (*m.*), 6
bomb bombardear, 12
bone hueso (*m.*), 6
book libro (*m.*), P
border limitar (con), 4; colindar con (*Méx.*), 4
borrow pedir (e:i) prestado(a), 13
boundary límite (*m.*), 4
box caja (*f.*), 16
botanical botánico(a)
boy niño (*m.*)
brackets corchetes (*m. pl.*)
brain cerebro (*m.*), 6
branchiae agallas (*f. pl.*), 8; branquias (*f. pl.*), 8
breakfast desayuno (*m.*), 9
breathe respirar, 7
brief breve, P
— conversation conversación breve (*f.*), P
bring traer, 2
broken roto(a), 3
bronchial tube bronquio (*m.*)
brown marrón, 2; café (*Méx.*), 2; carmelita (*Cuba*), 2
brush cepillar(se), 19
budget presupuesto (*m.*)
bull toro (*m.*)
bus autobús (*m.*), 10; ómnibus (*m.*), 10; camión (*m.*) (*Méx.*), 10; guagua (*f.*) (*Cuba, Puerto Rico*), 10
but pero, 1
butterfly mariposa (*f.*)
button abrochar, 16
by entre, 14; por, 14
bye chau, P

C

cabinet armario (*m.*), 5; gabinete (*m.*) (*Méx.*), 5
cactus cacto (*m.*), 10
cafeteria cafetería (*f.*), 2; comedor (*m.*) (*Méx.*)
cake pastel (*m.*)
calcium calcio (*m.*), 19
call llamar, 3
— on the telephone llamar por teléfono, 3
called llamado(a)
what is . . . called? ¿cómo se llama...?, 6
camel camello (*m.*)
camellia camelia (*f.*)
can poder (o:ue)
candy dulce (*m.*); golosina (*f.*), 18
cape cabo (*m.*)
capillary vaso capilar (*m.*), 7
capital (letter) mayúscula (*f.*), 3; **(city)** capital (*f.*), 4
capitalism capitalismo (*m.*)
carbohydrate carbohidrato (*m.*), 19
cardboard cartón (*m.*)
carnation clavel (*m.*)
carpet alfombra (*f.*), 16
carrot zanahoria (*f.*)
carry llevar, 1
— out llevarse, 10
case: in that — entonces, 11
cat gato(a) (*m., f.*)
celery apio (*m.*)
center centro (*m.*), 17
centimeter centímetro (*m.*)
Central America América Central; Centroamérica
century siglo (*m.*), 12
cerebellum cerebelo (*m.*)
chain of mountains cordillera (*f.*)
chair silla (*f.*), P
chalk tiza (*f.*), P
change cambiar, 9; cambio (*m.*), 15
characteristic característica (*f.*), 8
chart cartel (*m.*), 4
cheap barato(a), 12
check revisar, 11
cheese queso (*m.*)
chemistry química (*f.*), 15
cherry cereza (*f.*)
chest pecho (*m.*)
chew mascar, masticar, 5
chewing gum goma de mascar (*f.*), 5; chicle (*m.*), 5
chicken pollo (*m.*)
— pox varicela (*f.*)
child niño(a) (*m., f.*), 1; hijo(a) (*m., f.*), 9
children niños(as) (*m. pl., f. pl.*), 2; hijos(as) (*m. pl., f. pl.*), 9
chlorine cloro (*m.*), 15
chocolate chocolate (*m.*), 12
choose elegir (e:i), escoger
Christmas Navidad (*f.*), 5
— Eve Nochebuena (*f.*)
circle círculo (*m.*), 16
circulatory system aparato circulatorio (*m.*), 7
circumference circunferencia (*f.*), 17
citizenship conducta (*f.*)
city ciudad (*f.*)
civil civil, 12
class clase (*f.*), 1
classmate compañero(a) de clase (*m., f.*), 9
classroom aula (*f.*), P
clean limpiar, 5
cleanliness limpieza (*f.*), 19
clear claro(a), 3
clock reloj (*m.*), P
close cerrar (e:ie), 5
closed cerrado(a), 20
clothes ropa (*f.*), 6
cloudburst lluvia torrencial (*f.*)
coagulate coagular, 7
coast costa (*f.*), 12
coat abrigo (*m.*), 16
cold frío(a), 8
colon dos puntos (*m.*)
colonize colonizar, 12
colony colonia (*f.*), 12
color color (*m.*), 5; colorear, 2
colored pencils lápices de colores (*m. pl.*), 2
Columbus (Christopher) (Cristóbal) Colón, 12
come venir, 4
— back volver (o:ue), 6
— in pasar, P
comical gracioso(a), 16; cómico(a), 16
comma coma (*f.*)
common común
— noun nombre (sustantivo) común (*m.*)
communism comunismo (*m.*)
compass compás (*m.*)
compose componer, 15
composition composición (*f.*), 3
compound compuesto(a), 15
comprehension comprensión (*f.*)
concept concepto (*m.*), 17
condensation condensación (*f.*)
conduct conducta (*f.*)
cone cono (*m.*)
conference conferencia (*f.*), 9
congress congreso (*m.*), 12
congressional delegate representante (*m., f.*)
conjunction conjunción (*f.*)
connect unir
— the dots unir los puntos
conquer conquistar
considerate considerado(a)
consistent consistente
consonant consonante (*f.*), 11
constitution constitución (*f.*), 12
construction paper cartulina (*f.*)
consume consumir, 19
contagious contagioso(a)
contest concurso (*m.*), 11
continent continente (*m.*), 14
continue continuar, 5; seguir (e:i), 7
contraction contracción (*f.*)
conversation conversación (*f.*), P
converse conversar
cookie galletita (*f.*), 18; galleta (*f.*) (*Méx.*), 18
cooperation cooperación (*f.*), 20
copy copiar, 2
correct correcto(a), 3; corregir (e:i), 11
corn maíz (*m.*)
cotton algodón (*m.*), 5
council consejo (*m.*)
count contar (o:ue), 13
country país (*m.*), 4
cousin primo(a) (*m., f.*), 13
cover cubrir, 6
covered (with) cubierto(a) (de), 8
cow vaca (*f.*)
crab cangrejo (*m.*)
crocodile cocodrilo (*m.*), 8
cry llorar, 18
cube cubo (*m.*)
cubic cúbico(a)
— measurement medida cúbica (*f.*); medida de volumen (*f.*)
cultural cultural
cup taza (*f.*), 16

cure curar, cura (*f.*), 19
curved curvo(a), 17
cut cortar, 5; recortar, 5
cyclone ciclón (*m.*)
cylinder cilindro (*m.*)

D

daisy margarita (*f.*)
dark oscuro(a), 6
dash raya (*f.*)
date fecha (*f.*), 2
  what's the — today? ¿qué fecha es hoy?, P
daughter hija (*f.*), 9
day día (*m.*), 20
deal (with) tratar (de), 19
  a great — mucho
decade década (*f.*), 12
decimal decimal, 13
decimeter decímetro (*m.*)
declare declarar, 12
defeat vencer; derrotar
definite article artículo definido (*m.*)
definition definición (*f.*)
degree grado (*m.*), 17
democracy democracia (*f.*)
denominator denominador (*m.*), 14
dentist dentista (*m.*, *f.*), 20
depend depender, 6
depression depresión (*f.*), 12
desert desierto (*m.*), 10
desk escritorio (*m.*), P; pupitre (*m.*), P
diameter diámetro (*m.*), 17
dictation dictado (*m.*)
dictionary diccionario (*m.*), 3
die morir (o:ue), 13
diet dieta (*f.*), 19
difference diferencia (*f.*); resto (*m.*)
different diferente, 5; distinto(a), 6
difficult difícil, 11
difficulty dificultad (*f.*), 9
digest digerir (e:ie), 6
digestion digestión (*f.*), 6
digestive digestivo(a)
  — system aparato digestivo (*m.*)
digit dígito (*m.*), 13
dimension dimensión (*f.*)
diphtheria difteria (*f.*)
discover descubrir, 12
disease enfermedad (*f.*), 19
dismissal salida (*f.*), 6
dissolve disolver (o:ue)
disturb interrumpir
divided dividido(a), 8
dividend dividendo (*m.*)
divisible divisible, 13
division división (*f.*)
divisor divisor (*m.*)
do hacer, 5
doctor doctor(a) (Dr., Dra.) (*m.*, *f.*), P; (*M.D.*) médico(a) (*m.*, *f.*), 20
dog perro (*m.*)
doll muñeca (*f.*), 16
door puerta (*f.*), P
dot punto (*m.*)
dotted line línea de puntos (*f.*)
down abajo
downstairs abajo
draw (*a picture*) dibujar, 5; (*a line*) trazar, 5
drawer cajón (*m.*), 5; gaveta (*f.*) (*Cuba, Puerto Rico*), 5
drawing dibujo (*m.*), 5
dress vestido (*m.*)
drill práctica (*f.*), 4; simulacro (*m.*) (*Méx. y Puerto Rico*), 4
drink tomar, 5; bebida (*f.*)
duck pato (*m.*)
due
  is (are) — to se debe(n) a, 9
during durante, 12
dyslexia dislexia (*f.*), 9

E

each cada, 3
ear oreja (*f.*); (*inner*) oído (*m.*)
earth tierra (*f.*), 8
Earth Tierra (*f.*), 15
earthquake terremoto (*m.*)
east este (*m.*), 4
Easter Pascua Florida (*f.*)
easy fácil, 3
eat comer, 2
effort esfuerzo (*m.*)
  to make an — esforzarse (o:ue), 9
egg huevo (*m.*), 8
eighth (*fraction*) octavo (*m.*)
elbow codo (*m.*), 6
elect elegir (e:i), 12
election elección (*f.*), 12
electricity electricidad (*f.*), 15
electron electrón (*m.*), 15
element elemento (*m.*), 7
elephant elefante (*m.*)
eleventh (*fraction*) onceavo (*m.*)
emergency emergencia (*f.*), 3
empty vacío(a), 18
end: at the — of a fines de, 12
energy energía (*f.*), 15
England Inglaterra, 12
English (language) inglés (*m.*), 3
enough bastante
enroll matricular(se), 20
enrolled matriculado(a), 20
enter entrar (en), 2
envelope sobre (*m.*), 20
equal igual, 17
equilateral equilátero(a)
equivalence equivalencia (*f.*), 14
erase borrar, 2
eraser borrador (*m.*), P
esophagus esófago (*m.*)
essential esencial, 19
established establecido(a), 12
Europe Europa
evaluation evaluación (*f.*), 9
evaporation evaporación (*f.*)
even (number) par, 13
event acontecimiento (*m.*), 12
ever alguna vez
everybody todos(as), 2
exactly exactamente, 19
exam examen (*m.*), 3
example ejemplo (*m.*), 15
  for — por ejemplo, 11
excellent excelente, 11
exclamation mark signo de admiración (*m.*)
exception excepción (*f.*), 11
excursion excursión (*f.*)
excuse me con permiso, P; disculpar(se), 3
excuse the interruption perdonar la molestia, 2
exercise ejercicio (*m.*), 3; hacer ejercicio, 19
exist existir, 8
expensive caro(a), 20
experiment experimento (*m.*), 15
explain explicar, 8
expression expresión (*f.*)
eye ojo (*m.*), 16
  — doctor oculista (*m.*, *f.*), 9
eyeglasses anteojos (*m. pl.*), 9; lentes (*m. pl.*), 9; espejuelos (*m. pl.*) (*Cuba, Puerto Rico*), 9; gafas (*f. pl.*) (*España*), 9
eyesight vista (*f.*), 9

F

face cara (*f.*)
fact: the — is . . . es que..., 18
factor factor (*m.*)
fall otoño (*m.*), 10; caer(se), 18
farewell despedida (*f.*), 9
farm finca (*f.*)
  — animal animal de finca (*m.*)
fasten abrochar, 16
fat grasa (*f.*), 19
Father's Day Día del Padre (*m.*)
fear temer
feather pluma (*f.*), 8
feed alimentar, 10
feel sentirse (e:ie), 15
felt fieltro (*m.*), 5
fever fiebre (*f.*); calentura (*f.*)
field trip excursión (*f.*), 10
fifth (*fraction*) quinto (*m.*), 14
fight pelearse, 9; luchar
figure figura (*f.*), 17
fill (out) llenar, 20
film película (*f.*)
filter filtrar
find encontrar (o:ue), 10
  — out averiguar
fine bien, P
finger dedo (*m.*)
finish terminar, 1; acabar, 1
finished terminado(a), 3
fire fuego (*m.*), 4; incendio (*m.*), 4
first primero(a), 2
fish pez (*m.*) (*animal*), 8; pescado (*m.*)
fishing pesca (*f.*), 4

flood inundación (*f.*)
floor piso (*m.*), 16
flower flor (*f.*), 10
fly volar (o:ue), 8; mosca (*f.*)
fold doblar, 5
folded doblado(a), 5
following siguiendo, 5; siguiente, 11
food comida (*f.*), 6; alimento (*m.*), 10
foot pie (*m.*), 14
football fútbol americano (*m.*)
for para, 3; por
forget (to) olvidar(se) (de), 16
form formar, 11; forma (*f.*), 20; planilla (*f.*), 20; formulario (*m.*) (*Puerto Rico*), 20
formed formado(a), 6
formula fórmula (*f.*), 15
found fundar
fourth (*fraction*) cuarto(a), 14
fowl ave (*f.*), 8
fraction quebrado (*m.*), 13; fracción (*f.*), 13
frame armazón (*f.*), 6
France Francia, 12
free gratis, 9; libre
French fries papas fritas (*f. pl.*)
fresh (air) puro(a) (aire), 19
friend amigo(a) (*m., f.*), 20
friendly amistoso(a)
frog rana (*f.*), 8
from de, P
front frente (*m.*)
  in — of delante de, 18
  to the — (of) al frente (de), 7
fruit fruto (*m.*), 10; fruta (*f.*)
funny gracioso(a), 16; cómico(a), 16
furniture muebles (*m. pl.*), 10
further más
future futuro (*m.*)

G

galaxy galaxia (*f.*), 15
gallon galón (*m.*)
gander ganso (*m.*), 8
garden jardín (*m.*), 10
garlic ajo (*m.*)
gas gas (*m.*), 15
gaseous gaseoso(a), 15
generally generalmente, 17
gentleman señor (*m.*), P
geography geografía (*f.*), 4
geometric geométrico(a), 17
geometry geometría (*f.*), 17
germ microbio (*m.*), 6
German measles rubéola (*f.*)
get conseguir (e:i)
  — along llevarse bien, 9
  — angry enojarse, 16
  — better mejorar, 1; mejorar(se), 9
  — fat engordar, 19
  — hurt lastimarse, 18
  — in line ponerse en fila, 10
  — nourishment alimentarse
  — off bajar(se), 10
  — on subir(se), 10
  — out salir, 7
  — ready prepararse, 11
  — separated separarse, 10
  — together reunión (*f.*), 20; junta (*f.*), 20
gills agallas (*f. pl.*), 8; branquias (*f. pl.*), 8
giraffe jirafa (*f.*)
girl niña (*f.*)
give dar, 3
  — back devolver (o:ue)
gland glándula (*f.*)
  salivary — glándula salival (*f.*)
globe globo terráqueo (*m.*), 4
glue pegar, 5; goma de pegar (*f.*), 5
go ir, 3
  — away irse, 9
  — back regresar, 3; volver (o:ue)
  — on a tour (excursion) ir de excursión, 10
  — out salir, 7
  — to the bathroom ir al baño, 2
goat cabra (*f.*), chivo(a) (*m., f.*)
golden dorado(a)
good bueno(a)
  — afternoon buenas tardes, P
  — evening (night) buenas noches, P
  — morning (day) buenos días, P
  what are . . . — for? ¿para qué sirven...?, 7
good-bye adiós, P
goose gansa (*f.*), 8
government gobierno (*m.*)
governor gobernador(a) (*m., f.*)
grade grado (*m.*), 5
  at — level al nivel del grado, 9
  — school escuela primaria (elemental) (*f.*), 10
gram gramo (*m.*), 14
grammar gramática (*f.*)
grape uva (*f.*)
grapefruit toronja (*f.*); pomelo (*m.*)
gray gris
greater mayor, 13
green verde
greeting saludo (*m.*), P
group de grupo, 1; grupo (*m.*), 2
growth crecimiento (*m.*), 19
guardian tutor (*m.*)
guess adivinar, 16
gulf golfo (*m.*)
gum goma (*f.*)
  chewing — goma de mascar (*f.*), 5; chicle (*m.*), 5
gymnastics gimnasia (*f.*)

H

habit hábito (*m.*), 19
hair pelo (*m.*), 8; cabello (*m.*)
half mitad (*f.*), 5; (*fraction*) medio, 14
  in — por la mitad, 5
ham jamón (*m.*)
hamburger hamburguesa (*f.*)
hand mano (*f.*)
hang up colgar (o:ue), 16
happen pasar, 7; ocurrir, 11
happy contento(a), 4
hardworking trabajador(a)
have tener, 4
  — a seat tomar asiento, P
  — fever tener fiebre
  — just (done something) acabar (de) (+*inf.*), 13
  — to tener que (+*inf.*), 4
head cabeza (*f.*), 6
  — lice piojos (*m. pl.*)
health salud (*f.*), 19
hearing oído (*m.*)
heart corazón (*m.*), 7
  to have — trouble padecer del corazón, 7
heat calor (*m.*), 15
height altura (*f.*), 17
hello hola, P
help ayuda (*f.*), 1; ayudar, 9
hen gallina (*f.*)
here aquí, 1
  — is . . . aquí tiene..., 2
hexagon hexágono (*m.*)
hi hola, P
high alto(a), 4
hippopotamus hipopótamo (*m.*)
history historia (*f.*), 12
hit pegar, 9
hold sostener, 6
  — hands tomarse de las manos, 10
holiday día festivo (*m.*)
Holland Holanda, 12
home a casa, 1; casa, 13
  at — en casa, 3
homework tarea (*f.*), 1
hope esperar, 17
  I — . . . ojalá..., 17
horizontal horizontal, 17
horse caballo (*m.*)
hot caliente, 8; cálido(a)
  — dog perro caliente (*m.*)
hour hora (*f.*)
house casa (*f.*), 13
how cómo
  — are you? ¿cómo está Ud.?, P
  — easy! ¡qué fácil!, 17
  — happy! ¡qué contento!, 4
  — is it going? ¿qué tal?, P
  — many cuántos(as), 4
  — much cuánto(a)
  — nice! ¡qué bien!, 4
  — pretty! ¡que bonito!, 5
hundred centena (*f.*)
  — thousandth cien milésimo(a)
hundredth centésima (*f.*), 14
hurricane huracán (*m.*)
hurry up apurarse, 10; darse prisa, 10
hurt doler (o:ue), 8; lastimar(se), 18
husband esposo (*m.*), 9
hydrogen hidrógeno (*m.*), 15
hygiene higiene (*f.*), 19
hyphen guión (*m.*)

I

I am soy, P
ice cream helado (*m.*)
idea idea (*f.*)
if si, 2
— **only . . .** ojalá, 17
I'll be right back. Vuelvo enseguida., 6
ill enfermo(a), 20
illustration ilustración (*f.*), 4; lámina (*f.*), 4
imagination imaginación (*f.*), 16
important importante, 7
improper impropio(a)
improve mejorar, 1; **improve (oneself)** mejorar(se), 9
in en, 1; dentro (de), 4
— **fact** en realidad, 19
— **the shape of** en forma de, 8
inch pulgada (*f.*), 14
inclined inclinado(a), 17
— **plane** plano inclinado (*m.*), 15
income riqueza (*f.*)
indefinite article artículo indefinido (*m.*)
independence independencia (*f.*), 12
— **Day** Día de la Independencia (*m.*)
Indian indio(a)
industry industria (*f.*), 4
inexpensive barato(a), 12
information información (*f.*), 12
inhabitant habitante (*m.*), 4
inorganic inorgánico(a)
insect insecto (*m.*), 8
inside dentro, 4; adentro
instruction instrucción (*f.*), 1
instructor instructor(a) (*m., f.*), P
insurance seguro (*m.*), 20; aseguranza (*f.*) (*Méx.*), 20
intelligent inteligente, 4
interjection interjección (*f.*)
interrupt interrumpir, 12
intestine intestino (*m.*), 6
large — intestino grueso
small — intestino delgado
invertebrate invertebrado (*m.*), 8
iron hierro (*m.*), 19
irregular irregular, 11
island isla (*f.*), 4
isosceles isósceles
it's a pleasure (to meet you) mucho gusto, P
it's just that . . . es que..., 18
it's (*time*) ser las (+ *time*), 1

J

jacket chaqueta (*f.*), 16; chamarra (*f.*) (*Méx.*), 16
janitor conserje (*m., f.*)
Japan Japón (*m.*), 12
Japanese japonés(esa), 12
jelly jalea (*f.*); mermelada (*f.*)
join unir, 17
joining together unión (*f.*), 6
joint articulación (*f.*), 6; coyuntura (*f.*), 6
jump saltar, 16
— **rope** saltar a la cuerda, 18

K

keep guardar, 3; (*oneself*) mantener(se), 12
kilo(gram) kilogramo (*m.*), 14
kilometer kilómetro (*m.*)
kind clase (*f.*), 8
kindergarten jardín de infantes (*m.*), 16; jardín de niños (*m.*) (*Méx.*), 16; kindergarten (*m.*), 16
kingdom reino (*m.*), 8
kitchen cocina (*f.*), 15
knee rodilla (*f.*), 6
knit tejer
know saber, 2; conocer, 7
knowledge conocimiento (*m.*), 15

L

Labor Day Día de los Trabajadores (*m.*)
lady señora (*f.*), P
young — señorita (*f.*), P
lake lago (*m.*)
land tierra (*f.*), 8
— **suitable for farming** tierra cultivable (*f.*), 12
language lenguaje (*m.*)
large grande, 4
larger mayor, 13
last último(a), 11; durar, 12
late tarde
later más tarde, 2; luego, 13
see you — hasta luego, P
lathe torno (*m.*), 15
laugh reír(se), 19
law ley (*f.*)
leaf hoja (*f.*), 10
learn aprender, 3
learning aprendizaje (*m.*)
— **disability** problema de aprendizaje (*m.*), 9
leave irse, 9; dejar
— **alone** dejar en paz, 18
— **behind** dejar, 9
left izquierdo(a)
to the — a la izquierda, 5
leg pierna (*f.*)
lemon limón (*m.*)
lemonade limonada (*f.*)
lend prestar, 13
length longitud (*f.*), 14; largo (*m.*), 17
less menor, 13
lesson lección (*f.*), 3
today's — la lección para hoy, 3
let dejar, 18; permitir, 19
let's have lunch vamos a almorzar, 7
letter letra (*f.*), 3
lettuce lechuga (*f.*)
level nivel (*m.*), 9
lever palanca (*f.*), 15
liberate liberar
librarian bibliotecario(a) (*m., f.*)
library biblioteca (*f.*), 6
life vida (*f.*), 8
light luz (*f.*), P; claro(a)
— **year** año luz (*m.*)
like gustar, 8; como, 11
— **this** así, 3
line línea (*f.*), 5; fila (*f.*), 10
to get (stand) in — ponerse en fila, 10
linear lineal, 13
lion león (*m.*)
liquid líquido (*m.*), 15
list lista (*f.*)
listen escuchar, 1
liter litro (*m.*)
literature literatura (*f.*)
little (*size*) pequeño(a), 5; (*quantity*) poco(a), 6
a — un poco, 9
very — (*adv.*) muy poco
live vivir, 4
liver hígado (*m.*)
livestock ganadería (*f.*), 4
lizard lagartija (*f.*), 8
lobster langosta (*f.*)
located situado(a), 4
long largo(a), 4
— **wave** onda larga (*f.*)
look (at) mirar, 9
— **for** buscar, 3
— **out!** ¡cuidado!, 18
lose perder (e:ie), 20
low bajo(a), 9
lowercase letter minúscula (*f.*), 3
lunch almuerzo (*m.*), 20
to have — almorzar (o:ue), 7
lung pulmón (*m.*), 7

M

machine máquina (*f.*), 15
madam señora (*f.*), P
made up (of) formado(a), 6
main principal, 4
mainly principalmente, 12
maintain (oneself) mantener(se), 12
maintenance mantenimiento (*m.*), 19
make hacer, 5
— **an appointment** pedir (e:i) turno, 9; hacer una cita, 9
— **an effort** esforzarse (o:ue)
— **good use of** aprovechar, 20
mammal mamífero (*m.*), 8
man hombre (*m.*)
manner manera (*f.*), 11
many muchos(as), 1
— **times** muchas veces, 9
map mapa (*m.*), P
mare yegua (*f.*)
material material, 3
mathematics matemáticas (*f. pl.*), 12
matter materia (*f.*), 15
may poder (o:ue), 6

maybe quizá(s), 9
mayor alcalde (*m.*); alcaldesa (*f.*)
mean significar, 1
meaning significado (*m.*), 3
measles sarampión (*m.*)
measure medida (*f.*); medir (e:i), 17
measurement medida, 13
meet (each other) encontrarse (o:ue), 17
meeting reunión (*f.*), 20; junta (*f.*), 20
meridian meridiano (*m.*)
meter metro (*m.*)
metric system sistema métrico (*m.*), 14
mile milla (*f.*)
milkshake batido (*m.*); leche malteada (*f.*) (*Méx.*)
Milky Way Vía Láctea (*f.*), 15
millimeter milímetro (*m.*)
million millón (*m.*), 4
mineral mineral (*m.*), 19
mining minería (*f.*), 4
minuend minuendo (*m.*)
minus menos
minute minuto (*m.*), 2
misbehave portarse mal, 9
miss perder (e:ie), 20; señorita (Srta.) (*f.*), P
mixed mixto(a), 14
mixture mezcla (*f.*)
model modelo (*m.*), 5; patrón (*m.*), 5
molecule molécula (*f.*), 15
mom mamá (*f.*), 8; madre (*f.*), 8
moment momento (*m.*), 2
monarchy monarquía (*f.*)
money dinero (*m.*), 20
monkey mono (*m.*); chango (*m.*) (*Méx.*)
month mes (*m.*), 20
moon luna (*f.*), 15
more más, 1
  — carefully con más cuidado, 3
  — or less más o menos, 4
mosquito mosquito (*m.*); zancudo (*m.*) (*Méx.*)
mother madre (*f.*), 8; mamá (*f.*), 8
Mother's Day Día de la(s) Madre(s) (*m.*)
mount monte (*m.*), 4
mountain montaña (*f.*), 4
mouth boca (*f.*), 8
move mover (o:ue), 6
movie película (*f.*)
Mr. Sr. (*m.*), P
Mrs. Sra. (*f.*), P
much (*adv.*) mucho, P; (*adj.*) mucho(a)
  so — tanto(a), 17
multiple múltiplo (*m.*), 13
multiplicand multiplicando (*m.*)
multiplication multiplicación (*f.*)
multiplier multiplicador (*m.*)
multiply multiplicar, 1
mumps paperas (*f. pl.*)
muscle músculo (*m.*), 6
music música (*f.*)
must deber, 2

N

name nombrar, 7
nationality nacionalidad (*f.*), 12
natural natural
nature naturaleza (*f.*), 15
near (to) cerca de, 18
necessary necesario(a), 16
neck cuello (*m.*)
need necesitar, 1
needed necesario(a), 16
needle aguja (*f.*)
neighbor vecino(a) (*m., f.*), 20
neither tampoco, 9
nephew sobrino (*m.*), 20
nerve nervio (*m.*)
nervous nervioso(a)
  — system sistema nervioso (*m.*); 7
neutral neutral, 12
neutron neutrón (*m.*), 15
never nunca, 1
new nuevo(a), 2
next próximo(a)
  — to al lado de, 16
  — to-last penúltimo(a), 11
ninth (*fraction*) noveno (*m.*)
no no, P
  — one nadie, 18
nobody nadie, 18
noise ruido (*m.*)
none (not any) ninguno(a), 17
north norte (*m.*), 4
  — America Norteamérica, 4; América del Norte, 4
  — American norteamericano(a), 12
nose nariz (*f.*)
not no, P
  — to be feeling well no sentirse (e:ie) bien
  — to return the books no devolver (o:ue) los libros
note nota (*f.*)
notebook cuaderno (*m.*), P
noun nombre (*m.*), 3; sustantivo (*m.*), 3
nourish alimentar, 10
nourishing nutritivo(a), 19
nourishment alimento (*m.*), 10
  take — alimentarse, 10
now ahora, 3
number número (*m.*), 4; cifra (*f.*)
numerator numerador (*m.*), 14
nurse enfermero(a) (*m., f.*), 8
nutrient alimento (*m.*), 10
nutrition nutrición (*f.*), 19

O

object (*grammar*) complemento (*m.*)
observe observar, 9
obtuse obtuso(a)
ocean océano (*m.*), 4
octagon octógono (*m.*)
odd impar (*number*), 13; extraño(a)
office oficina (*f.*), 3
on en, 2; sobre, 5
once in a while de vez en cuando, 9
ones: the — who los (las) que, 12
onion cebolla (*f.*)
only único(a), 11; solamente, 11
open abrir, 2
opening abertura (*f.*), 17
operate operar, 7
operation operación (*f.*)
oral oral
  — reading lectura oral (*f.*)
orange anaranjado(a), 2; naranja (*f.*)
  — juice jugo de naranja (*m.*)
  — tree naranjo (*m.*), 10
orchid orquídea (*f.*)
order orden (*m.*)
  in — to para, 6
organ órgano (*m.*), 7
organic orgánico(a)
original original
other otro(a), 9
  the others los (las) demás, 1
ounce onza (*f.*), 14
outside afuera
oxygen oxígeno (*m.*), 6

P

Pacific Pacífico (*m.*), 4
padlock candado (*m.*), 20
page página (*f.*), 2
paint pintura (*f.*); pintar
pairs: in — de dos en dos, 10
pancreas páncreas (*m.*)
pansy pensamiento (*m.*)
pants pantalones (*m. pl.*)
paper papel (*m.*), 2
parallel paralelo(a), 17; paralelo (*m.*)
parallelogram paralelogramo (*m.*)
parentheses paréntesis (*m. pl.*)
parents padres (*m. pl.*), 20
part parte (*f.*), 3
  be a — (of) formar parte (de), 7
participate participar, 1
participation participación (*f.*)
past pasado(a), 11; pasado (*m.*)
pattern modelo (*m.*), 5; patrón (*m.*), 5
pay pagar
  — attention prestar atención, 1
peace paz (*f.*), 18
peanut butter mantequilla de maní (*f.*); mantequilla de cacahuete (*f.*) (*Méx.*)
pear pera (*f.*)
pen pluma (*f.*), P
pencil lápiz (*m.*), P
  — sharpener sacapuntas (*m.*), P
peninsula península (*f.*)
pentagon pentágono (*m.*)
penultimate penúltimo(a), 11
people gente (*f.*), 12
pepper (bell) ají (*m.*); chile verde (*m.*)
per day al día, 19
percent por ciento, 14
percentage tanto por ciento (*m.*), 14
perfect perfecto(a), 13
perhaps quizá(s), 9

perimeter perímetro (*m.*), 17
period punto (*m.*)
permit permitir, 19
perpendicular perpendicular, 17
persecution persecución (*f.*), 12
person persona (*f.*), 6
personal personal, 19
pet animal doméstico (*m.*)
phenomenon fenómeno (*m.*)
phone teléfono (*m.*)
phosphorus fósforo (*m.*), 19
photograph fotografía (*f.*), 8
physical education educación física (*f.*)
physics física (*f.*), 15
pick up recoger, 5; buscar
picture lámina (*f.*), 4; ilustración (*f.*), 4
pie pastel (*m.*), 19
piece pedazo (*m.*), 19; trozo (*m.*), 19
pig cerdo(a) (*m., f.*); cochino(a) (*m., f.*)
pigment pigmento (*m.*), 6
pilgrim peregrino(a) (*m., f.*), 12
pink rosado(a), 2; rosa, 2
pint pinta (*f.*)
pioneer pionero(a) (*m., f.*)
place lugar (*m.*), 13
plane plano (*m.*), 17
planet planeta (*m.*), 15
plant planta (*f.*), 10
platelet (blood) plaqueta (*f.*), 7
play practicar
playground patio (*m.*), 18
please por favor, P; gustar, 13; hacer el favor de..., 20
pleasure gusto (*m.*); placer (*m.*)
  it's a — to meet you mucho gusto, P
  the — is mine el gusto es mío, P
plus más (+)
point punto (*m.*), 14
pole polo (*m.*)
polite de cortesía
popular popular
population población (*f.*), 4
position posición (*f.*), 17
possible posible, 20
poster cartel (*m.*), 4
potato papa (*f.*), patata (*f.*) (*Spain*)
  — chip papita (*f.*)
pound libra (*f.*), 14
power potencia (*f.*), 12
practice practicar, 11
predicate predicado (*m.*)
prefer preferir (e:ie), 5
prefix prefijo (*m.*)
prepare (oneself) preparar(se), 11
prepared preparado(a), 11
preposition preposición (*f.*)
present presente, 2
president presidente (*m.*), 4
pretty bonito(a), 3
prevent prevenir, 19
prime primo(a), 13
principal director(a) (*m., f.*), 3
principal's office dirección (*f.*), 2
problem problema (*m.*), 1
product producto (*m.*), 4
professor profesor(a) (*m., f.*), P
progress adelantar, 17
progressing progresando
pronounce pronunciar, 11
proper propio(a)
  — noun nombre propio (*m.*), 3
property propiedad (*f.*)
prosperity prosperidad (*f.*), 12
protect proteger, 6
protected protegido(a), 6
protein proteína (*f.*), 19
proton protón (*m.*), 15
proud orgulloso(a), 15
psychologist psicólogo(a) (*m., f.*), 9
pulley polea (*f.*), 15
punish castigar, 9
puppet títere (*m.*), 16
purify purificar, 7
puritan puritano(a) (*m., f.*)
purple morado(a), violeta
push empujar, 18
put poner, 5
  — away guardar, 3
  — on ponerse, 16
  — together armar, 16
puzzle rompecabezas (*m.*), 16
pyramid pirámide (*f.*)

Q

quantity cantidad (*f.*), 6
quart cuarto (*m.*)
question pregunta (*f.*), 11
  — mark signo de interrogación (*m.*)
quiet callado(a), 16; calladito(a)
quotation marks comillas (*f. pl.*)
quotient cociente (*m.*)

R

rabbit conejo (*m.*)
radius radio (*m.*), 17
rain llover (o:ue), 10
raincoat impermeable (*m.*); capa de agua (*f.*) (*Puerto Rico*)
raise levantar
  — one's hand levantar la mano, 6
read leer, 1
  — more leer más, 1
reading lectura (*f.*), 1
  — book libro de lectura (*m.*), 2
  — hour hora de lectura (*f.*), 2
ready listo(a), 5
reality
  in — en realidad, 19
reason razón (*f.*), 20
receive recibir, 20
recess hora de recreo (*f.*), 3
reciprocal recíproco(a), 14
rectangle rectángulo (*m.*)
red rojo(a), 2
reduce reducir, 14
register matricular(se), 20
registered matriculado(a), 20
regular regular, 11
rejoice (at) alegrarse (de), 17
related relacionado(a)
religious religioso(a), 12
remain quedarse, 16
remainder residuo (*m.*)
remember recordar (o:ue), 6; acordarse (o:ue) (de), 19
remove quitar, 10
repair reparación (*f.*), 19
repeat repetir (e:i), 11
report card libreta de calificaciones (*f.*), 1; boleta de calificaciones (*f.*) (*Méx.*), 1; tarjeta de notas (*f.*) (*Puerto Rico*), 1
reptile reptil (*m.*), 8
request pedir (e:i), 8
resolve resolver (o:ue), 13
respect respetar
respiratory system aparato respiratorio (*m.*), 7
retain retener (e:ie), 19
return regresar, 3; volver (o:ue), 6; devolver (o:ue)
review repasar, 11; repaso (*m.*), 3
rhombus rombo (*m.*)
rhyme rimar
right derecho(a)
  — angle ángulo recto (*m.*), 17
  — away enseguida, 6
  — now ahora mismo, 3
  — ? ¿verdad?
  to the — a la derecha, 5
ring sonar (o:ue), 6
rise subir(se), 10
river río (*m.*), 4
Roman romano(a), 13
room cuarto (*m.*), 18
rooster gallo (*m.*)
root raíz (*f.*), 10
rope cuerda (*f.*), 18
rose rosa (*f.*)
rubella rubéola (*f.*)
rug alfombra (*f.*), 16
rule regla (*f.*), 11
ruler regla (*f.*), P
run correr, 16

S

salary sueldo (*m.*), 20
salivary salival
salt sal (*f.*), 15
salute saludar
same mismo(a), 11; igual
sand arena (*f.*), 18
sandwich sándwich (*m.*), 18; bocadillo (*m.*) (*España*), 18; emparedado (*m.*), 18; torta (*f.*) (*Méx.*), 18
satellite satélite (*m.*), 15
satisfactory satisfactorio(a), 1
say decir (e:i), 7
  — hello to saludos a, P
  how do you — . . . ? ¿cómo se dice...?, 3
  — good-bye to despedirse (e:i) (de), 11
saying dicho (*m.*), 19

scale escama (*f.*), 8
scalene escaleno
scarf bufanda (*f.*)
scholastic escolar, 20
school escuela (*f.*), 2; (*adj.*) escolar, 20
  — related escolar, 20
  — yard patio (*m.*), 3
science ciencia (*f.*), 8
scientific científico(a), 15
scissors tijeras (*f. pl.*), 5
sea mar (*m.*)
seasons of the year estaciones del año (*f. pl.*),
sealed cerrado(a), 20
seat asiento (*m.*)
  have a — tome asiento, P
secretary secretario(a) (*m., f.*), 2
second segundo(a), 6
see ver, 7
  let's see a ver, 11
  — you around hasta la vista, P
seed semilla (*f.*), 10
segment segmento (*m.*), 17
self mismo(a), 17
semicolon punto y coma (*m.*)
senator senador(a) (*m., f.*)
send enviar, 7; mandar, 18
sense sentido (*m.*)
sentence oración (*f.*), 3
separate separar(se), 10
serious serio(a), 1
serpent serpiente (*f.*), 8
serve servir (e:i), 7
seventh (*fraction*) séptimo (*m.*)
several varios(as), 5
sew coser
shall I go now? ¿voy ahora?, 3
shape forma (*f.*), 8
sheep oveja (*f.*)
shelf estante (*m.*), 5
shirt camisa (*f.*)
short bajo(a); corto(a)
  — story cuento (*m.*), 16
  — wave onda corta (*f.*)
should deber, 2
show enseñar, 8; mostrar (o:ue), 8
shrimp camarón (*m.*)
sick enfermo(a), 20
sickness enfermedad (*f.*), 19
side lado (*m.*), 17
sight vista (*f.*), 9
sign firmar, 1; signo (*m.*)
signify significar, 1
silence silencio (*m.*), 2
silent callado(a), 16; calladito(a)
silently (*reading*) en silencio, 2; con la vista, 2
silvered plateado(a)
silvery plateado(a)
simple simple, 15
simplify simplificar, 14
simultaneously a la vez, 11
sing cantar, 16
singular singular
sir señor (*m.*), P
sit down sentar(se) (e:ie), 9
situated situado(a), 4
situation situación (*f.*)
sixth (*fraction*) sexto (*m.*)
skeleton esqueleto (*m.*), 6
skin piel (*f.*), 6
skirt falda (*f.*)
skull cráneo (*m.*), 6
slave esclavo(a) (*m., f.*)
slavery esclavitud (*f.*), 12
sleep dormir (o:ue), 6
slowly despacio, 19
small pequeño(a), 5
  — letter minúscula (*f.*), 3
smaller menor, 13
smallpox viruela (*f.*)
smell olfato (*m.*)
smoothie batido (*m.*)
snail caracol (*m.*)
snake serpiente (*f.*), 8
snow blizzard tormenta de nieve (*f.*)
so así que, 9; así
  — much tanto, 17
  — that para que, 19
social studies estudios sociales (*m. pl.*)
soda refresco (*m.*)
sodium sodio (*m.*), 15
  — chloride cloruro de sodio (*m.*), 15
soil tierra (*f.*), 8
solar solar, 15
solid sólido(a), 15
solidification solidificación (*f.*)
solution solución (*f.*), 9
solve resolver (o:ue), 13
some algunos(as), 2
somebody alguien, 6
someone alguien, 6
something algo, 5, 8
  — else otra cosa
sometimes a veces, 1
son hijo (*m.*), 9
song canción (*f.*), 16
soon pronto, 13
sorry: I'm — lo siento, 20
sound sonido (*m.*), 11
  — (like) sonar (o:ue) (como), 11
source fuente (*f.*)
south sur (*m.*), 4
  — America Sudamérica
space espacio (*m.*), 15
Spain España, 12
speak hablar, 1
special especial
speed velocidad (*f.*)
spell deletrear, 11
  how do you — . . . ? ¿cómo se escribe...?, 3
spelling ortografía (*f.*), 3
  — bee concurso de ortografía (*m.*), 11
sphere esfera (*f.*)
spider araña (*f.*)
spine columna vertebral (*f.*), 8
spinal cord médula espinal (*f.*)
sport deporte (*m.*), 19
spouse esposo(a) (*m., f.*), 9
spring primavera (*f.*)
square cuadrado (*m.*); cuadrado(a)
  — measure medida cuadrada (de superficie) (*f.*)
stand (up) pararse, 16
  — for significar, 1
star estrella (*f.*), 15
start empezar (e:ie), 5; comenzar (e:ie), 12; (*war*) estallar, 12
state estado (*m.*), 4
stay quedarse, 16
steal robar, 20
stem tallo (*m.*), 10
step paso (*m.*)
still todavía, 11
stockings medias (*f. pl.*)
stomach estómago (*m.*), 6
stop parada (*f.*), 20
story cuento (*m.*), 16
straight recto(a), 17
strawberry fresa (*f.*)
stress acento (*m.*), 11
student alumno(a) (*m., f.*), P; estudiante (*m., f.*), P
study estudiar, 1; estudio (*m.*), 17
subject materia (*f.*), 1; tema (*m.*), 20; sujeto (*m.*)
subtract restar, 1
subtraction resta (*f.*), 13
subtrahend substraendo (*m.*)
success éxito (*m.*)
suffer (from, with) padecer (de), 7
sufficient suficiente, 9
suffix sufijo (*m.*)
sugar azúcar (*m.*), 4
suggest sugerir (e:ie), 16
summer verano (*m.*)
sun sol (*m.*), 10
sunlight luz del sol (*f.*), 10
supervision supervisión (*f.*), 20
support sostener, 6
suppose suponer, 15
sure seguro(a), 4
surname apellido (*m.*)
swallow tragar, 6
sweet dulce (*m.*), 18; golosina (*f.*), 18
swimming natación (*f.*)
swing columpio (*m.*), 18
syllable sílaba (*f.*), 11
symbol símbolo (*m.*)
synonym sinónimo (*m.*)

T

table mesa (*f.*), 5; tabla (*f.*)
  multiplication — tabla de multiplicación (*f.*), 1
tadpole renacuajo (*m.*), 8
take llevar, 1; tomar, 7
  — a trip hacer un viaje, 15
  — advantage of aprovechar, 20
  — away llevarse, 10; quitar, 10
  — out sacar, 16
  — part in sports practicar deportes, 19
  — roll (attendance) pasar lista, 2
tall alto(a), 4

taste gusto (*m.*)
tea té (*m.*), 16
teach enseñar, 10
teacher maestro(a) (*m., f.*), P; profesor(a), P
telephone teléfono (*m*)
tell decir (e:i), 7; contar (o:ue), 16
temperate templado(a)
ten decena (*f.*), 13
— **thousandth** diez milésimo(a)
tennis tenis (*m.*), 16
tenth décima (*f.*), 14; (*fraction*) décimo (*m.*)
territory territorio (*m.*)
tetanus tétano (*m.*)
than que, 4
thank agradecer, 20
— **you** gracias, P
— **you for coming** gracias por venir, 1
Thanksgiving Day Día de Acción de Gracias (*m.*)
that que, 4; ese(a) 8; eso, 8
then entonces, 11; luego, 13
there allí, 4
— **is (are)** hay, 2
— **was (were)** había, 12; hubo, 12
these estos(as)
thing cosa (*f.*)
think pensar (e:ie), 6; creer, 9
— **so** creer que sí, 11
third (*fraction*) tercio (*m.*)
thirsty: to be — tener sed, 5
this este(a), 7
thousand millar (*m.*)
thousandth milésima (*f.*)
thread hilo (*m.*)
throughout por todo, 6
throw tirar, 18
— **up** vomitar
tiger tigre (*m.*)
time tiempo (*m.*), 12; vez (*f.*), 19; época (*f.*)
at that — en esa época, 12
at the same — a la vez, 11
from — to — de vez en cuando, 19
— **to go** hora de salida (*f.*), 5
what — is it? ¿qué hora es?, 1
tissue tejido (*m.*), 19
to school a la escuela, 2
today hoy, P
toe dedo del pie (*m.*)
together juntos(as), 20
tomato juice jugo de tomate (*m.*)
tomorrow mañana, 4
ton tonelada (*f.*), 14
tongue lengua (*f.*)
too también, 16
that's — bad! ¡qué lástima!, 20
— **much** demasiado(a), 16
tooth diente (*m.*), 19
top arriba, de arriba, 5
on — of sobre, 5; encima de
topic tema (*m.*), 20
tornado tornado (*m.*)
total suma (*f.*); total (*m.*)
touch tacto (*m.*)
tour excursión (*f.*)
toward hacia, 16
trace trazar, 5; calcar
trachea tráquea (*f.*), 7
transform transformar, 10
trapezoid trapecio (*m.*)
trash can basurero (*m.*), 18
travel viajar
tree árbol (*m.*), 5
triangle triángulo (*m.*)
trim recortar
trip viaje (*m.*)
true verdadero(a)
— **?** ¿verdad?, 1
trunk (tree) tronco (*m.*), 10
try tratar (de), 9; esforzarse (o:ue), 9
T-shirt camiseta (*f.*)
tuna fish atún (*m.*), 18
turkey pavo (*m.*), guajolote (*m.*) (*Méx.*); guanajo (*m.*) (*Cuba*)
turn turno (*m.*)
— **in** entregar
— **into** transformarse, 10; convertir (e:ie) (en), 19
— **off** apagar, 16
— **on** encender (e:ie); prender
to be one's — tocarle a uno(a), 16
turtle tortuga (*f.*), 8
T.V. set televisor (*m.*)
two dos
— **by —** de dos en dos, 10
type clase (*f.*), 8

U

uncle tío (*m.*), 4
under bajo, 13; debajo de
underline subrayar, 3
understand entender (e:ie), 5; comprender, 20
unfold desdoblar
unfortunately desgraciadamente, 17
union unión (*f.*), 6
unit unidad (*f.*), 13
unite unir, 17
United States Estados Unidos, 4
unless a menos que, 19
until hasta, 5
up arriba
upper de arriba, 5
— **case letter** mayúscula (*f.*), 3
upstairs arriba
urgent urgente
use usar, 3
useful útil

V

vacation vacaciones, (*f. pl.*), 13
vaccination vacunación (*f.*)
Valentine's Day Día de los Enamorados (*m.*)
vanilla vainilla (*f.*)
various varios(as), 5
VCR videograbadora (*f.*)
vein vena (*f.*), 7
velocity velocidad (*f.*)
ventilation ventilación (*f.*), 19
verb verbo (*m.*), 3
verify comprobar (o:ue), 15
versus contra, 12
vertebrate vertebrado (*m.*), 8
vertical vertical, 17
vertex vértice (*m.*), 17
very muy, P
— **little** muy poco, 1
— **well, and you?** muy bien ¿y usted?, P
Veteran's Day Día de los Veteranos (*m.*)
vice principal subdirector(a) (*m., f.*); vicedirector(a) (*m., f.*), 20
video video (*m.*)
violet violeta (*f.*)
visiting de visita, 20
vitamin vitamina (*f.*), 19
vocabulary vocabulario (*m.*), 2
volcano volcán (*m.*), 4
volleyball vóleibol (*m.*)
volunteer voluntario(a) (*m., f.*), 20
vote votar
vowel vocal (*f.*), 11

W

wait esperar, 2
walk caminar, 10
want querer (e:ie), 5
war guerra (*f.*), 12
warm cálido(a)
wash lavar(se), 19
wasp avispa (*f.*)
watch vigilar, 18; reloj (*m.*)
water agua (*f.*), 5
— **color** acuarela (*f.*)
way manera (*f.*), 11
this — por aquí, 10
weak débil, 19
weather clima (*m.*)
week semana (*f.*), 4
weight peso (*m.*), 14
well bien, P; bueno..., 1
west oeste (*m.*), 4
what qué, 1; cuál(es), 3
— **a pity!** ¡qué lástima!, 20
— **are . . . good for?** ¿para qué sirven...?, 7
— **for?** ¿para qué?, 5
what's the date today? ¿qué fecha es hoy?, P
what's new? ¿qué hay de nuevo?, P
— **time is it?** ¿qué hora es?, 1
when cuándo, 6
where (to) dónde, 1; adónde, 3
where (from)? de dónde?, P
which cuál(es), 3
while mientras
white blanco(a), 7
who que, 9; quién(es)

whole entero (*m.*), 14
whom quién(es)
whooping cough tos ferina (*f.*)
why? ¿por qué?, 5
width ancho (*m.*), 17
winter invierno (*m.*)
wish querer (e:ie), 5
wife esposa (*f.*), 9
window ventana (*f.*), P
windpipe tráquea (*f.*), 7
wish querer (e:ie), 8
with con, 1
  — me conmigo, 6
  — you contigo, 17
without sin, 7
wood madera (*f.*), 10
word palabra (*f.*), 2
work trabajo (*m.*), 1; trabajar, 1
workbook cuaderno de ejercicios (*m.*), 2
world mundo (*m.*), 4; (*adj.*) mundial, 12
  —wide mundial, 12
worry preocuparse
wow! ¡uy!, 4
write escribir, 2
written escrito(a), 13
wrong mal, 3

Y

yard yarda (*f.*), 14
yarn estambre (*m.*), 5; lana de tejer (*f.*), 5
year año (*m.*), 10
yellow amarillo(a), 2
yes sí, 1
yesterday ayer, 11
yet todavía
  not — todavía no, 2

Z

zebra cebra (*f.*)

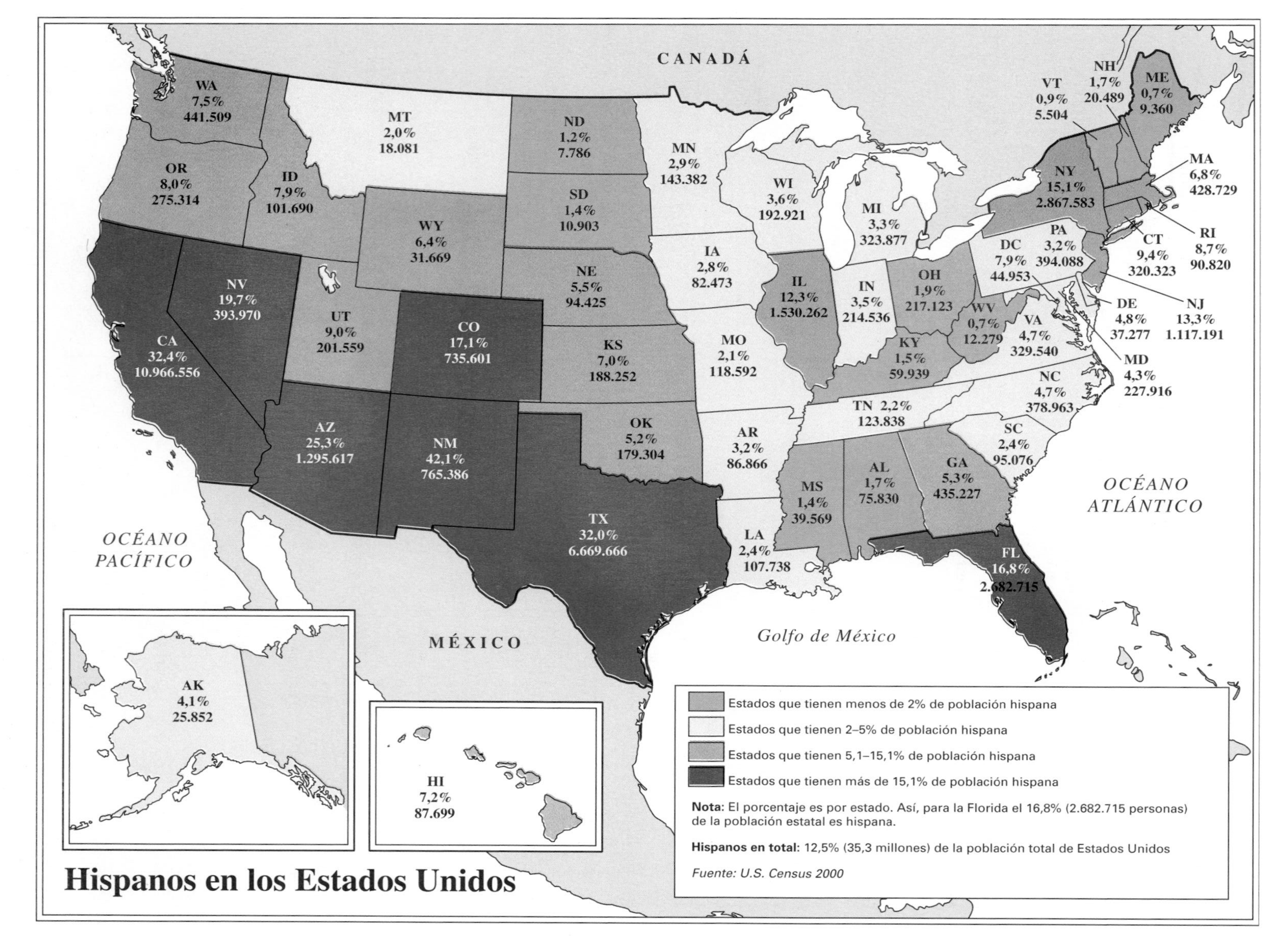

CANADÁ
WA 7,5% 441.509
OR 8,0% 275.314
CA 32,4% 10.966.556
NV 19,7% 393.970
ID 7,9% 101.690
MT 2,0% 18.081
WY 6,4% 31.669
UT 9,0% 201.559
CO 17,1% 735.601
AZ 25,3% 1.295.617
NM 42,1% 765.386
ND 1,2% 7.786
SD 1,4% 10.903
NE 5,5% 94.425
KS 7,0% 188.252
OK 5,2% 179.304
TX 32,0% 6.669.666
MN 2,9% 143.382
IA 2,8% 82.473
MO 2,1% 118.592
AR 3,2% 86.866
LA 2,4% 107.738
WI 3,6% 192.921
IL 12,3% 1.530.262
MI 3,3% 323.877
IN 3,5% 214.536
OH 1,9% 217.123
KY 1,5% 59.939
TN 2,2% 123.838
MS 1,4% 39.569
AL 1,7% 75.830
GA 5,3% 435.227
FL 16,8% 2.682.715
SC 2,4% 95.076
NC 4,7% 378.963
VA 4,7% 329.540
WV 0,7% 12.279
DC 7,9% 44.953
PA 3,2% 394.088
NY 15,1% 2.867.583
VT 0,9% 5.504
NH 1,7% 20.489
ME 0,7% 9.360
MA 6,8% 428.729
RI 8,7% 90.820
CT 9,4% 320.323
NJ 13,3% 1.117.191
DE 4,8% 37.277
MD 4,3% 227.916
OCÉANO PACÍFICO
OCÉANO ATLÁNTICO
MÉXICO
Golfo de México
AK 4,1% 25.852
HI 7,2% 87.699
Estados que tienen menos de 2% de población hispana
Estados que tienen 2–5% de población hispana
Estados que tienen 5,1–15,1% de población hispana
Estados que tienen más de 15,1% de población hispana
Nota: El porcentaje es por estado. Así, para la Florida el 16,8% (2.682.715 personas) de la población estatal es hispana.
Hispanos en total: 12,5% (35,3 millones) de la población total de Estados Unidos
Fuente: U.S. Census 2000
Hispanos en los Estados Unidos